A Reader's Guide to Modern American Drama

A Reader's Guide to Modern American Drama

Sanford Sternlicht

Syracuse University Press

First Edition 2002
02 03 04 05 06 07   6 5 4 3 2 1

The paper used in this publication meets the minimum requirements of
American National Standard for Information Sciences—Permanence of
Paper for Printed Library Materials, ANSI Z39.48–1984.∞™

Library of Congress Cataloging-in-Publication Data

Sternlicht, Sanford V.
A reader's guide to modern American drama / Sanford Sternlicht.— 1st ed.
p. cm.
Includes bibliographical references and index.
ISBN 0-8156-2939-7 (pbk. : alk. paper)
1. American drama—20th century—History and criticism—Handbooks,
manuals, etc. 2. Theater—United States—History—20th
century—Handbooks, manuals, etc. I. Title.
PS350 S74 2002
812'.509—dc21
2002002049

Manufactured in the United States of America

Contents

Backgrounds

Playwrights and Plays

Sanford Sternlicht was the chairperson of the Theatre Department of State University of New York at Oswego. He currently teaches drama theory and dramatic literature in the English Department of Syracuse University. His books on drama include *A Reader's Guide to Modern Irish Drama* and *Selected Plays of Padraic Colum.* He has co-edited *New Plays from the Abbey Theatre: 1993–1995* with Christopher Fitz-Simon and *New Plays from the Abbey Theatre: 1996–1998* with Judy Friel. All were published by Syracuse University Press.

Acknowledgments

My thanks to my research assistants, Jennifer Dee and William Donahue. Thanks also to Dr. Wendy Bousfield of Syracuse University's Bird Library for ordering many of the books I needed to complete my work. I am grateful to Frances Parks for information about Suzan-Lori Parks. I especially wish to thank my partner, Mary Beth Hinton, for editorial advice and patient, ongoing editing of the manuscript of this book.

Backgrounds

• • •

1
•••

The Nineteenth-Century Inheritance

During the nineteenth century, melodrama dominated the American stage. Farce came second, and grand revivals of Shakespeare ran a close third. No great American drama arose in the century, but the American theater thrived, and its technical advances were spectacular indeed. Professional theater was not as centered in New York City as it would be for much of the twentieth century. Boston and Philadelphia competed with New York for theatrical dominance. In 1819 the Chestnut Street Theatre in Philadelphia was the first American theater to replace oil lamps and even candles with gas lighting, allowing for sophisticated lighting effects not possible previously. It took ten years for gas lighting to be employed in a New York theater. But by the advent of the Civil War, New York dominated American theater production. That domination has continued ever since.

Melodramas were a nineteenth-century phenomenon and staple. They offered a simple, moral view of life compatible with residual American Puritanism. Right and wrong are clearly discernible. Villains are congenitally evil, and they do bad things in elaborately contrived plots. In the end they suffer for their misdeeds. The good people, generally bland, two-dimensional characters, live happily ever after, or at least from the barely avoided catastrophic climax to the almost immediate final curtain. Suspense alternates with surprise. Emotion flows copiously. Special effects often are the chief attractions as American stagecraft and technology promote breathtakingly realistic spectacles such as shipwrecks, floods, conflagrations of various sorts, and fierce battles.

Pocahontas by George Washington Parke Custis (1781–1857) is an early historical drama that helped promulgate the John Smith-Pocahontas legend. *Superstition* by James Nelson Barker (1784–1858) is set in seventeenth-century New England, and it connects to the Salem witchcraft trials in a way similar to Arthur Miller's *The Crucible* a century later.

The first American megahit was *She Would Be a Soldier, or The Plains of Chippewa* by Mordecai M. Noah (1785–1851). It held the boards for almost fifty years and introduced several attributes of nineteenth-century American melodrama: patriotism, close escape from death by the heroine, noble Indians, and a good-hearted American farmer, often a Yankee, who has both wit and wisdom. *The Forest Rose* by Samuel Woodworth (1785–1842) offered an American pastoral in which a clever Yankee farmer bests a dim-witted Englishman. It held the stage for forty years. Unfortunately, it introduced the comic African American in a demeaning portrayal akin to early minstrel shows. *Brutus, or The Fall of Tarquin* by John Henry Payne (1791–1852) introduced a classical, tragic, faux Shakespearean model into American drama.

In *Metamora* by John Augustus Stone (1800–1834) a Native American is portrayed as a tragic hero for the first time. Performances of *The Gladiator* by Robert Montgomery Bird (1806–1854) depict the Spartacus legend. It was much admired for a spectacular slave revolt. Perhaps the second most frequently performed American play of the nineteenth century (second only to *Uncle Tom's Cabin*) was *The Drunkard* by W. H. Smith (1808–1872), a preposterous melodrama about a young husband, an alcoholic, who is saved by religion and the help of a temperance worker. Of course the play received great support from the nineteenth-century temperance movement.

By far the most popular American play of all time is the great, melodramatic, antislavery narrative *Uncle Tom's Cabin* by Harriet Beecher Stowe (1812–1896), rewritten as a play. Beginning in 1852 the novel was dramatized by at least thirty authors, all without the consent of Stowe, who disapproved of play-going and who earned nothing from the story pirating. At one time five hundred traveling companies of *Uncle Tom's Cabin* were on the road simultaneously. Performances, often taking great liberty with Stowe's narrative, were given the world over in many languages, until finally the early film industry took interest and shot at least ten versions. As late as the 1930s there was still a hinterland American audience for *Uncle Tom* companies.

Still read and sometimes performed today is the comedy *Fashion* by Anna Cora Mowatt (1819–1870). It is an American version of a Restoration comedy without the bawdy, and, of course, the hero is a straight-arrow American army officer.

Perhaps the greatest melodramatist was the Irish-born Dion Boucicault (1820–1890), whose career was largely spent in America. Two of his most famous plays have American settings. *The Octoroon,* like *Uncle Tom's Cabin,* shows the suffering that slavery created as well as its cruel injustice. In terms of spectacle, characterization, and theme, *The Octoroon* may be the perfect melodrama. *The Poor of New York* purported to show the growing mercantile city and the power of villainous bankers. It also contrived to have a great city fire scene. The play was so successful that the wily Boucicault toured it and drew in vast crowds by changing the title to include the city in which the play was being performed. Thus *The Poor of San Francisco, The Poor of London,* and so forth.

Francesca da Rimini by George Henry Boker (1823–1890) played on the American stage for the entire last half of the nineteenth century. The star-crossed love of Paolo and Francesca made well-written romantic tragedies a staple of nineteenth-century American drama.

Like Stowe's *Uncle Tom's Cabin,* Washington Irving's (1783–

1859) beloved *Rip Van Winkle* was ripe for conversion to melodrama by theatrical pirates. Stage versions began to appear as early as 1828, only nine years after Irving wrote the story. When the actor Joseph Jefferson III put together some of the versions, he went on to perform the title role continually for thirty-nine years.

As the nineteenth century came to a close, the Victorian affinity for melodrama and sentimental comedy was mitigated by a new realism in the portrayal of character, plot, and mise-en-scène. But the audience's desire for the expected ending—happy couples marrying, families reunited, and evil punished—could not be totally ignored. Until the end of the century, the audience expected a restitution of order as the only conclusion acceptable in its literature and drama. In 1891 *Margaret Fleming*, by James A. Herne (1839–1901), shows the influence of Henrik Ibsen on American drama at last. The family in the play is middle class and it has a serious social problem to deal with: marital infidelity in a society that permits the double standard.

Young Mrs. Winthrop, written by Bronson Howard (1842–1908), called in his time "the dean of American drama" and reputedly the first American dramatist to earn a living by his playwriting, depicted the dangers of devoting one's life to business and social climbing. The American audience at the end of the nineteenth century saw these activities as the main preoccupations of the new American rich.

After success with *Beau Brummell* and the patriotic historical drama *Barbara Frietchie,* William Clyde Fitch (1865–1909), called the finest American dramatist at the century's end, produced his masterpiece, *The City,* in which the politics, social climbing, and sexual indiscretions of the New York upper class are savagely addressed.

2
...

America and the Themes of Early Modern American Drama

In 1898, with the quick and easy victory over Spain in the Spanish-American War and the obtaining of some of the former Spanish colonies (Puerto Rico, Guam, and the Philippine Islands, despite the resistance of the Philippine people), the United States entered twentieth-century history as an imperialistic world power. The pugnacious, chauvinistic president Theodore Roosevelt won the Nobel Peace Prize by bringing the Russo-Japanese War to a conclusion in 1905. Then he built the Great White Fleet to sail around the world and impress it with the new American might.

The nation swelled with immigration. The new Americans brought vitality, strong arms, diversity, European culture, and a great desire to participate in the political life of the world's greatest democracy. Cities with a theater tradition, New York and Philadelphia, now had populations of over a million people each. American industry, manufacturing, and invention competed with European counterparts. During World War I (1914–18) America began to dominate world trade. Wealthy citizens who had accumulated vast fortunes in the Gilded Age of the late nineteenth century now found that society expected, from them and their businesses, ethical behavior and some compassion for their workers.

Meanwhile, nationwide electrification, the automobile, motion pictures, and the airplane presaged a twentieth century that would bear little resemblance to the nineteenth. The new drama would be very different too.

3
...

Modernism

The realistic, sometimes naturalistic (ultra realistic) drama that is the staple of what is now called modern drama had its origins in a vast intellectual and creative European-centered movement now called modernism, referring not to a time so much as to a cultural milieu and style. Modernism came to the drama before any other art form. Its father was the Norwegian Henrik Ibsen (1828–1906), and its birth date was the production of his shocking play *The Doll's House* in 1878. In it a middle-class woman is treated like a brainless pet by her husband. But then in a family crisis she is viciously subjected to verbal abuse by her insensitive, vain, unappreciative, patriarchal husband. So she walks out on him and their children.

From Ibsen on, world drama was irrevocably changed. Social dramas about problems faced by contemporary middle-class people and performed for middle-class audiences would dominate serious modernist drama for more than a century.

The Swedish playwright August Strindberg (1849–1912) followed Ibsen in his brutally realistic portrayal of the war between the sexes with *The Father* and *Miss Julie*. In the intellectual and artistic circles that had become fascinated with the psychoanalytic theories of Sigmund Freud, Strindberg found a ready audience for his misogynistic dramas with their sexually motivated characters.

The Irish master George Bernard Shaw (1856–1950) used comedy to address such social problems as prostitution, militarism, institutionalized religion, suffragism, the "threat" of the New Woman, political corruption, Victorian hypocrisy, and even predatory slum landlords. *Widowers' Houses, Mrs. Warren's Profession, Arms and the Man, Candida, Major Barbara,* and *Saint Joan* address these issues.

Anton Chekhov (1860–1904) first made his literary reputation with short stories that featured brilliant characterization. Repudiating the centrality of plot, he wrote plays that depicted the psychological turmoil that tormented and depressed so many middle-class people who were bored and could find no meaning in their lives. *Uncle Vanya, The Three Sisters,* and *The Cherry Orchard* addressed the ennui and predicted the demise of the Russian middle class.

Modern dramatists from Ibsen to the present time valorize character development and eschew the model play structure of the nineteenth century, the "well-made play," in which exposition was followed by intensifying scenes that bring a central conflict to a climax late in the play, and then to a quick, sometimes surprising but always satisfying closure. The "well-made play" was manipulative: protagonists experienced sudden reversals, important information was withheld, and suspense took precedence over probability.

4
...

Early Experimental Drama
and the Little Theater Movement

Founded on Grand Street in New York City's Jewish ghetto in 1915, the Neighborhood Playhouse, an offshoot of the Henry Street Settlement House, began as a community theater, but five years later it turned professional. Although the company disbanded in 1927, the theater continued to produce the works of modern playwrights well into the 1930s. The Neighborhood Playhouse was the forerunner to the Off-Broadway movement that reached its zenith in the 1950s.

Simultaneous with the Neighborhood Playhouse, the Washington Square Players, founded in 1914 and disbanded in 1918, performed some early O'Neill one-acts and plays by Elmer Rice.

Founded in 1916 (originally based in Cape Cod), the Provincetown Players on McDougal Street in Greenwich Village brought Eugene O'Neill himself to the New York theater scene, first with his nautical one-act plays and then with major full-length naturalist dramas such as *The Emperor Jones, The Hairy Ape,* and *Desire Under the Elms.* Other writers whose early work was produced by the Provincetown Players include Edna St. Vincent Millay, Edna Ferber, Edmund Wilson, and Paul Green. When the players disbanded in 1929, O'Neill was a world-class playwright.

One of the early twentieth century's most successful producing organizations was the Theatre Guild. It was founded in 1919 and lasted into the 1950s, but its most successful years were the 1920s and 1930s. In those years it premiered Elmer Rice's expressionist drama *The Adding Machine* as well as plays by O'Neill, William Saroyan, Sidney Howard, S. N. Behrman, Robert E. Sherwood, and Maxwell Anderson.

In 1926 the great actor Eva Le Gallienne founded the Civic Repertory Theatre on Fourteenth Street, the northern boundary of New York City's Lower East Side. The idea was to provide its audience with the opportunity to see a company of actors performing a variety of classical plays and new plays in rotation. It failed financially in 1933. Le Gallienne tried the repertory idea again in 1946 along with the director Margaret Webster and the producer Cheryl Crawford. The new theater, named the American Repertory Theatre, lasted one year. Neither it nor the Civic especially encouraged new American writers. Shakespeare, Ibsen, and Chekhov provided the main menu.

The Group Theatre was founded in 1931 by famed acting teacher Lee Strasberg and others. Its model was Konstantin Stanislavski's Moscow Art Theatre, where method acting was invented and where Chekhov built his reputation. The Group's most famous dramatist was Clifford Odets, whose realistic, proletarian plays, the most famous of which is *Golden Boy*, were perfect for the radical 1930s. Other important playwrights whose work was performed by the Group Theatre included Maxwell Anderson and Sidney Kingsley. Elia Kazan was the company's best director. The Group dissolved in 1941, but Strasberg went on to direct the Actor's Studio and create the American school of acting, a version of Stanislavski's "method." The Actors Studio was the premier acting school in the United States for more than twenty-five years, succeeding the American Academy of Dramatic Arts, the oldest American school for acting, which had been established in 1884.

5
...

Drama in the American University

Drama in the universities contributed to the development of generations of American dramatists. In 1904 Professor George Pierce Baker of Harvard University established a playwriting course at Radcliffe College. In 1913 the course, open now to Harvard students, included an extracurricular production workshop, the 47 Workshop. Playwrights Eugene O'Neill, S. N. Behrman, Philip Barry, Sidney Howard; the director George Abbott; the critics Robert Benchley and John Mason Brown; and the first great American scene designer, Robert Edmund Jones, trained under Baker, who later transferred to Yale University, where he founded the distinguished Yale School of Drama.

In 1914 the Carnegie Institute of Technology offered America's first degree in theater. Other colleges and universities followed suit, so that today drama and theater departments abound in American academe.

Yale established the Yale Repertory Theatre in 1966 under the critic Robert Brustein, who in 1979 moved to Harvard and the American Repertory Theatre in Cambridge. Lloyd Richards, the outstanding African American stage director, took over at Yale when Brustein departed. The American theater benefited greatly by the collaboration of August Wilson, the premier African American dramatist, and Richards. The latter left Yale in 1992 for freelance directing.

13

6
...

The Federal Theatre

During the Great Depression of the 1930s, the American government actually became involved in American theater through the Works Project Administration. This experiment in government-subsidized theater was called the Federal Theatre Project. It began under a 1935 act of Congress, and its expressed purpose was to provide free theater to the people and employment to theater professionals—actors, dramatists, designers, and others. It was political, radical, and multiracial. There was a Negro theater unit, and another unit put on plays in Yiddish. Thousands were employed and millions entertained throughout the country. Hallie Flanagan, who had assisted George Pierce Baker at Harvard University and who was professor of drama and director of experimental theater at Vassar College, was the intrepid, resourceful, and beleaguered head of the project.

Although many new playwrights contributed original dramas, the Federal Theatre discovered no playwrights of distinction; but twenty-one year old Orson Welles made his reputation as a director and actor in the project. It also led to Welles and John Houseman's Mercury Theatre. The outstanding production of the project was Nobel Laureate Sinclair Lewis's dramatization of his novel *It Can't Happen Here*. The Federal Theatre Project was closed down in 1939 by a politically conservative Congress.

7
...

Off-Broadway Producing Companies

Off-Broadway theater refers to plays, original or otherwise, produced in generally small venues that are not located in the Times
Square area of New York City. The Off-Broadway movement, meaning an avant-garde, less expensive, less commercial kind of theater,
really began in Greenwich Village with the Washington Square
Players (1914) and the Provincetown Players (1915). But the term
came into general usage to note and celebrate the explosion of creativity just after World War II in the experimental little theaters of
New York City, especially in Greenwich Village and surrounding
areas.

The Playwright's Company evolved out of the Theatre Guild in
1938. It was founded as a producing organization by and for
Maxwell Anderson, S. N. Behrman, Sidney Howard, Elmer Rice,
and Robert E. Sherwood. The Company produced many if not most
of the finest American plays of the late 1930s and 1940s, from Sherwood's *Abe Lincoln in Illinois* in 1938 (the best play ever written
about Lincoln) through Tennessee Williams's *Cat on a Hot Tin Roof* in
1955. The Company disbanded in 1960, as the founders had either
passed on or were no longer writing.

The American Negro Theatre (1940–51), cofounded by Abram
Hill and Frederick O'Neill in Harlem, provided professional training and produced plays about African American life.

15

Located in Sheridan Square in the heart of Greenwich Village, The Circle in the Square was founded by the director José Quintero and others in 1950. The circle part of the name refers to the arena stage. The staples of the company were plays by O'Neill and Williams. Its greatest triumph was the production of O'Neill's *The Iceman Cometh* in 1956. In 1960 the company moved to Bleecker Street.

The Phoenix Theatre, located on the Lower East Side's Second Avenue in a former Yiddish theater house, competed with the Circle in the Square for the title of the best-known Off-Broadway venue in the 1950s. Founded by the director Norris Houghton, it specialized in high-quality productions of Ibsen, Shaw, Pirandello, and absurdists such as Ionesco. But it also produced plays by Sidney Howard, George S. Kaufman, O'Neill, and William Saroyan. The Phoenix's greatest success was the 1962 production of Arthur Kopit's *Oh Dad, Poor Dad, Mamma's Hung You in the Closet and I'm Feelin' So Sad*. The Phoenix performed from 1953 to 1982.

The Living Theatre Company first began playing in 1952 in Greenwich Village. Later the company moved uptown to various venues. The founders, Julian Beck and Judith Malina, set out to be the most radical and experimental American theater company, and to a large extent they succeeded. The Living Theatre epitomized counterculture performance. The company had no interest in material success, and the members lived as a family. The company's controversial fame extended beyond America when it made European and South American tours. Jack Gelber's 1959 play about drug addiction, *The Connection*, proved to be the company's most famous production. The second great hit was Kenneth Brown's play about Marine Corps life, *The Brig* (1963). The company disbanded in 1973.

Founded in 1954 by the controversial but brilliant impresario Joseph Papp, and performing in venues such as the Delacorte Theatre in Central Park and the former Astor Library in Lower Manhattan, the New York Shakespeare Festival is the most successful of all Off-Broadway producing companies, having presented nearly five hundred plays to date. Galt MacDermot's *Hair* and David Rabe's Vietnam War drama, *The Basic Training of Pavlo Hummel,* are the most outstanding original productions of the festival. The playwright George C. Wolfe is the current artistic director.

Café La Mama (the La Mama Experimental Theatre Club) opened in 1962 under the direction of the designer Ellen Stewart. It became famous for giving full scope to radical playwrights and absurdist productions, to the delight of the hippie generation.

Joseph Chaikin, an actor who had worked with the Living Theatre, founded the Open Theatre in 1963. It was primarily an experimental workshop that Americanized the theories of the Polish director Jerzy Grotowski. The company's best-known playwright was Jean-Claude van Itallie. The Open Theatre performed for ten years.

In 1964 the American Place Theatre was founded by Sidney Lanier and Wynn Handman to promote new American playwrights. Sam Shepard and Ed Bullins are the two most successful playwrights the company featured. Women dramatists received special encouragement.

The Negro Ensemble Company was founded in 1967 by Douglas Turner Ward, a playwright, actor, and director. Outstanding dramas such as Joseph A. Walker's *The River Niger* and Charles Fuller's *A Soldier's Play* were produced by the company.

The Ridiculous Theatrical Company, presenting a gay and lesbian humorous perspective on the relativity of gender and sexuality, was energized in 1967 by the playwright and actor Charles Ludlum.

Richard Schechner popularized "environmental theater" with the Performance Group, founded in 1968. It shocked the New York theater audience with the sexually explicit *Dionysus in 69.* Sam Shepard's *The Tooth of Crime* was the company's greatest critical success.

Playwrights Horizons in New York began in 1971 under the leadership of the director Robert Moss, now artistic director of Syracuse Stage. Most of Wendy Wasserstein's plays have premiered at Playwrights Horizons as well as plays by Christopher Durang and A. R. Gurney.

The Roundabout Theatre Company, founded in 1974, is the most mainstream of the Off-Broadway producing organizations, with many annual subscribers.

Outside of New York City the Arena Stage in Washington, D.C., the Alley Theatre in Houston, the Tyrone Guthrie Theatre in Minneapolis, the Long Wharf Theatre in New Haven, the Mark Taper Forum in Los Angeles, the Steppenwolf Theatre and the Goodman Theatre (first home of David Mamet drama) in Chicago, and many other regional theaters, most outstandingly the Actors Theatre of Louisville (Kentucky), became the starting point for American playwrights as Broadway shrank, and Off Broadway, and even the tiny venues of Off-Off-Broadway, could not fully accommodate the creativity of American drama and theater in the last quarter of the twentieth century.

8

African American Drama

African American actors were first given access to Broadway projects with Eugene O'Neill, whose *Emperor Jones* initially starred Charles S. Gilpin in 1920, and the greatest African American actor of his time, Paul Robeson, in a revival. But the first African American dramatist to receive national attention was Langston Hughes, whose plays, such as *Mulatto* in 1935, were popular with black and white audiences—but in Harlem, not on Broadway. The Broadway breakthrough for African American playwrights came in 1941 with Richard Wright's stage adaptation of his famous novel *Native Son*, with the African American star actor Canada Lee as Bigger Thomas. In the 1950s Broadway welcomed Louis Peterson's *Take a Giant Step* in 1953, and Lorraine Hansberry's *Raisin in the Sun* (1959) became the most successful and most often performed African American play up through the present.

In the 1960s the second emancipation, the African American civil rights revolution, brought African American dramatists to the forefront of American drama both on and Off Broadway right through to the present. It started with Ozzie Davis's *Purlie Victorious,* James Baldwin's *Blues for Mister Charlie,* Imamu Amiri Baraka's *The Dutchman,* James A. Walker's *The River Niger,* Charles Gordone's *No Place to Be Somebody,* Ntozake Shange's *For Colored Girls Who Have Considered Suicide/When the Rainbow Is Enuf,* Adrienne Kennedy's *A Movie Star Has to Star in Black and White*, Charles Fuller's *A Soldier's Play*, George C. Wolfe's *The Colored Museum*, and Suzan-Lori Parks's *Venus*. Of course the greatest living African American dramatist is August Wilson, whose series of plays referred to as the *Pittsburgh Cycle* are already an important part of the history of American drama. After Arthur Miller, Wilson is the most significant living American playwright.

9
...

Feminist Drama

Although Zona Gale, Rachel Crothers, Susan Glaspell, Zoe Akins, Lulu Vollmer, Edna Ferber, Lillian Hellman, Carson McCullers, and Lorraine Hansberry made significant contributions to American drama in their time, it was not until the women's movement in the late 1960s and 1970s that a feminist agenda reached the American stage. This agenda included defining issues of gender, studying sex and power, supporting equality for women, differentiating the language and experience of woman, empowering women writers in a patriarchal and sexist society, and contradicting the often distorted depiction of women in plays written by men. Additionally, women dramatists strove to create a contemporary canon of women's plays. Feminist drama foregrounds a woman's struggle for autonomy. Arguably, however, it does not have to be written by a woman.

Outstanding among the women dramatists inspired by and participating in the women's movement are the African American Ntozake Shange, whose 1976 play *For Colored Girls Who Have Considered Suicide/When the Rainbow Is Enuf* symbolized the connection with, and the debt to, the Civil Rights movement of the 1960s; Beth Henley *(Crimes of the Heart,* 1977); Marsha Norman *('Night Mother,* 1983); Tina Howe *(Painting Churches,* 1983); and Wendy Wasserstein *(The Heidi Chronicles,* 1988, and *The Sisters Rosensweig,* 1992).

21

10
...

Gay and Lesbian Drama

As early as 1934 the possibility of a lesbian relationship is broached on the American stage in Lillian Hellman's *The Children's Hour.* But it was not until Mart Crowley's *The Boys in the Band* in 1968 that the pleasures and the pains, the humor and the pathos of gay life in the United States entered the mainstream of American drama (and film). The next year, after the police raid on the Stonewall Inn in Greenwich Village, a gay bar, the Gay Liberation movement went into high gear. Activists fought for decriminalization of sexual acts between consenting adults, the end of discrimination against homosexuals in employment and public accommodations, fair representation in the arts, and acceptance in the general American community.

Dramas and comedies with gay themes proliferate, but the outstanding efforts have been some of the plays of Terrence McNally *(The Ritz,* 1975), Harvey Fierstein *(Torch Song Trilogy,* 1981), Tony Kushner *(Angels in America,* 1991, 1992), and more than two dozen wonderfully outrageous plays such as *Camille* (1973) and *The Mystery of Irma Vep* (1984) that Charles Ludlam wrote for the Ridiculous Theatrical Company.

The American Musical Play from Operetta to Sondheim

The history of the popular modern American musical theater has three phases: operetta, musical comedy, and musical drama. Early-twentieth-century operetta began with Ireland-born Victor Herbert (1859–1924), who came to New York before the twentieth century began because his wife signed a contract to sing with the Metropolitan Opera Company. European trained, Herbert studded his operettas with waltzes and marches. But it is the beautiful sentimental songs, including "Every Day Is Ladies' Day with Me," "I'm Falling in Love with Someone," and "Ah, Sweet Mystery of Life," that endeared his operettas to the American public. *The Red Mill* and *Naughty Marietta* are his most enduring musical treats.

Herbert's American-born contemporary, John Philip Sousa (1854–1932), the March King, also had success with operetta. His most famous is *El Capitan,* best remembered for its title number.

Like Herbert, European-trained Rudolph Friml (1879–1972) came to the United States from Bohemia. He composed musical comedies as well as operettas, but his most memorable work is the operetta *Rose-Marie,* with its title song and "Indian Love Call."

Sigmund Romberg (1887–1951) immigrated to America from

23

Hungary at the age of twenty-two. *Maytime* with "Will You Remember," *The Student Prince* with "Deep in My Heart" and "Golden Days," *The Desert Song* with "One Alone," and *The New Moon* with "Lover, Come Back to Me" and "One Kiss" are Romberg's great gifts to American musical theater and American song.

The American musical comedy of the first forty years of the twentieth century was influenced by the less-objectionable elements of the old minstrel shows, ragtime, African American spirituals, and, most of all jazz. The first master of the American musical comedy was George M. Cohan (1878–1942), whose raucous, chauvinistic plays delighted American audiences. His most famous works are *Little Johnny Jones,* with "Give My Regards to Broadway" and "The Yankee Doodle Boy," and *Forty-Five Minutes from Broadway.* Cohan also wrote nonmusical plays.

The golden age of American musical comedy was the Jazz Age, the 1920s and the early Depression years, 1931–36. Among the outstanding productions were George (1898–1937) and Ira Gershwin's (1896–1983) *Porgy and Bess* with DuBose Heyward (1885–1940); Cole Porter's (1891–1964) *Anything Goes;* Richard Rodgers (1902–1979) and Moss Hart's (1904–1961) *On Your Toes;* as well as Irving Berlin (1888–1989) and Moss Hart's *As Thousands Cheer.* But the landmark musical of the period, based on a novel by Edna Ferber, is *Showboat* (1927) by Jerome Kern (1885–1945) and Oscar Hammerstein II (1895–1960). The prototypical popular musical drama, *Showboat* was the first time a powerful story was set to music. This long-running and continually revived musical drama eventually led to *Oklahoma* (1943) by Richard Rodgers and Oscar Hammerstein II and the great Broadway musicals of the 1950s and 1960s: moving stories with plausible characters told with appropriate and beautiful music.

Oklahoma is not only recognized as the outstanding American musical of the 1940s, it is universally seen as the show that finally inaugurated the realistic, fully integrated American musical drama. But other 1940s musicals remain popular, such as the German-

Jewish refugee Kurt Weill's (1900–1950) *Lady in the Dark* and *Lost in the Stars* (with Maxwell Anderson, 1888–1959), which lent gravity and introduced expressionism and Freudianism to the American musical stage; Richard Rodgers and Lorenz Hart's (1895–1943) *Pal Joey;* Leonard Bernstein (1918–1990), Betty Comden (1915–), and Adolph Green's (1915–) *On the Town;* Berlin's *Annie Get Your Gun;* and Cole Porter's *Kiss Me Kate,* an adaptation of Shakespeare's *Taming of the Shrew.*

If the golden age of American musical comedy was the 1920s, the 1950s and early 1960s marked the golden age of American musical drama. At this time, and prior to the ascendancy of rock music and Motown rhythm and blues, the songs of Broadway shows were the popular radio music of the time. Outstanding American musicals of the period include Alan J. Lerner (1918–1986) and Frederick Loewe's (1904–1988) *My Fair Lady* and *Camelot* with Moss Hart; Rodgers and Hammerstein's *South Pacific, The King and I,* and *The Sound of Music;* Berlin's *Call Me Madam,* and, with Stephen Sondheim (1930–), *Gypsy;* Bernstein, Lillian Hellman (1905–1984), Richard Wilbur (1921–), John Latouche (1917–1956) and Dorothy Parker's (1893–1967) *Candide;* Bernstein, Sondheim, and Laurents's (1918–) *West Side Story;* Jerry Herman's (1932–) *Hello Dolly!* and *Fiddler on the Roof,* with Joseph Stein (1912–) and Jerry Bock (1928–); and John Kander (1927–), Fred Ebb (1932–), and Joe Masteroff's (1919–) *Cabaret.*

The debut of the rock musical, with *Hair* in 1968 by Galt MacDermot (1928–), changed the American musical again. Now the strong, often literature-based plot was replaced by a representation of a milieu, a stratum of society, an age group, or an art form. The most successful musicals of this subgenre were the 1970s hits *Company, A Little Night Music,* and *Sweeney Todd,* all by Sondheim; and Michael Bennett (1943–) and Marvin Hamlisch's (1944–) *A Chorus Line.* Sondheim continued his dominance of the American musical stage into the 1980s with *Sunday in the Park with George.*

In the 1980s at long last the American musical stage offered a sympathetic presentation of gay life with Harvey Fierstein (1954–) and Jerry Herman's *La Cage aux Folles*. But the late 1970s saw the invasion and near coup d'état of the Broadway musical drama scene by imports from London such as *Evita, Cats, Les Miserables, Phantom of the Opera, Miss Saigon,* and *Sunset Boulevard*. These huge, spectacular productions became an integral part of the New York City tourism industry in the 1980s and 1990s.

Fortunately American creativity in musical drama has not dried up. The late 1980s and the 1990s saw the Disney-produced, Anglo-American *The Lion King* by Tim Rice (1944–), Elton John (1947–), Roger Allers, and Irene Mecchi; E. L. Doctorow (1931–), Lynn Ahrens (1948–), and Stephen Flaherty's (1960–) *Ragtime;* Jonathan Larson's (1960–1996) radical *Rent;* and Maury Yeston (1945–) and Peter Stone's (1930–) megashow *Titanic*. It appears that a healthy competition will endure between British and American musical dramas in the 2010s. Audiences around the world will continue to enjoy the modern musical-dramatic art form that originated in, and has been dominated by, the American theater.

Playwrights and Plays
• • •

Themes in Modern American Drama

Many themes structure the almost one-hundred-year history of modern American drama. It seems clear at the beginning of the twenty-first century that the overall and most pervasive theme in modern American drama is the desire of American dramatists to play back the American experiment and the American experience to the American audience. They employ the stage as microcosm for the American "place," and the drama as canvas on which to paint the scope, subtleties, contradictions, hopes, and dreams of the variegated yet somehow composite American character.

From the beginning of the twentieth century, and under the influence of Ibsen and Shaw on one hand, and the French playwright Alfred Jarry (1873–1907) on the other, American drama followed two paths: the path of realism and naturalism—its extreme sociological and deterministic form—and the antirealism path of expressionism and absurdism. The main road has been realism, a mode of writing and performing that most values verisimilitude. It is mimetic. The ratio is one to one. In the usual theatrical process of invoking suspension of disbelief, realism attempts to produce the illusion of what actually happens in real life. Of course realism is an artistic convention, like romanticism or expressionism. It achieves its "slice of life" effects by selecting themes representing the problems of ordinary people, avoiding direct address to the audience, employing conversational dialogue, and using linear narrative as a basic architectonic, although characterization takes precedence over plot.

The major works of our greatest dramatists, Eugene O'Neill, Tennessee Williams, and Arthur Miller, are in the realistic mode, even when the plays have flashback scenes, dream episodes, or passages of psychological revelation. An arrow shot down the straight road from O'Neill's *Desire Under the Elms* (1924) would strike the heart of the drama of August Wilson today. And because Wilson, a superb dramatist, has situated his epic work on the broad avenue of realism, he is the most likely future addition to the first rank of American dramatists: O'Neill, Williams, and Miller.

The Paradox of the American Family: Nurturer and Destroyer

Playwrights the world over have found subject and theme in the family. It is not surprising. The home is a theater. The family is the basic sociological and political unit. It is an emotional foundry where we learn about women, men, fidelity, trust, risk, love, hate, control, myth, values, and culture. The family is our legacy of the good and the bad in our lives.

Some American dramatists have chosen to portray the family as a site for oedipal conflict. O'Neill's *Long Day's Journey into Night* and Miller's *Death of a Salesman*—the two greatest American tragedies—play out the archetypal struggles between fathers and sons and the suffering of women caught in the cross fire.

Other dramatists have seen the family as a place where helpless love, the child's lot, is endured almost beyond endurance. Williams's *The Glass Menagerie* is such a play, rich in the agony of love. *The Glass Menagerie* also reminds the viewer, as does Sam Shepard's *Fool for Love,* of the vanishing American father, a man in love with space.

Edward Albee sees the family as a site for terror and terrorizing when he is not portraying it as an exercise in absurdism. *Who's Afraid of Virginia Woolf?* is a study in family hatred as is Lillian Hellman's *The Little Foxes* and Sam Shepard's *True West*. These kinds of plays imply that it is impossible to survive in a traditional family without fighting successfully for space, power, hegemony, and life itself. The best that can be hoped for is an armistice.

On the other hand, some major American dramatists have portrayed the family as a place of peace and refuge—the site of value accretion—a paradise of childhood or youth recalled nostalgically from a merciless real world stripped of illusion. Interestingly, O'Neill, who painted one of the darkest pictures of family life in *Long Day's Journey into Night,* created one of the most idyllic views of early-twentieth-century American life in *Ah, Wilderness!* Surely the play is a portrait of a family life O'Neill dreamed about. Nostalgia for a lost America, or an America that never really existed, is a secondary theme in the onstage saga of the American family.

Thornton Wilder's *Our Town,* like *Ah, Wilderness!*, is set in a small town in the first decades of the twentieth century. *Our Town* is so profoundly emotional, reaching as it does a place in our psyche where our longing for a "return" to a familial paradise we never knew resides, that it is the most popular American drama. Yet unlike *Ah, Wilderness!* the "family values" are so blatantly presented that the play seems ideological and can be read by a jaundiced eye as propaganda.

A Raisin in the Sun, Lorraine Hansberry's magnificent portrait of African American ghetto life, portrays the black family as a strong unit able to survive economic deprivation and loss, as well as white prejudice. It argues that all families are potentially indestructible if unity and love are present.

Tina Howe's outstanding feminist drama *Painting Churches* shows the privileged white family at the point of diminishing significance, but does so lovingly, as a competing mother and daughter, facing the decline of the father, come to an understanding that bridges the values of two generations.

Trashing the American Dream

Immigrants flocked to America from Europe in the nineteenth and early twentieth centuries, as indeed they flow in from Latin America and Asia today. Almost all saw this country as a golden land. Opportunities seemingly abounded. A person had only to work hard and eventually this person or his or her children would be rich. With riches came luxury, power, respect, and of course happiness. Many were ruthless, climbing over the bodies of those who did not compete successfully or have the necessary luck. It didn't matter what a person did to get ahead as long as the person prospered. Economic Darwinism—the survival of the fittest in the world of money-making—deeply offended many American dramatists, especially during the 1930s and 1940s.

Before and after those decades, American drama was less critical of the American economic system, with the battle line drawn between a traditional American respect for the individual and the right of all members of the community to equal opportunity and justice. Lately some dramatists foreground the need of the community to protect the health of its members and the environment in which all live. Providing for the poor and the helpless has been an issue in drama from the beginning of the twentieth century.

Clifford Odets supported unionization in *Waiting for Lefty* and depicted the plight of the urban worker in *Awake and Sing!* Elmer Rice saw workers of the future reduced to automatons in his expressionistic drama *The Adding Machine*. Sidney Kingsley showed how the system turned slum children into criminals in *Dead End.*

In *All My Sons* Arthur Miller savaged war profiteers, who were willing to let a generation of young men die so that they could make money. In *Death of a Salesman* Miller showed that the drive to achieve the American dream of happiness through material gain at all costs leads to disaster for the young exposed to immoral, opportunistic, and misogynistic values. Miller also excoriated bosses' indifference to the needs and natural rights of old workers. Edward Albee ripped apart the American family's impossible demands on the young in *The American Dream*. And in *Colored Girls* Ntozake Shange sang the sad song of the plight of women in the ghetto, whom American prosperity excluded.

Appearance Versus Reality

The conflict between appearance and reality is not only a pervasive theme in modern American drama, it is one of the great themes of Western literature. Shakespeare, Cervantes, Goethe, Austen, Dickens, Ibsen, Shaw, Joyce, Beckett, and so many other giants of literature have felt compelled to illustrate the dangers of illusion as well as the great human need for it in order to endure the pain of living. Eugene O'Neill and Arthur Miller are surgeon-dramatists, cutting away at the debilitating illusions and fantasies of their protagonists yet pitying them all the while.

The Search for Justice in America

Ever since Ibsen and Shaw, the stage in Euro-American modern culture has often been used as a pulpit in disguise. American playwrights have preached that even in a democracy, justice is frail and often unattainable. Richard Wright's adaptation of his classic novel *Native Son* cried out against the oppression of African Americans. Herman Wouk reminded us in his adaptation *The Caine Mutiny Court-Martial* that judicial decisions often are far from clear-cut. In *The Brig* Kenneth H. Brown showed audiences that the American military, in its senseless torture of American servicemen, could be as cruel as any fascist state. James Baldwin in *Blues for Mister Charlie* bitterly indicted Southern "justice" as applied to African American men. *The Indian Wants the Bronx* by Israel Horowitz condemned the mindless brutality inflicted on those who are different or helpless.

On the satiric side Amiri Baraka's *Jello* has the radio and television personality Jack Benny under fire for oppressing his chauffeur, Rochester, who is now a black militant. And August Wilson in *Ma Rainey's Black Bottom* targeted the economic injustice that white society in the 1920s, represented by the music recording business, inflicted on African American musicians.

In many modern American plays plot reveals character instead of, as in the nineteenth century and earlier, character revealing plot. Even when dramatists have chosen to objectify the hidden unconsciousness of their characters, and even when, as in most cases, modern American dramatists have abandoned dramatic heroes, they still imbue their protagonists with the desire to obtain or sustain human dignity, the foundation of Western individualism. In Williams's *A Street Car Named Desire,* all his broken and pathetic heroine wants is to be permitted her self-respect. In John Steinbeck's adaptation of his novel *Of Mice and Men,* it is better for the slow-witted, accidental killer to die unknowingly at the hands of his friend than be murdered by a lynch mob because his dignity as a human being deserves an end without terror, torture, and humiliation. In *A Raisin in the Sun* Lorraine Hansberry has her protagonist, an African American chauffeur, nearly destroy his family until he places self-respect over money. A place in the sun must not be bought at the cost of black pride. Amiri Baraka portrayed, in *The Dutchman,* a middle-class, assimilated African American man teased and tormented to the point that he is ready to murder. The American stages of the twenty-first century will echo resoundingly with demands for justice, equality, and respect for women, minorities, the handicapped, gays and lesbians, Latinos, Asian Americans, immigrants, and all those who have not shared fully in the growing wealth of the country.

The great dramatic themes of the twenty-first century may come to differ from those that dominated the American stage in the twentieth. But the archetypal presence of the family, the close connection between the idea of the sanctity of human dignity within Western democracy and the continual need to temper capitalistic greed with compassion and social action will insure the continuation of these themes, until the American dream becomes more than a dream.

13
...

Early-Twentieth-Century Playwrights
Eugene O'Neill (1888–1953)

In the eyes of much of the world, Eugene O'Neill is America's greatest playwright. Born in the nineteenth century, he dominated the American stage until the arrival of Tennessee Williams and Arthur Miller. In 1936 he was awarded the Nobel Prize for literature; he is one of the few dramatists to receive the award and the only American playwright so honored. His only competitors for primacy in American drama are Arthur Miller and Tennessee Williams. Beyond controversy is that O'Neill wrote two of the greatest American dramas: *The Iceman Cometh* (1946) and *Long Day's Journey into Night* (produced 1956). The latter may be *the* American tragedy, challenged only by Miller's *Death of a Salesman*. The primary difference is that O'Neill's drama is the tragedy of a family, while Miller's play is a tragedy of a man in his family, as well as a man trapped in a merciless economic system. O'Neill's power as a dramatist lies in his narrative skills, his understanding of the human need for either vicarious or empirical catharsis, and his intuitive feeling for the paradoxical beauty of tragedy.

Eugene O'Neill was the first American playwright, and one of the few, to do profound battle with ideas. He wrestled with the fate of humankind and saw it as tragic. Human beings are powerless in the vast universe. At best, our struggles are like those of heroic ants. As a patriarchal man he feared what he saw as the castrating power of women and the pitfalls of sexual relationships. His female characters portray a spectrum of women's roles: mothers, submissive wives, aggressive daughters, lovers, heartbreakers, adulterers, prostitutes, and addicts. Significantly, unlike many modern American dramatists, he does not relegate women to the background of the drama or make them mere passive pleasure bearers for men or units for homosocial exchange. Sometimes cruel, selfish, cunning, or vengeful, they nevertheless are often modern Electras and Medeas, and they must be respected.

O'Neill envisioned theater as an educational opportunity in which the American audience could confront, intellectually and emotionally, the fragility of relationships, the biological continuity of life, and the inevitability of death. He introduced Greek mythology and the values of classical Greek drama into the American theater with the Aeschylean trilogy *Mourning Becomes Electra* (1931), the Euripidean *Desire Under the Elms* (1924), and the use of masks in *The Ancient Mariner* (1924—adapted from Coleridge), *The Great God Brown* (1926), and *Lazarus Laughed* (1927). In the latter play O'Neill returned the rituals of Dionysian worship to drama by also employing choruses, great spectacle, and the theme of the individual triumph of life over death through the rebirth of the human spirit.

Eugene Gladstone O'Neill was born in a hotel on Broadway at Forty-Third Street. His father, James O'Neill, was one of the most successful and unhappiest actors of his day. Until he was seven Eugene, his mother, and his older brother James O'Neill Jr. followed James O'Neill around the country on his annual tours of the profitable production he had bought, *The Count of Monte Cristo*. This fabulously successful melodrama made James rich and ruined his career as a serious actor, for the theater audience so identified him with Cristo that they could not accept him in any other role. The family, like a small flock of migratory birds, returned each summer to New London, Connecticut, where James Sr. had bought a summer cottage near the seashore. There Eugene became fascinated with ships and sailors.

Eugene's mother, born Ella Quinlan, had been a young bride from a small Ohio town. She gave birth to three children. A middle child, also a son, had died of measles long before Eugene was born, but Ella never got over the loss. She took solace in devout Catholicism and morphine addiction and had to undergo institutional treatment from time to time. Ella was a failure as a homemaker.

Eugene's elementary schooling took place in Catholic boarding schools in New York City. During his secondary education, at the nondenominational Betts Academy in Stamford, Connecticut, O'Neill began his serious reading of Tolstoy, Dostoyevsky, Kipling, Conrad, Wilde, and the adventurous Jack London. After Betts, O'Neill entered Princeton University. He learned little there, except to drink heavily and to admire the plays of Ibsen. He withdrew after only nine months.

O'Neill, full of Conrad, Kipling, and London, would have chosen an adventurer's life, but instead his father got him a job in 1908 as a clerk in a mail-order jewelry house in New York City. There O'Neill found Greenwich Village, Bowery dives, and characters he would later revivify in his plays. James O'Neill Sr. decided to give Eugene a small allowance that permitted him to live independently for a while and share a studio with two friends so that Eugene could try to develop as a poet. Eugene became a playboy, and in the social swirl he met Kathleen Jenkins, a debutante, who found the handsome, poetic son of a famous actor fascinating. Soon the pair believed they were in love.

Learning of the affair, James Sr. was furious. He was sure Kathleen was a fortune hunter, and since she was a Protestant he could not condone a marriage. James Sr. arranged for his son to join an expedition to Honduras to hunt for gold. The adventure fascinated Eugene, but first he had to get back at his father. Eugene and Kathleen eloped in 1909. O'Neill was not quite twenty-two. Still he sailed to Honduras, where he contracted malaria. Returning to the United

States nine months later, still sick, he learned of the birth of his son, Eugene Gladstone O'Neill Jr., from a newspaper. The senior O'Neill was again angry with Eugene both for having married and for having concealed the marriage. James Sr. made arrangements for a divorce, while Eugene, under his father's strict control, was made stage manager of a touring company.

Back in Connecticut, Eugene could not face his wife or his father, and his mother was in a sanitarium. He decided to ship out to sea on a sailing vessel bound for Buenos Aires. He loved the idea of adventure. Finding the South American city a wide-open place, O'Neill stayed on, working at several dull jobs until he shipped out again in a steamer bound for South Africa. There, because of lack of cash, he was not allowed to land, so he sailed back to Buenos Aires. Totally impoverished, he became a hungry, homeless beggar. Fortunately, he was able to obtain another berth on a steamer, and he made it back to New York. There O'Neill lived in a waterfront saloon until the sea called him back. Now rated as an able-bodied seaman, he sailed on a merchant vessel to Southampton, England, and then back to New York and the saloons.

Now O'Neill's sailing days were over, but they remained fixed in his memory. Meanwhile, his father had pushed through the divorce of Eugene and Kathleen late in 1912. Kathleen neither asked for nor received alimony or child support. After the divorce O'Neill saw Eugene Jr. only once before the child reached age eleven.

O'Neill was malarial, malnourished, and alcoholic. He attempted suicide. Finally, he had to crawl back under his father's wing. He was relegated to playing a bit part in the vaudeville version of *The Count of Monte Cristo*. Returning to the family's Connecticut summer home, O'Neill went to work for the New London *Telegraph*, but he was ill. The hard living of the past had damaged his immune system, and he came down with tuberculosis. In 1912 he was sent to a tuberculosis sanitarium with a death sentence. Frightened at the prospect of an early and painful demise, O'Neill began to take care of himself. He rested, ate well, did not drink alcohol, read extensively in classic literature, and began to write in the genre he liked most: drama.

Released from the sanitarium with the warning that he needed at least another year of rest, O'Neill convinced his father that he should stay on in New London while the family departed for New York City and the theatrical season. With several one-act plays written, O'Neill convinced his father that he had some playwriting talent, and James Sr. sent him to Harvard University in 1914 to enroll in Professor George Pierce Baker's famous playwriting course, 47 Workshop, for one year. After Harvard, O'Neill was a full-time writer. In 1915 O'Neill was back in Greenwich Village, but the following summer he joined the Provincetown Players on Cape Cod, and his professional career as a dramatist was underway with a series of one-act plays based on O'Neill's experiences as a sailor.

O'Neill's one-act dramas showed so much promise that the Washington Square Players in Greenwich Village did one of his plays. The success of *In the Zone* (1918) encouraged the Provincetown Players to move to Greenwich Village and continue productions of O'Neill's manly, stirring, often tragic dramas. Meanwhile, O'Neill met Agnes Bolton, a short-story writer, and they married early in 1918. The next year their son, Shane, was born.

In 1920 O'Neill was ready for Broadway. His first full-length Broadway play was *Beyond the Horizon* (1920), a play in which a heartbroken New England farmer looks forward to the freedom of death. It was awarded a Pulitzer Prize, the first of four that O'Neill would win. Shortly after the play opened, James O'Neill Sr., proud of his younger son for the first time, died of cancer. O'Neill's morphine-addicted mother took hold of herself and gave up the drug, but she died one and one-half years after her husband. Only one and one-half years after that sad event, O'Neill's only surviving sibling, James O'Neill Jr., part-time actor and full-time drunk, died too, at the age of forty-five. In a little over three years Eugene O'Neill had lost all his close relatives. He returned to heavy drinking and his marriage suffered. The couple quarreled continually. In fact, both Eugene and Agnes were heavily into alcohol. O'Neill seems to have connected his alcoholism with his Irishness, and, partly because of this conception, he portrayed the Irish in America as a doomed people.

In 1925 Agnes gave birth to a daughter, Oona. She was O'Neill's last child. Meanwhile, O'Neill's reputation as a playwright grew. In the 1920s his major successes included *The Emperor Jones* (1920), an expressionist drama of an African American—played first by Charles S. Gilpin and then by Paul Robeson—who escapes prison and makes his way to an island in the West Indies, where he meets death as a corrupt leader; *Anna Christie* (1921), the story of a defiant prostitute in a New York waterfront dive; the expressionist drama *The Hairy Ape* (1922), a grim drama about a brutish man who can find no place in society; *All God's Chillun Got Wings* (1924), a sympathetic discussion of the problems of miscegenation that starred Paul Robeson as an African American attorney who marries a white woman; *Desire Under the Elms* (1924), an O'Neill masterpiece of father-son conflict; *The Fountain* (1925), a play about Ponce de Leon; *The Great God Brown* (1926), in which actors speak from behind and to their masks, and which O'Neill is reputed to have named his favorite play; *Marco's Millions* (1928), a satiric study of the eternal businessperson who places commercial success over personal relationships; *Strange Interlude* (1928), a nine-act masterpiece in which a heroine, seemingly out of the pages of Virginia Woolf, sees the relationships in her life as interludes in the journey toward God or oblivion; and *Dynamo* (1929), an unsuccessful satire on the American worship of science that featured a hydroelectric plant on stage.

In 1926, while living in Bermuda, O'Neill had an affair with the actor Carlotta Monterey, a great beauty. He left his wife in the winter of 1927, and the next March he eloped with Carlotta, fleeing to France, where they spent the next three years. They married as soon as the divorce from Agnes was finalized in 1929. The divorce was acrimonious. As a result O'Neill was estranged from Shane and Oona, both of whom he cut out of his will.

Eugene Jr., of whom O'Neill was proud, had a brilliant career as a Harvard University professor of classical Greek literature, especially drama, but his life was unhappy, and he committed suicide three years before his father's death in 1953. Carlotta and Eugene's marriage was difficult and unstable, but they managed to stay together for the rest of his life.

O'Neill's greatest play before *The Iceman Cometh* and *Long Day's Journey into Night* commenced production in the 1930s. *Mourning Becomes Electra* (1931), O'Neill's version of *The Oresteia* of Aeschylus, set at the time of the American Civil War, was O'Neill's last triumph until *The Iceman Cometh* in 1946. O'Neill's sentimental comedy *Ah, Wilderness!*, his most successful attempt at a genre he seldom tried, followed in 1933. Although frequently revived, it is not a great play, for O'Neill's artistic vision was essentially a tragic one. *Days Without End*, a miracle play, failed in 1934, just as O'Neill fell ill with Parkinson's disease, which became progressively worse until finally, in 1944, the shaking prevented him from writing.

The Iceman Cometh in 1946 did little to bring O'Neill to the public eye. A 1956 revival Off Broadway did that. *A Moon for the Misbegotten* (first produced in 1947 but written in 1941) connects with the later-produced *Long Day's Journey into Night* in that the older brother character of the latter play, James Tyrone Jr., first appears here. His oedipal relationship with his mother is explored. *A Moon for the Misbegotten* was the last new O'Neill play produced in his lifetime. Posthumously produced dramas not only rescued his reputation but carried it to a height surpassing what it was when he received the Nobel Prize in 1936. The great American family tragedy *Long Day's Journey into Night*, O'Neill's dramatic autobiography, was produced in 1956. *A Touch of the Poet* (1957), the story of a vain and overly proud Irish American who is humiliated, presents a hero who lives off his past as did both James O'Neill Sr. and O'Neill's brother, James O'Neill Jr. *More Stately Mansions* (1962) looks back to America in the 1830s. *Hughie* (1964), a long one-act monologue in which a small-time gambler faces entropy, ennui, and the fact of life's randomness, has proved fresh for new generations.

At the time of his death from Parkinson's disease, Eugene and Carlotta were reduced to living in a Boston hotel. Supposedly, O'Neill's last words were a sardonic epitaph: "Born in a hotel room, and—Goddammit—died in one!"

O'Neill's plays, full-length and one-act, number nearly sixty. Besides his four Pulitzers and the 1936 Nobel Prize, O'Neill received an honorary doctorate of literature from Yale University in 1926 and many other honors.

Along with one or two of his realistic plays such as *Anna Christie* and *The Iceman Cometh*, O'Neill's autobiographical plays in which, perhaps out of guilt, he tried to repossess time passed and mend relationships long beyond repair, are his finest achievements. Whatever may be said of O'Neill as the twenty-first century moves on, the first modern American playwright was indeed loved by Melpomene, the muse of tragedy.

• • •

O'Neill's dramas can be categorized in different ways: by subject, chronology, thematic order, and stylistic pattern. Here the plays are organized and discussed in a manner that employs all four categories, moving from one to another to aid understanding of the nature, scope, and direction of the O'Neill canon.

Sea Plays

Bound East for Cardiff (1916)

Bound East for Cardiff is a spellbinding one-act play about Yank, a sailor dying from a fall on the SS *Glencairn*, a tramp steamer, who talks to his friend, an Irishman named Driscoll, and other shipmates about the life ashore that he had always wanted to live. Death comes in the guise of a pretty woman dressed in black. This play was O'Neill's first produced drama.

Thirst (1916)

Written in 1914 or earlier and considered by many to be O'Neill's first completed play, *Thirst* is a one-act play in which three survivors of a shipwreck, a beautiful dancer, a gentleman passenger, and a black sailor, are going mad from thirst as their raft floats on a shark-infested sea. The plot is melodramatic, but the characterization is strong and economical. The racist gentleman and the woman believe the sailor has hidden some drinking water, but he hasn't. She tries to bribe the sailor with jewelry and sex to no avail. When she dies, the sailor wants to use her body to save the gentleman and himself, but, horrified, the gentleman fights with the sailor, and when the former is stabbed, they both fall into the sea, where the sharks are waiting for their meal.

Fog (1917)

Three people are adrift in a lifeboat off the Grand Banks of Newfoundland in *Fog,* a one-act play. They are the survivors of a passenger steamer sunk by a collision with an iceberg. One person is a socialistic poet who is tired of life. The second person is a selfish business man. The third is a silent woman whose baby cried when the ship went down and so she and the baby were heard and picked up.

The baby has died in the night and the men soon find out that the women has also died from the cold. The boat drifts into a field of icebergs. They hear a rescue ship in the fog. The businessman wants to shout for help, but the poet insists that they remain quiet so as not to endanger the people on the searching vessel. A boat comes to them anyway and the businessman, ashamed of his cowardice, takes credit for not endangering the ship. Supernaturally, the rescuing sailor heard the baby crying long after the infant was dead. The poet, despairing of life, chooses to stay in the lifeboat with the dead.

In the Zone (1917)

In the Zone, a one-act play, is about a sailor aboard the SS *Glencairn* who has a small black box that his shipmates think contains evidence that he is a spy and that the ship could be torpedoed. They go through his gear and find the box, but, to their embarrassment, it only contains sentimental letters from a girl he loved but who left him because of his drinking.

The Long Voyage Home (1917)

The crew of the SS *Glencairn* in this one-act play have been paid off in London and are drinking in a waterfront dive. Olson, a Swede trying to stay sober, is happy that his sailing days are over and is planning to go home, but he is given a drugged drink and shanghaied aboard the SS *Aminda*, a hell ship bound for Cape Horn and two years at sea.

Ile (1917)

The captain's cabin of a whaling ship locked in ice is the setting of this one-act play. The crew, desiring to get home, attempts a mutiny, but the indomitable captain puts it down. His wife, accompanying him on the voyage, is driven mad by the ice and loneliness when he refuses to turn back.

Where the Cross Is Made (1918)

In a room in a California seaside house fitted out like a captain's cabin, an old captain awaits the return of a treasure ship, which in fact has been lost at sea. His son is about to have him committed to an insane asylum because he and the neighbors are afraid of him. When the captain hallucinates that the treasure ship has returned, the also unstable son "sees" his father's long-drowned shipmates and believes the old man, who suddenly dies of shock. The son then becomes the madman to be committed. In 1921 O'Neill wrote and produced a full-length version of *Where the Cross Is Made* under the title *Gold.*

The Moon of the Caribbees (1918)

The crew of the SS *Glencairn* in this one-act play joyously await prostitutes from a West Indian Island coming out to the anchored ship with rum. When the women arrive they provoke a fight, and a sailor is knifed to death. The women are shuffled off the vessel, and the seamen sadly listen to singing coming from the island they will not visit. Here and elsewhere in the early one-act plays O'Neill depicts the hard drinking and the hard living of "fo'c'sle" (forecastle) shipmates, making use of the experiences of his adventurous youth.

Realistic Plays

Before Breakfast (1916)

O'Neill's first-produced, nonseafaring, realistic play is a one-act dramatization of a dysfunctional marriage that is reminiscent of August Strindberg's *The Father* (1887). The cruelly nagging, controlling wife succeeds in driving the husband to suicide.

The Sniper (1917)

The Sniper, a slight one-act drama, is an antiwar play in which a peasant youth is drawn into the maelstrom of battle.

The Rope (1918)

In *The Rope,* a one-act play, a miserly, old, religious fanatic battles with his married daughter and hates his son-in-law and grand-daughter because they are Catholics. The daughter was the product of his first marriage. His first wife died, and a second marriage produced a son, but he ran off as did his mother. The grandfather has strung a rope in his barn for the renegade son, who has stolen some of his money. He wants his son, Luke, to hang himself if he ever returns.

When the son shows up, it turns out he has been to sea for five years, and now he plans to torture his father so he will reveal the hiding place of the rest of his money. The son has taught his niece to skip coins into the ocean. She accidentally discovers the gold coins and skips them all into the sea. The money is gone, and the play ends with the old man about to be tortured by the son and son-in-law.

The Dreamy Kid (1919)

This one-act play is the story of a black gangster, who has killed and is fleeing from the law, and his relationship with his disappointed mother, who is on her death bed. *The Dreamy Kid* was the first play to give African American actors access to the white professional theater. *All God's Chillun Got Wings* and *The Emperor Jones* continued O'Neill's groundbreaking attempts to liberalize and integrate the American stage.

Beyond the Horizon (1920)

Beyond the Horizon, O'Neill's first Broadway play and first Pulitzer Prize winner is the tragedy of a young New England farmer, Robert Mayo, who is a dreamer. His brother, Andrew, is stronger, better looking, and more competent. Robert hopes to find O'Neill-like adventure on his uncle's sailing vessel. The brothers are in love with the same woman, Ruth Atkins, and the day prior to Robert's departure she prevails upon him to marry her. Andrew then takes Roger's berth and departs.

After three years Andrew returns. Meanwhile Robert has made a mess of his life. The farm is failing, his marriage is a disaster, and he only cares for his daughter, Mary. His wife compares him unfavorably to his brother, but, in fact, Andrew has not profited from his adventure, and he has turned into a hard character. Ruth tells him that she has made a mistake and should have married him, but Andrew informs her that he forgot about her long ago.

Five years go by. The child has died, and Robert is fatally ill with tuberculosis. Ruth cares for nothing. The farm is ruined. Andrew returns and castigates Ruth for her behavior, for he has always loved his brother. He insists that she tell her dying husband that she has loved only him, but she defers until it is too late. The play ends with Andrew's curse on Ruth for not telling his brother the lie that would have eased his death.

New York audiences were enthralled by the raw language, the stark realism of the play, the verisimilitude of the characterization, and the certainty of the young writer's philosophical convictions.

Anna Christie (1921)

O'Neill's tough, defiant, and complex heroine Anna is a remarkable portrait of a prostitute in that for the first time on the American stage a woman in the sex trade is presented sympathetically and as a real human being. The role is an outstanding one in the repertoire for women. O'Neill was awarded his second Pulitzer Prize for *Anna Christie*.

Anna is the daughter of Chris Christopherson, a New York barge captain who hangs out in a South Street dive, Johnny-the-Priests. A letter arrives from twenty-year-old Anna, stating that she is on her way to join him in New York. She was raised on a farm in

Minnesota and at the age of sixteen was seduced by a cousin. Fleeing the farm, she became a prostitute and a heavy drinker in a Midwestern city. Now she wants to be with her father.

Chris takes her onboard the barge, and she is regenerated by life on the water. Her health improves, and she begins to have some faith in men again. One day, off Provincetown, Massachusetts, Chris rescues a group of seamen who have been drifting in an open boat after their ship went down. One of the men, a rough, burly Irishman named Mat Burke, falls in love with Anna and asks her to marry him. Chris is jealous. He doesn't want to lose his daughter, and he precipitates a fight with Mat.

Anna realizes that the two patriarchal rivals are fighting over her as if she were property. Distressed because the fight reminds her of her previous experiences with men, Anna decides to confess that she was seduced on the farm and had worked in a house of prostitution. She tells Mat that she loves him, but he, unable to deal with the news, is disgusted with her and goes ashore. Chris joins him and they drink together. Anna waits on the barge for a decision about her life and finally plans to resume her old profession as the only way she can survive.

In order to prevent that, Chris signs on a vessel sailing to Capetown, South Africa, with his wages going to Anna. Meanwhile, Mat has signed on to the same vessel. The news that her father and former suitor would be sailing on the same steamer amuses Anna. Mat comes back, and she informs him that she hated the men who bought her services. All she wants is the true love of one man. Chris realizes that in abandoning his child, he was responsible for her fate, and now he is glad that she and Mat are reconciled. Anna will await their return and make a home for father and husband, but the sea may have tragic plans for them all.

Anna Christie is a raw, slice-of-life drama. Marriage and a possible happy ending does not cleanse the waterfront or the world of filth, nor does it compensate for cruelties perpetrated in the past.

Exorcism (1920), *Diff'rent* (1920), *The Straw* (1921),
The First Man (1922), and *Welded* (1924)

Five one-act plays that were unsuccessful were produced in the early 1920s. *Exorcism,* whose hero fails in a suicide attempt, shows how life can be appreciated after one almost loses it. *Diff'rent* portrays a spinster whose life declines after she rejects a suitor when she was young because he had not led a sexually pure life. In the end she falls prey to a con man.

The Straw, actually written in 1918 but not produced until 1921, chronicles in a fictional way O'Neill's experience with romance in the tuberculosis sanitarium. *The First Man* finds a young couple unable to deal with the problem of an unwanted pregnancy. The husband is a scientist who hates the idea that his important work will be disturbed by a child. The mother dies, and relatives blacken her name by hinting that she was immoral. *Welded* indicates some autobiographical influence as a moody young playwright and a flighty actor engage, à la Strindberg again, in the war of the sexes.

All God's Chillun Got Wings (1924)

An African American, Jim Harris, and a white woman, Ella Downey, marry and have problems. But *All God's Chillun Got Wings* is not really about miscegenation. It is a psychological drama, showing the way a man may be destroyed by possessiveness. Again there is a debt to Strindberg's misogyny. Jim and Ella grew up in innocence together as friends in a city slum area. When they mature, Jim, an intelligent man and a good student, is trying to become a lawyer. Ella has become the mistress of a gangster named Mickey. When she gives birth to an illegitimate child, he deserts her.

Compassionate Jim marries Ella, but instead of feeling gratitude, Ella's inherent racism emerges, because she must exert some superiority over her achieving husband and racial bigotry is her means. She attempts to prevent him from rising high and becoming an attorney. Jim needs her love and is affected by her racial attacks to the point that he doubts his abilities and fails. She goes mad and tries to murder Jim. Then she regresses into childhood. Now she is Jim's childhood girlfriend in the slums and in love with him. She is fully dependent on him, and he is tied for life to a mentally ill person. O'Neill, here the naturalist, makes no social judgment on mixed marriage. Ella and Jim are ordinary human beings caught up in the tidal flow of modern urban life. Paul Robeson was the first actor to play Jim.

The Iceman Cometh (written in 1939; produced in 1946)

One of O'Neill's greatest dramas, *The Iceman Cometh* is a New York waterfront drama set in Harry Hope's establishment, the Last Chance Bar, where derelicts and those defeated by life drink and dream. The play is four hours long.

Harry is a former ward heeler politician. A young man, Dan Parritt, new to the seedy environment, is a beachcomber like O'Neill was in his youth. He struggles to find truth and to deal with his hatred for his mother along with concomitant feelings of guilt. Other regulars in this alcoholic dream factory include a newspaper man, a Harvard-educated lawyer, and an anarchist. A fast-talking traveling hardware salesman named Hickey joins the ensemble, determined to strip the gathering of its illusions. He is drunk because his wife is with the Iceman, implying she is having an affair.

Hickey finally reveals that he has killed his wife. The Iceman is death. Hickey really sells self-deception, equivocation, hypocrisy, and death. He has talked himself into believing that he murdered his wife to save her from the pain of living with him. In other words, he killed his wife because he loved her, but the truth is that he did it because he hated her. He tries to get the anarchist to talk the young man into suicide, which O'Neill had tried as a youth. In O'Neill's barroom, as in Jean-Paul Sartre's hotel room in *No Exit* (1944), conversation is confession and hell is a confined space. The ultimate tormented confession is the author's.

The Iceman Cometh is a naturalistic drama about the self-destructive impulses that lead to disintegration, something O'Neill understood quite well. Harry Hope's bar is like the flophouse of Maxim Gorky's *Lower Depths* (1902), a dumpster for the broken.

In the end the police arrest Hickey, but the derelicts have learned nothing, although the audience indeed has learned much about life. This last play of O'Neill's produced in his lifetime is a crescendo of despair. It shares with the plays of Bertolt Brecht a degree of audience alienation. There is no love or caring within the dramatic triangle of author, characters, and audience. Yet the power and the truth of the drama draws us into the vortex of understanding.

A Touch of the Poet (1957)

A Touch of the Poet is set in 1828 in a village tavern near Boston. As with *Long Day's Journey into Night,* the subject is family relations. Cornelius Melody, the tavern owner, struggles to find the lie that can convince him to keep on living. Melody is an Irish-born immigrant of peasant background who once was an officer in the British army. He is married to Nora, a widow who he feels is his social inferior. Yet she works very hard keeping the tavern operating.

Con thinks of himself as an aristocrat, and he tries to speak like one. Nora supports him in his fantasy, as she would do anything to make him happy. Con's beautiful daughter, Sara, is disgusted with him because he mistreats her mother and because he is a drunkard.

Con also dresses like an English aristocrat, and he owns a valuable thoroughbred mare that symbolizes his "aristocratic background." When his daughter is spurned as a possible daughter-in-law by rich Yankee neighbors, the Harfords, he sets out to avenge his honor with violence but is beaten by Harford servants and the police. Humiliated, his fantasy is destroyed. Con shoots the horse. He would have shot himself too, but he didn't think he was worth a bullet. He is no longer an aristocrat in his own mind. The romantic Irishman is gone too. Now he returns to his peasant roots and dialect.

Nora is unhappy that her husband, whom she dearly loves, has lost all spirit. Cornelius needs her love. Now he is more caring toward his "peasant" wife, but his daughter secures her own future by seducing Simon Harford. They will marry despite their parents. Simon, at least, is not coarse, for he has "a touch of the poet in him."

O'Neill is saying that everyone needs a touch of the poet. Illusion is risky, but stark, existential reality is unbearable. Perhaps the only future worth living for is the past.

Hughie (produced 1958)

Partly because of its concision, *Hughie* is arguably O'Neill's finest one-act drama. Set in 1928 in the lobby of a run-down mid-Manhattan hotel, *Hughie* is an obituary-like semimonologue in which a small-time gambler named Erie Smith talks to a new night clerk about the deceased night clerk, Hughie. Smith likes to think of himself as one of "the big shots," and he boasts of his gangland connections. Smith misses Hughie, who was his listener. He feels that his gambling luck has changed for the worse because Hughie was a good luck charm for him. Also, Hughie enjoyed a vicarious life, identifying himself with Smith's world. But Hughie's replacement is uninterested until Smith mentions a big-time gangster whose name the new clerk knows. Now he is impressed, and Smith's luck changes for the better as now he has a listener again. All people needs friends on whom they may project their idealized lives, knowing that the friends understand the need.

More Stately Mansions (1962)

The title comes from a line in the introspective poem "The Chambered Nautilus" by Oliver Wendell Holmes: "Build thee more stately mansions, O my soul." *More Stately Mansions* is a sequel to *A Touch of the Poet*. It is October 1832, four years after *A Touch of the Poet*. Con has just died. Sara Melody, who has parlayed her beauty and sexuality into a wealthy and prestigious marriage, is rich now, but she has savaged her husband by scheming and caused him to lose that touch of the poet that distinguished him from most other men. She has treated Simon in much the same way she dealt with Con.

Simon, not seen in *A Touch of the Poet*, is a major figure in *More Stately Mansions*. Buffeted by the battle over him waged by his mother and his wife, he is a sensuous man in need of, and subject to, the sexual power his wife has over him. Erotically, Sara plays the role of prostitute and receives payment in the form of shares in his business, a practice that ruins the company. As in other instances, O'Neill portrays a young man torn by the Madonna/whore complex. Like Sara, Simon's mother played roles for him when he was a child, alternating from good queen or fairy to evil queen or fairy. In the end, the mother and wife join forces against him and seem as one to Simon. The playwright's misogyny manifests itself in the Strindbergian view that a male-female relationship is always a power war, with the woman, the more ruthless of the pair, dominant and not bound by notions of chivalry or gentility. O'Neill's women seem to have most of the advantages.

In the end Sara has become corrupt and dissipated. She has grown into her father: a caricature of the gentry. Simon and his mother are near to madness, and Sara, now realizing how she has harmed the father of her children, vows to care for him as her mother did for Con after his fall.

Because of the complexities of this play and the limited use of thoughts spoken as asides, directors have developed several different versions of it.

Expressionistic Plays

Eugene O'Neill expressed his inner tensions and the problems of modern humankind by breaking realism into dissolving images and fragmentary scenes that represent the confusions of troubled minds and the aimlessness of deracinated individuals.

The Emperor Jones (1920)

O'Neill's first long expressionist play, with offstage drums beating the rhythm of the drama, *The Emperor Jones* symbolizes the fall of modern man in the jungle that is contemporary society. Brutus Jones, an African American sleeping car porter who has been imprisoned in the United States because of a fight, has escaped to an island in the West Indies, where, presumably because of his intelligence, great physical strength, and wider knowledge, he has made himself emperor of the island during a revolution. Jones has appointed a disreputable white trader, Smithers, as his advisor.

Jones becomes a tyrant, but he has convinced the native people that he can only be killed by a silver bullet. Of course, this is how he dies in the end. A series of fantasy scenes enrich the theatricality of the drama. Charles S. Gilpin and Paul Robeson, great African American actors who first played Jones, did much to make this play an American classic and to make O'Neill famous.

The Hairy Ape (1922)

A nightmarish drama, *The Hairy Ape* is the story of a rough-hewn coal stoker who works in the hellish boiler room on a luxury liner. Yank Smith is almost a part of the machines he serves. Like Brutus Jones, he is an outcast from American society. He represents an "other"—someone suspect, dangerous, and thought of as less than human. When a do-gooding society woman, Mildred Douglas, on a "slumming" visit to the liner's boiler room, sees Yank she shouts:

"Take me away! Oh! The filthy beast!" In a phrase she dehumanizes Yank. Not only is he not of her class, he is not of her exalted species.

Yank is hurt by the young woman's reaction to the sight of him. He hurls his shovel at the hastily departing visitors from the world above. Although Yank is angered, he is sensitized by the event, and he wonders just what he is worth in the world. He had taken pride in his work, in his ability to move the tons of coal that powered the mighty vessel.

Ashore, Yank roams Fifth Avenue, looking for Mildred so he can revenge himself in some way, so he can find his dignity and self-worth again. He gets into a street fight and is clubbed down by the New York police. Taken to prison, the other prisoners mock him and call him "ape." The cell he is in symbolizes the confinements of his life: class, lack of education, work in a boiler room.

Yank is advised to find revenge by joining the Wobblies, the Industrial Workers of the World, and he goes to a union meeting. He vents his anger and, misunderstood, is thrown out of the union hall.

Yank goes to the zoo, tries to commune with the gorilla in his cage, and attempts to release the animal. The gorilla misunderstands, crushes Yank in a vicious hug, and throws the broken Yank into the cage. He dies in his final cage.

The Hairy Ape is a bleak expressionist drama depicting the animosity some of the privileged have for those they consider beneath them. The play provokes deep sympathy for the trapped human whose "crimes" are ugliness, lack of education, and poverty. O'Neill's rough language and powerful characterization create a rumble of anger against privilege.

The Fountain (1925)

The Fountain, a play about Ponce de Leon's pursuit of the fountain of youth, begins in Granada as a young, ambitious de Leon accepts the surrender of the Moors. A woman who loves him feels disdained because he loves Spain above everything, and he intends to sail with Columbus and conquer foreign lands for his country. His comrades are not as noble as de Leon. They are cruel, ignorant, and without a true understanding of Christianity.

Ponce de Leon does sail with Columbus, and after twenty years he becomes governor of Puerto Rico. Now he is old and gray. He falls in love with a beautiful eighteen-year-old girl and is intrigued when a captured Indian chief tells him of a fountain of youth waiting to be discovered. He thinks that if he can restore his youth the girl will love him. He orders the Indian chief tortured to reveal the location of the fountain. The chief, Nano, pilots de Leon's fleet to the Florida coast. Later, de Leon realizes he has been betrayed. Indians attack and he is wounded but survives. In the end, back in Cuba, he has become spiritual. A courtyard fountain turns into a gushing edifice and becomes a symbol of the immortality of life itself.

The Fountain is a panoramic, sometimes expressionistic, epic drama whose theatricality masks its lack of profundity. Presenting the search for the fountain of youth as a man's search for a purpose to his life is hardly original or provocative. To O'Neill's credit he portrays Spanish occupiers as they were, rapacious, and he portrays the native Caribbean people as noble.

The Great God Brown (1926)

The Great God Brown is a highly literary play as well as a visually fascinating drama. In this play, a favorite of O'Neill's, the characters wear masks. Two young businessmen, William A. Brown and Dion Anthony, destined to inherit the business of their fathers, are in love with Margaret. She loves the Dion she sees in the cynical mask he wears, but in reality he is a poetic, tortured soul. Without his mask on he is repulsive to her. They marry, and Dion gives up the business world to become a painter.

Dion is plagued with wondering who the real Dion is. He fails as an artist and returns to the world of commerce to work for Brown. Dion soon dies, and Brown takes Dion's mask and his wife.

The sexuality of their embracing of what seemed illicit love shocked the audience of the 1920s. When the deception is revealed Brown is killed. Margaret, blind to the nature and qualities of the two men with whom she has lived, one good and one evil, now reveres the mask of Dion. Bidding the real world good-bye, she devotes the remainder of her days to memories of her life before marriage.

The great god Brown is neither great nor a god. The title is ironic. Brown—such an ordinary name—is a lusting, jealous, common philistine, filled with envy for the creative soul that his alter ego, Dion, possessed.

Lazarus Laughed (1928)

O'Neill called *Lazarus Laughed* "a play for the imaginative theater." It is his version of the ritual theater of fifth-century Athenians. In *The Great God Brown* O'Neill had experimented with the possibilities of variegated personae in the donning, exchanging, and doffing of masks. *Lazarus Laughed* is a continuation of the former play in that it is based on Dion's last speech on the hope of resurrection. But unlike *The Great God Brown*, *Lazarus Laughed* is both a religious play and a spectacle requiring 150 actors for a Greek chorus, a crowd, and at least 200 masks. The play calls for 420 roles. In John 11:1–44, Jesus comes to the body of Lazarus, and because Jesus is "the resurrection and the life," Lazarus returns from the world of the dead.

Lazarus Laughed begins after the resurrection, opening in the home of the restored man. He and Miriam, his wife, must confront a hateful crowd that wants his life because he is a follower of the already crucified Jesus. When he learns that the Romans have not only executed Jesus but also Lazarus's parents and sisters, Lazarus laughs as he is led away to prison.

People begin to think that Lazarus is the Greek god Dionysus, a god that can come back to life. In Rome the emperor, Tiberius, calls the Senate together because of the seeming threat from Lazarus and his followers, who are just outside the city.

Miriam fears that the Romans will kill her husband, who, strangely, appears to be growing younger. But Miriam is poisoned by a courtesan who loves Lazarus and is jealous. She laughs with Lazarus as she dies, for she knows the faithful have eternal life.

A main function of *Lazarus Laughed* is to affirm and promulgate O'Neill's belief in the eternal life of the individual soul. At the play's end the tortured Lazarus is a martyr in an amphitheater, tied to a stake and burned alive. He laughs as he is dying. The courtesan jumps into the flame, and Tiberius seems converted to the martyr's faith, and so he laughs as Lazarus's worst enemy, Caligula, strangles him to death. Caligula is instantly repentant and begs Lazarus to save him from death. The expiring Lazarus says, "There is no Death."

Laughter is a life force. It unifies humanity. It is a gift from God. Love and laughter always go hand in hand.

Strange Interlude (1928)

Pulitzer Prize-winning *Strange Interlude,* a nine-act play that takes most of a full day or two evenings to perform, is the masterpiece of O'Neill's expressionistic plays. Through Freudian imagery and situations, as well as asides and soliloquies that reveal thoughts and feelings, the playwright creates the theatrical equivalent of a modern stream-of-consciousness novel. Instead of physical masks, the face a character presents to the world is her or his mask, and the true self is revealed by soliloquy. In *Strange Interlude* O'Neill broke new ground in discussing abortion and adultery, then socially taboo subjects.

Nina Leeds has fallen out with her father because he persuaded Gordon, her fiancé, to postpone marriage until he returns from army service in World War I. An aviator, he is shot down and killed. Gordon was the only man whom Nina could love fully. She grieves because they never had a chance to consummate their love. She is bitter and sometimes irrational.

While serving as a nurse in a military hospital, she becomes sexually promiscuous with young soldiers she feels are about to be killed. There she finds that three men have fallen in love with her. One is Edmund, a doctor primarily devoted to his career. Another is Charles, a writer who is overly shy. The third is Sam, a weak man whom Nina marries. He has a family history of mental illness, and Nina secretly aborts her pregnancy, and then becomes pregnant with Edmund's child. Edmund wants her to divorce Sam and marry him. She declines, and her son grows up fond of Sam. When Sam dies eleven years later, she marries Charles the writer because it is too late to marry Edmund. The relationship with Charles reverts back to her earliest relationship, that of a father and daughter. For all the characters, and for O'Neill, the happenings in the past are merely interludes, as all human beings only wait for desire to pass.

Like an onion being peeled, Nina Leeds's character is revealed in its several facets as manifested through her relationships. She is by turns daughter, wife, mistress, and mother. The stimuli for the psychological development of these roles are the different men in her life, each of whom she experienced in a different way. Nina's psychological fragmentation comes about because of the death of her first love, Gordon. He was the only man who aroused all facets of her personality. The rest of her life is a pursuit of a fulfillment that is impossible for her to achieve. Her husband, Sam, her lover, Edward, and her timid friend, Charles, can only meet her needs in parts. In her middle age Nina's son, also named Gordon, seemingly is able to provide the kind of love she needs, but he must perforce find his own life with a young woman.

Nina's consolation for her realization that no love is all-fulfilling is found in prayer and a Buddhistic acceptance of fate.

Days Without End (1934)

Days Without End is O'Neill's attempt to come to grips with his early indoctrination into Catholicism. He wanted to dramatize the struggles between faith and science, between belief in God and the skeptical reasoning mind, and, ultimately, between good and evil. The play was not a success.

The main character, John Loving, is dichotomized into two different men, John and Loving, instead of a man and his mask. John is a superego, the idealistic persona. Loving is the base id. The two versions of John Loving, the two personalities, are in conflict with each other.

The binary John Loving works for a business firm that is doing poorly in the Depression. John is an orphan, the son of devout Catholics. He was once religious but has fallen away from religion. John's uncle, a priest, visits the office. Father Baird was John's guardian for a while, but had to leave him at an early age, and John has grown up without much supervision. He has been a writer and has married Elsa. Love is his religion now, as he, as Loving, has been avoiding God. Elsa has been married before, unhappily, and she believes that John has healed her wounds. But when Elsa learns of her husband's personal story and his past infidelities, she falls seriously ill. Like an angel and a devil, John and Loving struggle, but John embraces the cross and Elsa is saved.

Days Without End is a tortured play by a tortured writer. Despite reason, religion must be embraced. Only God can save despairing human beings and the writer himself.

Classical Plays

Classical Greek tragedy influenced O'Neill in various ways, but two of his greatest plays relied heavily on his knowledge of Aeschylus, Sophocles, and Euripides. O'Neill found tragedy to be his most natural mode.

Desire Under the Elms (1924)

Based on both Euripides' *Hippolytus* and *Phèdre*, Racine's version of the father-son-young stepmother triangle, *Desire Under the Elms* moves that explosive mixture to nineteenth-century New England. Seventy-five-year-old Ephrian Cabot, a hardworking, hard-driving farmer, has been married and widowed twice. He works the farm with two lumpish sons from his first marriage and a sensitive son from his second. The play implies that Cabot has worked his first two wives to death. The youngest son, Eben, is sure that is how his mother died.

Cabot marries a third wife, a young widow determined to inherit the valuable farm upon the death of her elderly bridegroom. Like two Esaus with a Jacob, the older brothers sell their shares in a potential inheritance for enough money to get them to the gold rush in California. Cleverly, the young wife, Abbe, seduces Eben and becomes pregnant, expecting that she and her child will become Cabot's heirs. Cabot brags to his neighbors about his seeming virility when the child is born, but the community is sure that he has been cuckolded.

Infuriated because Abbe used him, Eben denounces her, but she now loves him and to prove that love she murders her child. Eben calls the sheriff in, but he has come to love Abbe and wishes to share her fate. He falsely confesses that he had a hand in the death of the child, and he and Abbe are taken off to prison, trial, and probable execution, while Cabot, like an Old Testament patriarch, is left to struggle alone on the stony fields.

The tragedy seemed so palpable and sexually charged to early audiences that productions got into trouble with police. But the father-son conflict, so universal and archetypal, has rarely been better portrayed than in O'Neill's drama. Cabot, Eben, and Abbe are choice acting roles.

Mourning Becomes Electra (a Trilogy) (1931)

Mourning Becomes Electra is O'Neill's most ambitious dramatic effort. It is a milestone and a monument of modern American drama. Again O'Neill adapts a classical Greek tragedy to nineteenth-century New England. This time the model is the *Oresteia*, Aeschylus's trilogy about the murder of Agamemnon upon his return from the Trojan War by his wife and her lover, and the revenge of his son and his daughter on the murderers. Now the war is the Civil War and the location is New England.

The first play, *The Homecoming*, has the wife of the rich businessman-war hero-Union Army general Ezra Mannon, Christine, having a love affair with the sea captain Adam Brant, a young cousin of the general. The daughter of the Mannons, Lavinia, hates her mother but reveres her father. Lavinia suspects that an affair is going on between her mother and Brant. Cleverly, she gets Brant to confess the liaison.

The Mannons also have a son, Orin, who is much closer to his mother than to his father, a fact the elder Mannon resents. Upon the general's return, he is poisoned by his wife. But Lavinia discovers that her father has been murdered, and she cries out to his spirit to help her with the dreadful situation she is in.

In the second play, *The Hunted*, Lavinia informs her brother, who has also returned from the war, that their mother has poisoned their father so she could marry her lover. With great difficulty she convinces Orin that they must avenge their father by killing Brant and thus destroying their mother's life. Orin will only agree if there is proof. Orin and Lavinia follow Christine to Brant's ship, docked in Boston harbor, where they overhear the lovers making future plans. When Christine leaves the vessel, Orin, convinced of the affair, shoots Brant to death. The brother and sister make the murder look like the result of a robbery. When Christine learns of her lover's death, she has nothing to live for and so takes her own life with a gun. Orin is filled with guilt, believing himself the murderer of his beloved mother.

In the third play, *The Haunted*, Orin is overwhelmed with guilt, despite the fact that a year has passed and he and his sister have made a long sea voyage. He believes that his overly close relationship with his mother has been a cause for her hatred of his father and the ensuing deaths. Lavinia tries to convince her brother, whom she now controls, that he has actually saved his mother, a poisoner, from hanging. Meanwhile Lavinia has become engaged to a cousin, but Orin is so attached to his sister now that he threatens to expose her if she marries. Orin is deranged, as if he were pursued by the Furies. He fears that Lavinia will now poison him so that she can marry. Finally, Lavinia convinces Orin that he must take his own life. He shoots himself, making it look like his death was an accident.

But Lavinia cannot marry after all. There are too many ghosts in her life. She sends her fiancé away, boards up the windows of the family mansion, and, again in mourning attire, awaits her own death as the last of the Mannons.

The play's situations are melodramatically exciting, and O'Neill's dialogue, and especially the soliloquy, are at their best. Puritan New England is shown as a place of hypocrisy, destructive passion, and psychological incest. Perhaps *Mourning Becomes Electra* is an Irish Catholic's revenge on the "Yankees" who looked down their noses at his family when he was a youth. The full *Mourning Becomes Electra,* written in the trilogy format as Aeschylus, Sophocles, and Euripides wrote their tragedies, takes at least five hours to perform.

Autobiographical Plays

Many of O'Neill's plays have autobiographical aspects and disguised family portraits. His mother, father, and brother are often present in various roles. But two of O'Neill's late plays are very close to his family story, and they are among his very best work.

Long Day's Journey into Night
(written 1939–42; produced 1956)

Long Day's Journey into Night, O'Neill's penultimate masterpiece, won him, posthumously, his fourth Pulitzer Prize. Unified in time, place, and action, like a classical or neoclassical drama, the play takes place during one day and evening in the Tyrone family summer home near the beach in New London, Connecticut, in 1912. James Tyrone Sr. (based on O'Neill's actor-father James O'Neill Sr.) is a successful Irish-born actor who drinks excessively. His wife, Mary (based on O'Neill's mother), is a religious woman who is a morphine addict because, after the difficult birth of her last-born son, Edmund, she was given too much morphine by a quack doctor called in by her miserly husband. Jamie Tyrone (based on O'Neill's older brother James O'Neill Jr.) is a drunkard, a womanizer, and a wastrel with a strong oedipal fixation and consequently a hidden hatred for his younger, sickly, but brilliant and sensitive brother, Edmund (Eugene O'Neill). The men are addicts too—alcoholics—but neither they nor the author really acknowledge this fact.

In the course of the play Edmund comes to know why his mother is an addict, how complicated and disappointing his father's life has been, and that his brother both loves and hates him simultaneously. Edmund will, as O'Neill did, go to a sanitarium to recover from tuberculosis. The great Irish American family nightmare ends at midnight and in despair. But during the Tyrone *Walpurgisnacht*, Edmund will come to understand and pity his family, and also love them as never before.

Moon for the Misbegotten (written 1941; produced 1947)

Written at the same time as *Long Day's Journey into Night*, the tragicomedy *A Moon for the Misbegotten* is a part of O'Neill's personal family saga. Set in 1923, it is a sequel to *Long Day's Journey into Night*. The central character, Jim Tyrone, is Jamie from *Long Day's Journey into Night* and is again based on O'Neill's brother, James O'Neill Jr. The story of the Tyrone family picks up after Mary Tyrone's death. Jim is in his forties, dissolute from alcohol, and desperately lonely. Still he has some of his Irish good looks left. He is seen as a person who has squandered his education and his opportunities, a wastrel who has done very little work in his life except to act in a few of his father's plays. Jim is a shattered shadow of the robust thirty-two-year-old Jamie in *Long Day's Journey into Night*.

The grieving Jim winds up on a Connecticut farm owned by Phil Hogan, a miserly widower who has a sharp-tongued, over-sized daughter, Josie. The twenty-eight-year-old woman, with a reputation for promiscuity, falls for the still-handsome Jim. She and her father try to bring Jim out of the depression brought on by his mother's death, but to no avail.

Josie would like Jim to love her, and he is sexually attracted to her, but he is an incurable alcoholic, searching for a mother figure, not a life partner. He wants maternal warmth and comforting, not sex. He is really searching for death, and O'Neill drapes Jim in death imagery. Josie gives up on Jim and prepares to marry a suitor who has been after her for a long time, while Jim goes off to find his death.

A Moon for the Misbegotten is a fine drama, even if it does not compare to the power and the profundity of *Long Day's Journey into Night*. But then, hardly any other American drama does.

Comedy

Comedy was not O'Neill's forte. Still, he attempted a few comedies with some success, especially *Ah, Wilderness!*, his nostalgic rendition of the kind of youth he would have liked to have had.

The Movie Man (1914)

O'Neill subtitled *The Movie Man* "A Comedy in One Act." It is an antiwar satire, set in Mexico, about how the nascent film industry covered foreign events for newsreels. Henry Rogers and Al Devlin are two Americans working for the Earth Motion Picture Company, which is filming the revolution south of the border. Rogers helps a beautiful Mexican girl save her father from death at the hands of the villain, a rebel general. But the Americans are more interested in good footage than they are in the lives of the people they are filming.

The Sniper, first performed in 1917, is another early antiwar one-act play. All his life O'Neill hated war, seeing it as the worst of collective human activities, and as proof of the indifference if not the absence of God.

Marco's Millions (1928)

In O'Neill's satire, Marco Polo is a greedy, opportunistic, conscienceless capitalist. The author is talking as much about the business ethic in late capitalism as he is about an Italian adventurer in the Cathay court of the great khan. Indeed, at the end of the play, when the house lights rise, Polo is in the audience and on his way to his waiting limo.

Beginning in Venice, the play shows a fifteen-year-old Marco pledging his troth to a twelve-year-old girl from a wealthy family. A marriage to her would be financially advantageous to the Polos, and Marco vows fidelity to her. Subsequent scenes are set in Syria, Persia, India, Mongolia, and then by the Great Wall of China. Polo spends fifteen years in Cathay. The khan's granddaughter, Kukachin, falls in love with Marco, although she is to marry a cousin and become queen of Persia. But Marco is insensitive to this love and is only interested in accumulating wealth. When he goes home, Kukachin, in the style of grand opera, pines away her life.

Back in Venice, Donata, now rather plump, has her fabulously wealthy hero-lover back, and he is admired as a great businessman. During an expressionist moment, the khan, at the bier of his beloved granddaughter, sees all that is happening in materialistic Venice, and he concludes that Kukachin died for a fool.

The attack on early-twentieth-century Babbittry dressed in medieval and oriental clothing is humorous indeed, but *Marco's Millions* is marred by a certain didacticism and by awkward dialogue that seems the product of trying to sound exotic.

Ah, Wilderness! (1933)

Ah, Wilderness! is one of the two famous nostalgic stage representations of the idealized American family. The other, Thornton Wilder's *Our Town* (1938), is derivative of O'Neill's earlier play. O'Neill's portrayal of an American family living in the Connecticut of the early decades of the twentieth century is in stark contrast to his later presentation of another Connecticut family in *Long Day's Journey into Night*.

The year is 1906, and the Miller family is preparing to celebrate the Fourth of July. Richard Miller, a wishful, autobiographical projection of the author, is a naïve youth moving from adolescence to adulthood, who thinks, as in the Omar Khayyám poem *(The Rubáiyát)* from which the title is taken, that all he needs is a book of verse and the company of his first girlfriend to be happy. But life is neither simple nor complying. His path is toward the loss of innocence as he learns about the real world's corruption. Wilderness is not pastoral; it is filled with thorns and other dangers. Muriel, his love, breaks with him on her father's orders after showing him Richard's passionate love letters. Richard's father does not agree with his son's idealistic radicalism, although he defends the honorable intentions of his son when they are impugned by Muriel's father. Richard's mother is not happy with his addiction to poetry, nor does she appreciate his reading choices: Algernon Swinburne, Oscar Wilde, George Bernard Shaw, Henrik Ibsen, and other radical and "decadent" writers. His uncle Sid, a family favorite, has lost his job as a reporter because of alcoholism. Sid is the counterpart in *Ah, Wilderness!* to Jamie in *Long Day's Journey into Night*.

Richard and a friend determine to experience "life." They pick up two prostitutes in a hotel, and one of them wants Richard as a customer. Fortunately, Richard demurs, but he gets drunk and is brought home in a terrible state, having been thrown out of the hotel bar.

The next day, Richard swears never to drink again and to lead a moral life. But he is determined to see Muriel again after she sends a note begging him to meet her that night. They meet on a beach, and Richard discloses his "evil" past of one day's duration. The couple plan to marry one day. When his father confronts him upon his return, Richard is warned about predatory women. His punishment is that he will not be allowed to go to Yale in the fall. But Richard is delighted. Now he can marry Muriel right away. This is not what Mr. Miller wants to hear, so the punishment is reversed: Richard must go to Yale in the fall.

The play is simple. In the end it is about a father, a son, and learning "the facts of life." No wonder it remains one of the author's most frequently performed plays. Richard in *Ah, Wilderness!* possesses the youth O'Neill never had. Writing the comedy must have caused the author pain as well as pleasure.

Additional Reading

Floyd, Virginia. *The Plays of Eugene O'Neill: A New Assessment.* New York: Frederick Ungar, 1985.

Gassner, John. *Eugene O'Neill.* Minneapolis: Univ. of Minnesota Press, 1965.

Gelb, Arthur, and Barbara Gelb. *Eugene O'Neill.* New York: Harper, 1974.

———. *Eugene O'Neill: Life with Monte Cristo.* New York: Applause, 2000. First of three projected volumes.

Hirsch, Foster. *Eugene O'Neill: Life, Work, Criticism.* Fredericton, N.B.: York, 1986.

O'Neill, Eugene. *The Complete Plays of Eugene O'Neill.* Edited by Travis Bogard. New York: Viking, 1998.

Sheaffer, Louis. *O'Neill: Son and Playwright.* Boston: Little Brown, 1968.

———. *O'Neill: Son and Artist.* Boston: Little Brown, 1973.

Maxwell Anderson (1888–1959)

In his time, Maxwell Anderson was Eugene O'Neill's greatest rival. Author of thirty produced plays, Maxwell Anderson was born in

Atlantic, Pennsylvania. His father was an itinerant Baptist minister; his mother helped his father with church duties. In North Dakota Anderson attended the state university, graduating and marrying in 1911. A fellowship to Stanford resulted in an master of arts degree in English literature and a teaching job at Whittier College in Southern California. As a radical pacifist he was not at home at Whittier, and he was dismissed.

The Anderson family moved to San Francisco and then to New York City, where Anderson worked as a journalist until he tried his hand at playwriting. His first play, *The White Desert* (1923) was not successful, but when he teamed up with wounded World War I veteran Laurence Stallings to write *What Price Glory?* (1924), a play about the disillusion felt by soldiers in combat, his reputation as a dramatist concern with the human condition was well established.

Like George Bernard Shaw, Anderson always stood for individual freedom and for the poor against the wealthy. Also, like Shaw, he often found his texts in history. Blank verse dramas like *Elizabeth the Queen* (1930), *Mary of Scotland* (1933), and *Anne of the Thousand Days* (1947) proved popular and provided showcases for star actresses. *Winterset* (1935), based on the infamous Sacco-Vanzetti case that resulted in the execution of possibly wrongly convicted immigrant anarchists, endeared Anderson to American liberals. *Both Your Houses* (1933), a political satire, brought the playwright a Pulitzer Prize.

Anderson also wrote screenplays, including *All Quiet on the Western Front* (1930)—based on Erich Maria Remarque's magnificent novel—the greatest antiwar film ever made. Maxwell Anderson was a playwright with a conscience.

What Price Glory? (1924)

What Price Glory? is set in World War I. Two marines, Captain Flagg and Sergeant Quirt, unheroic professional warriors, fight each other a lot and the Germans a little. Their prize is Charmaine, the object of their lust. They each have their romantic triumphs and defeats. In the end they march off together to the front, once more comrades in arms. The 1920s audience was shocked by the soldier's lack of traditional patriotism and their raw language. Today's readers and audiences see the play as a sentimentalized view of war.

Mary of Scotland (1933)

A blank verse tragedy in the Shakespearean tradition, *Mary of Scotland* has Catholic Mary struggle with her cousin, Protestant Elizabeth I of England, who uses Scottish nobles to betray and overthrow the Scottish queen. True to history, Mary, who believes she should be Queen of England as well as Scotland, flees to England and is imprisoned by Elizabeth. Mary realizes that she will be executed one day if she does not bow to her cousin's will. But she exults in the realization that Elizabeth had a lonely, childless life, and she has James, her son, who not only is King of Scotland, but upon Elizabeth's death, will be King of England too. Mary, believing she is right, chooses resistance over surrender.

Anderson's *Mary of Scotland* is partially derived from Friedrich Schiller's *Mary Stuart* (1800).

Winterset (1935)

Winterset, Anderson's most controversial drama, is set beneath the Brooklyn Bridge. It was his second dramatization of the Sacco-Vanzetti case. In the blank verse play, a young man named Mio believes that his father was wrongly convicted and sentenced to death for the murder of an official. In fact, gangsters have done the killing, the judge is mentally unbalanced, and the system is corrupt.

Mio needs the help of a young woman named Miriamne, because her brother, a witness to the murder, could help him prove that his father was innocent. The young couple fall in love, but both are cut down in a hail of bullets by the gangsters. In the midst of the Depression, Anderson saw American democracy threatened.

High Tor (1937)

In *High Tor*, a light fantasy verse drama, a young man named Van is fed up with modernity. He refuses to sell to business people a hill overlooking the Hudson River that his family has owned since Dutch colonial times. Even his girlfriend, Judith, wants him to sell out. In the company of an American Indian, Van spends the night on his hill. He dreams of the explorer Hendrik Hudson and the crew of the Half Moon. Bank robbers appear and in the end are apprehended. The Native American wisely tells his friend that all that people make eventually turns into "good ruins." Van no longer fights progress, and he and Judith make peace. Van's idealism has diminished, and he says that people are complicated, human motivations are complicated, and change is inevitable. Today, Van seems a sell-out. Maturing no longer means accepting material progress.

Key Largo (1939)

Made into a memorable movie starring Humphrey Bogart, *Key Largo*, a verse tragedy, is in fact a drama about the Spanish Civil War (1936–39). King McCloud, an American fighting with the losing Spanish Republican Loyalists, the antifascists, realizes that the Republic is doomed. He deserts, leaving his soldiers behind, and is beset with guilt when he returns home. In a small hotel on Key Largo, McCloud sacrifices his life for the family of one of his men, who are being victimized by gangsters. The play reflected the guilt feelings of many liberals over the abandonment of Spain to Franco, Hitler, and Mussolini.

Anne of the Thousand Days (1947)

Returning to sixteenth-century English history, Anderson chose to write a blank-verse play about Henry VIII's second wife and the mother of Elizabeth I, Anne Boleyn. Henry, still married to Catherine of Aragon, has Mary Boleyn as a mistress, but he wants her younger sister, Anne, who is in love with the Earl of Northhumberland. Anne is portrayed as a spirited girl who would consider only marriage, not mistresshood. Henry forces Northumberland to marry elsewhere, and then the earl suddenly and mysteriously dies. Anne thinks Henry has caused the death of Northumberland, and yet she falls in love with the all-powerful despot.

Besotted with Anne, Henry divorces Catherine and marries Anne, with the result that he is excommunicated by the Pope and must establish an English church of his own. Henry needs a son and heir, and Anne makes the "mistake" of giving birth to a girl. Henry then wants Anne out of the way so he can remarry. Her choice is exile from England or death. Bravely, almost with visionary foresight, she chooses death, so that her child, Elizabeth may have a chance at the crown.

Henry deeply regrets Anne's death, for he still loves her. Anderson's eloquent farewell to Tudor royalty contains some of his finest characterizations.

Additional Reading

Gould, Jean. "Maxwell Anderson." In *Modern American Playwrights*, 118–34. New York: Dodd, Mead, 1966.
Shivers, Alfred S. *The Life of Maxwell Anderson.* Briarcliff Manor, N.Y.: Stein and Day, 1983.

George S. (Simon) Kaufman (1889–1961)

George S. Kaufman was born in Pittsburg. He was a journalist prior to becoming a playwright and director. Kaufman was the wittiest, funniest dramatist of his time. He has been equaled or perhaps surpassed a generation later only by Neil Simon. Kaufman was American drama's greatest collaborator. With a very few exceptions, such as *The Butter and Egg Man* (1925), he preferred to bounce ideas off another writer or supply the topical allusions, funny lines, and wise cracks for a situation or a plot provided by another dramatist.

Kaufman enjoyed sending up egotistic actors, the movie industry, politicians, modern business, Tin Pan Alley, critics, the rich, the nouveau riche, the upwardly mobile, and middle-class American life. But Kaufman was never cruel with his comedy. Most of all, Kaufman, like Neil Simon, wanted laughs. He defined high brow satire thus: "Satire is what closes Saturday Night."

With Marc Connelly Kaufman wrote *Dulcy* (1921), *To the Ladies* (1922), *Merton of the Movies* (1922), *The Deep Tangled Wildwood* (1923), and *Beggar on Horseback* (1924). With best-selling novelist Edna Ferber he wrote *Minick* (1924), *The Royal Family* (1927), *Dinner at Eight* (1932), and *Stage Door* (1936). With short story writer Ring Lardner he wrote *June Moon* (1929). After writing the libretto for *Cocoanuts* (1925) with Irving Berlin, he worked with Morrie Ryskind on the Marx Brothers musical *Animal Crackers* (1928), *Strike Up the Band* (1930), and the Pulitzer Prize-winning *Of Thee I Sing* (1931). With the critic Alexander Woolcott he wrote *The Dark Tower* (1933), and with Katherine Dayton *First Lady* (1935).

In his most successful set of collaborations, with Moss Hart, Kaufman wrote *Once in a Lifetime* (1930), *Merrily We Roll Along* (1934), the Pulitzer Prize-winning *You Can't Take It with You* (1936), the musical *I'd Rather Be Right* (1937), *The Man Who Came to Dinner* (1939), and *George Washington Slept Here* (1940). The last two and *You Can't Take It with You* are still frequently performed. With his biographer, Howard Teichmann, he wrote *The Solid Gold Cadillac* (1953).

Several of Kaufman's plays were made into successful movies, and he also wrote for Hollywood. *A Night at the Opera* (1935) was the Marx Brothers's greatest success. Kaufman was a member of the Algonquin Round Table, a famous gathering of New York writers who carried on a conversation at the Algonquin Hotel for two decades. Fellow Algonquinites included Dorothy Parker, Robert E. Sherwood, Heywood Broun, Marc Connelly, and Robert Benchley.

The Royal Family (1927)

In *The Royal Family*, Kaufman pokes good-natured fun at the Barrymore and Drew families. Here the royal family of acting is called Cavendish. The head of the great American acting family is Fanny. Her daughter Julie is a star, and Julie's daughter, Gwen, is an up-and-coming young actress. Fanny's son, Tony, has wasted his great talent as a stage actor to pursue film celebrity and chase women. Fanny's brother is a fading leading man. All of the Cavendishes complain about the price of fame. Julie and Gwen consider retiring into marriage, but they know that like all the Cavendishes, they could never leave the theater as long as they have breath.

Dinner at Eight (1932)

Socialite Millicent Jordan has a dinner party. Unbeknownst to her, the lives of her family members and her guests are entwined. Her young daughter, engaged to an eligible young man, is the secret mistress of an alcoholic matinee idol—a celebrity invited to the party—who kills himself. Millicent's husband is seriously ill and his business is failing, but Millicent is oblivious to his problems in light of her own difficulty in bringing off a dinner party. Mr.

Jordan's former mistress, an aging actress, appears and complicates Mr. Jordan's financial troubles by needing to sell her stock in his company. A corporate raider, having trouble with an unfaithful wife, is going to ruin him. All sit down to dinner unaware that their lives are collapsing. The plot of *Dinner at Eight* is brilliant and wryly satisfying.

You Can't Take It with You (1936)

You Can't Take It with You is about the idiosyncratic, crack-brained family headed by Mrs. Sycamore's father, Grandpa Vanderhof. She is an aspiring dramatist. Her husband madly experiments with fireworks in the basement of the house. Their daughter Essie has ambitions to be a ballet dancer, and she is forever practicing. The "message" of the Depression-era madcap comedy is simple: Lighten up. You can't take it with you. Zany characterization is what causes the play to succeed.

The Man Who Came to Dinner (1939)

Sheridan Whiteside, the selfish, egotistical, mean-spirited, conniving celebrity-critic who comes to dinner at the home of an admiring provincial family, falls and breaks a leg. While he is recuperating in the house, he takes over and demolishes the family and the household. Sheridan Whiteside was based on Kaufman's friend, the critic Alexander Woolcott. In the end, Whiteside brings lovers together and proves to have a heart of gold, even if it is a very small one.

Additional Reading

Goldstein, Malcolm. *George S. Kaufman: His Life*. New York: Oxford Univ. Press, 1979.

Teichmann, Howard. *George S. Kaufman: An Intimate Portrait*. New York: Atheneum, 1977.

Marc Connelly (1890–1980)

Marc Connelly was born in McKeesport, Pennsylvania. He first worked as a journalist and then became a dramatist and a screenwriter. He is best remembered for *The Green Pastures* (1930), a Pulitzer Prize play with an African American cast. His career as a dramatist centered on collaboration with George S. Kaufman. Their best known comedies include: *Dulcy* (1921); *To the Ladies!* (1922); *Merton of the Movies* (1922); a musical, *Helen of Troy* (1923); and *Beggar on Horseback* (1924).

The Green Pastures (1930)

Today this fantasy play in Southern black dialect seems patronizing to African Americans and others because it presents early-twentieth-century Southern black religion as naïve. But in its time, *The Green Pastures* was loved by black and white audiences alike. It was written with sympathy, admiration, and good will. Connelly depicts the Bible as if it were a celebration written by a black country preacher. Indeed, "de Lawd God Jehovah" *is* a black minister.

Part one of the play tells the biblical story from the Creation to the Flood. Part two covers the biblical story from Moses to the Crucifixion. The audience is amused by the "primitive" interpretation of the Bible, but, more significantly, it is moved by the deep religious belief of rural African Americans. The play gave many black actors work during its long popularity.

Additional Reading

Nolan, Paul T. *Marc Connelly.* New York: Twayne, 1969.

George Kelly (1890–1974)

Born in Philadelphia, George Kelly was the brother of a stage comedian and the brother of an athlete and wealthy builder who was the
father of Grace Kelly. George Kelly trained as an actor and then
began to write plays. His early plays were successful, most notably
Craig's Wife (1925), which received a Pulitzer Prize and which is
sometimes revived today.

Other successful plays include: *The Torch-Bearers* (1922), a comedy that makes fun of the popular amateur theater movement in
America; *The Show-Off* (1924), a very funny play about a lower-class
young man who seems to be a phony and who marries above his
station, but proves to be quite a catch after all; and *Behold the Bridegroom* (1927), in which a rich, spoiled young woman foolishly and
vainly rejects her suitors, only to fall in love with a man who rejects
her and breaks her heart. A half-dozen other plays had little success.
Kelly was a theater craftsperson who carefully constructed his
plots. His main subject was the weakness of human nature, but he
seemed to lack compassion for his characters.

Craig's Wife (1925)

Craig's Wife is the cynical and biting story of an unlovable woman.
Harriet Craig is a woman who cares more for her home and her
other material possessions than for people. Her meek husband,
Walter, is henpecked but does not seem to mind it. Others are made
miserable by her obsession for things. When a neighbor has a
tragedy, Walter wants to help but Harriet refuses to let them get involved. Furious at last, Walter breaks a knickknack, smokes a cigarette in the living room, and walks out on Harriet, who is left alone
with her precious things. For many years the term "a Craig's Wife"
was used to indicate a women pathologically obsessed with her
home.

Sidney Howard (1891–1939)

Born in Oakland, California, Sidney Howard attended university in his home state and then studied playwriting with Professor George Pierce Baker at Harvard in the famous 47 Workshop.

In 1918 Howard fought with the United States Army Air Corp in France. Back home, he worked as a journalist and a magazine writer until he succeeded as a playwright. Howard's finest play was *They Knew What They Wanted* (1924), which won a Pulitzer Prize. *Lucky Sam McCarver* (1925) depicts a bootlegging nightclub owner whose heart is broken by a beautiful socialite. *Ned McCobb's Daughter* (1926) shows how a strong woman who has made a bad marriage fights her way out of it. *The Silver Cord* (1926) portrays an overly possessive mother. *The Late Christopher Bean* (1932) demonstrates what happens to his family when a deceased artist becomes famous. *Alien Corn* (1933) shows how a talented woman pianist survives an awful teaching job and unsuitable suitors to make her own way in the world.

Howard adapted Sinclair Lewis's novel *Dodsworth* for the stage in 1934. He collaborated on the screenplay for Margaret Mitchell's *Gone with the Wind.*

They Knew What They Wanted (1924)

Set in the Napa Valley vineyards of Northern California, an area Howard knew from childhood on, *They Knew What They Wanted* is an erotically charged drama about an aging Italian immigrant wine grower named Tony, who seeks a bride via mail. He deceives the young woman, Amy, by sending her a photo of a young man named Joe and passing it off as his own likeness. When Amy arrives, she is dismayed to find she is engaged to an old man whom she can only shun. Soon she and Joe have an affair, and she becomes pregnant. Tony turns out to be a real human being. He is willing to adopt the child. Amy realizes how good Tony is and finds herself wanting to marry him after all.

In 1956 Frank Loesser, the composer and lyricist, turned *They Knew What They Wanted* into a fine musical play, *Most Happy Fella*.

The Silver Cord (1926)

Howard knew about overly possessive mothers from his own experience as a youth and a husband; a dispute he had with his wife over the raising of their daughter led to their parting. *The Silver Cord* is a Freudian drama of a mother's excessive need to keep control of the sons she loves almost to the point of psychological incest.

The cord is the umbilical cord. Mrs. Phelps, who has destroyed her husband, will do anything to keep her son Robert from marrying. She also wants to wreck the marriage of her married son, David. Mrs. Phelps has perverted motherhood. She succeeds so well in controlling Robert that his fiancée kills herself. But David, backed by his strong wife, breaks the silver cord to his mother. The psychological situation and believable characters have kept *The Silver Cord* alive on the American stage.

Additional Reading

White, Sidney H. *Sidney Howard*. Boston: Twayne, 1977.

Elmer Rice (born Leopold Reizenstein) (1892–1967)

Early in the twentieth century Elmer Rice, along with Maxwell Anderson, was considered a challenger to Eugene O'Neill for the title of America's leading dramatist. Rice was born in a tenement in Jewish Harlem in New York City. He apprenticed at his uncle's law office and studied law at night at New York University before commencing his career as a playwright. His initial stage effort, *On Trial* (1914), a courtroom melodrama, made use of his experience

in the law. It was the first American drama to employ the device of a flashback.

Rice's expressionistic play *The Adding Machine* (1923), with its depiction of a dehumanized worker, made a great impact on American drama. Rice experimented with theatrical form. He designed a rotating set so scenes could juxtapose in the way films cut from location to location. *The Subway* (1929) is another expressionistic play, with a disgruntled white-collar employee as the main character. The Pulitzer Prize-winning *Street Scene* (1929) brought the sidewalks of New York onto the New York stage in a realistic manner. *Counselor-at-Law* (1931) is another successful play based on Rice's legal background. Rice's later plays were generally unsuccessful. He is remembered in part for the variety of his work and because he saw people as victims of economic forces over which they have no control.

The Adding Machine (1914)

The Adding Machine, a drama of social protest, predicts that in the future humans will become slaves to the machines they have created. The protagonist, appropriately named Mr. Zero, stands as a symbolic indictment of the spiritual isolation and dehumanization of modern human beings. For twenty-five years Zero has been a faithful bookkeeper in a company, but he is replaced by an adding machine and fired. Furious, frustrated, and maddened, he kills his employer, is tried and executed. In the Elysian Fields things are little better. He is put to work on a giant adding machine, and then sent back to earth. He learns that he has been a slave to machines for many reincarnations and will continue to be so forever.

Street Scene (1929)

A realistic drama of the slums and the poor people of New York City, *Street Scene* presents the story of Rose, a young Irish American woman, whose father murders her mother because she is having an affair. Rose has to make a painful choice either to stay single and raise her younger brother or to marry one of her two suitors, the wealthy and cheerful Harry Easter, or Sam Kaplan, a serious Jewish friend. In the end she elects for duty, rejects her suitors, and intends to devote her life to caring for her orphaned brother.

Kurt Weil and Langston Hughes turned *Street Scene* into an opera in 1947.

Additional Reading

Durham, Frank. *Elmer Rice.* Boston: Twayne, 1970.
Hogan, Robert. *The Independence of Elmer Rice.* Carbondale, Illinois: Southern Illinois Univ. Press, 1965.
Rice, Elmer. *Minority Report.* London: Heinemann, 1963.

S. N. (Samuel Nathan) Behrman (1893–1973)

S. N. Behrman was born in Worcester, Massachusetts, the child of impoverished immigrant Jewish parents. After Clark University he went to Harvard to study with Professor George P. Baker in the 47 Workshop in playwriting. Moving to New York City, Behrman was awarded a master of arts degree at Columbia University. He worked as a journalist until he achieved success as a dramatist.

In more than thirty plays Behrman primarily wrote witty comedies that gave audiences something to think about after the show. Often the message was political, for Behrman favored socialism. He was almost as popular as George S. Kaufman, but he differed from Kaufman and was closer to Philip Barry in that there was more of an underlying seriousness to his work than was to be found in Kaufman's comedies. Also, Kaufman generally eschewed the lavish drawing room settings of Behrman and Barry.

The Second Man (1926) is a play about a hedonist writer who wants to marry a rich woman, but whose girlfriend is pregnant. In the end he gets the rich woman, and the girlfriend is happier with an earlier lover. The brilliant dialogue and risqué plot made for Behrman's first success.

Three of Behrman's plays still may be seen: *Biography* (1932), *No Time for Comedy* (1939), and the more serious but still humorous *Jacobowsky and the Colonel* (1944), adopted from a story by Franz Werfel. In the last, a Jewish refugee fleeing Paris as the Germans arrive hooks up with a quixotic, anti-Semitic Polish Army colonel, and they join forces and abilities to get away from the deadly enemy. Along the way they become friends.

Behrman wrote the book for the successful 1950s musical *Fanny* (1954). He was a tolerant, urbane, and humane person and writer who excelled in the comedy of manners.

Biography (1932)

Successful painter Marion Froude can't help herself: she loves people regardless of their faults. A young, outspoken, radical editor, Richard Kurt, wants to publish her autobiography. She likes the young man very much and agrees to the book. An old flame, Leander Nolan, a lawyer and politician running for the Senate, learns of the book and is upset because certain revelations will mean the end of his political career.

Nolan now realizes that he is still in love with Marion, but Richard has fallen in love with her also. Wisely, Marion realizes that neither the conservative politician nor the angry, radical editor, is a good candidate for a peaceful marriage. After destroying the autobiography, she goes on with her contented single life. *Biography* has current appeal because of its strong, successful, independent heroine, who prefers a happy single life and a career to a contentious marriage.

No Time for Comedy (1939)

Gaylod Esterbrook is a comic playwright who, because times are serious, is encouraged by his married mistress, Amanda Smith, to write serious drama. This advice angers Esterbrook's actress wife, Linda, who has starred in his hits. Gaylord makes a terrible mess of his first serious drama. He and Amanda plan to walk out on their spouses, but in the end all sense that their actions are like those in a comedy, and the marriages remain intact. The appeal of the play is in the delicious revelation of the "travails" of the theatrical life.

Additional Reading

Behrman, S. N. *People in a Diary.* Boston: Little, Brown, 1972.
Reed, Terry. *S. N. Behrman.* Boston: Twayne, 1975.

Robert E. (Emmet) Sherwood (1896–1955)

Robert E. Sherwood was a writer concerned with his times. He wanted to help create a better world. He was born in New Rochelle, New York, and attended Harvard College, where he took a drama course with Professor George Pierce Baker, but not his famed playwriting workshop. During World War I, he served with the Canadian Army in France and was severely wounded. After the war he worked as a critic for several magazines until his first play, *The Road to Rome* (1927), an antiwar play, established his reputation as a promising playwright.

Other successes included the romantic dramas *Waterloo Bridge* (1930) and *Reunion in Vienna* (1931), the philosophical *The Petrified Forest* (1935); the Pulitzer Prize-winning *Idiot's Delight* (1936), the first of three plays to be so recognized; and his most famous drama, the biographical *Abe Lincoln in Illinois* (1938), in which Sherwood's pessimism dissipated in light of Lincoln's humanity and sacrifice. The Lincoln play brought Sherwood his second Pulitzer. His drama about the 1939 Russo-Finnish War, *There Shall Be No Night* (1940), achieved his third Pulitzer.

Sherwood was a life-long liberal, who fought for the downtrodden and the oppressed. He was descended on his mother's side from the Irish martyr Robert Emmet who, early in the nineteenth century, gave his life attempting to free Ireland from English rule.

The Road to Rome (1927)

The great Carthaginian general Hannibal is close to a final victory over Rome, but he abandons his siege of the city because of a woman. He is seduced by the wife of the Roman leader, Fabius Maximus; she convinces him that it would be folly to destroy Rome. She persuades him that war is always a waste of human beings, and that true greatness is achieved when a general learns that fact.

Waterloo Bridge (1930)

An antiwar melodrama about a World War I American soldier and a London prostitute, *Waterloo Bridge* explores the psychological and emotional damage war does to women. The soldier is suffering from what is now called traumatic stress syndrome, but he musters enough compassion to save the girl from suicide and bring meaning back to his own tortured life. The play appealed to women, who could identify with the "wounded" girl.

Reunion in Vienna (1931)

In the comedy *Reunion in Vienna* Anton Krug, an arrogantly over-confident psychoanalyst, throws his wife, Elena, into the arms of a former lover, an Austrian prince in exile who has become a taxi driver on the Riviera. Anton is aware that his wife still carries a torch for Prince Rudolph, and he "scientifically" deduces that he will cure Elena of her affection for Rudolph by bringing them together for a reunion in Vienna. The romance between wife and lover ignites to such an intensity that Rudolph consults with Anton the analyst. In the end, the lovers part and go back to their separate lives, Elena to a chastised Anton and Rudolph to exile in France.

The Petrified Forest (1935)

For the first time Sherwood wrote a play about his own country in his own time. A writer is the central character of *The Petrified Forest*. Alan Squire has wasted a part of his life dallying with a rich woman on the French Riviera. Disillusioned with himself and depressed, he travels to the American West where he finds something useful to do with his life by sacrificing it to a gangster in order to save Gabby Maple, a fine young woman with the possibility of a happy life ahead of her.

Humphrey Bogart played the gangster, Duke Mantee, in the original Broadway production and then the film version. *The Petrified Forest* brought Bogart to stardom.

Idiot's Delight (1936)

The antifascist play *Idiot's Delight* is set in a Central European hotel where a group of guests hang out in the bar while the map of Europe is about to be changed radically. American entertainer Harry Van and his troupe of chorus girls are in the hotel. He recognizes a former chorus girl passing herself off as a Russian countess and now the mistress of a wealthy munitions maker. They were lovers once and, with the war about to begin, they renew their love over a bottle of champagne. Love, so tender and fragile a plant, will bloom even in the face of terror and mass death.

Sherwood showed his pessimistic view of the world's fate on the eve of the Spanish Civil War and World War II in *Idiot's Delight* when he shows a pacifist labor union leader succumbing to jingoism and war hysteria and a German-born physician doing research on cancer returning to Germany to work on poison gas. Sherwood had seen such idiocy at the outbreak of World War I in 1914 and had been swept up in it.

Abe Lincoln in Illinois (1938)

The early volumes of Carl Sandburg's biography of Lincoln influenced the great stage biography *Abe Lincoln in Illinois,* for Sherwood had come to realize, perhaps because of Franklin Delano Roosevelt, that intellect, compassion, and vision could exist in a politician.

In *Abe Lincoln in Illinois* the Great Emancipator is portrayed first as a troubled youth struggling with his feelings of inferiority because of his lack of education, homeliness, and outbreaks of depression. The great love of his youth, Ann Rutledge, dies, and he finally marries a strong woman, Mary Todd, who drives him on to the political destiny he tries to avoid. The play is truly an American classic.

Additional Reading

Brown, John Mason. *The Ordeals of a Playwright.* New York: Harper and Row, 1970.

———. *The Worlds of Robert E. Sherwood.* New York: Harper and Row, 1965.

Philip Barry (1896–1949)

Like S. N. Behrman, Philip Barry wrote drawing-room comedies. Barry especially liked to write about divorce in upper-class circles. Philip Barry was born in Rochester, New York, the son of an Irish Catholic immigrant father who died when Barry was one year old and an Irish Catholic mother who came from an established Irish Catholic family in Philadelphia. After parochial schools, and service with the State Department during World War I, he graduated from Yale in 1919. Barry also studied playwriting with Professor George Pierce Baker at Harvard in Workshop 47. His first plays were failures but Barry was neither embittered nor discouraged. Barry hit his stride with *Holiday* (1928). His greatest success was *Philadelphia Story* (1939). His best efforts include *The Animal Kingdom* (1932). All these plays are witty and smartly sophisticated. Barry's philosophical and heavily psychological dramas, *Hotel Universe* (1930), *Bright Star* (1935), and *Here Come the Clowns* (1938) did not succeed.

Holiday (1928)

Holiday is a romantic comedy in which, Julia, a young woman from an upper-class New York family, is engaged to marry a young lawyer who has worked his way up from poverty to success in his profession. He does not love money, and he hopes to stop battling for it and relax and enjoy life while he and his bride are young. But Julia and her millionaire father are appalled by his irreverence for money. Fortunately, Julia's younger sister, Linda, is not a materialist and as Johnny leaves alone for his holiday from the rat race, Linda joins him and they will enjoy life together.

The Animal Kingdom (1932)

A big hit, *The Animal Kingdom* presents a turnabout marriage in a seriocomic way. A husband named Tom Collier finds that his mistress, Daisy, a sensitive artist, is more like a wife in that she is interested in his soul, and his beautiful wife, Cecelia, is more like a mistress in that she is a selfish woman disinterested in his artistic bent and intellectual ideas. She interferes in his business activities, is surly with employees, and is prone to headaches and locking him out of her bedroom. In the end he goes to his "real wife," his mistress, Daisy. The true "marriage" is one in which the relationship is based on unselfish love, affection, and mutual respect.

Philadelphia Story (1939)

A brilliant comedy of manners, *Philadelphia Story* is also a study in psychology. A beautiful "goddess," Tracy Lord, —a lord indeed—is worshiped by men, who put her on a pedestal. She is a catch, the divorced daughter of wealthy socialites. Tracy is not loved as a woman, however, because she is cold, too proud, and seemingly incapable of loving anyone else, including her former husband, Dexter. She is to be married to George, an affected man. A radical journalist, Mike Connor, arrives on the scene to report on the wedding. He provides needed leavening, including swimming nude with Tracy in the family pool, which sends George packing. Dexter, who has shown up for the wedding and has caused Tracy to doubt that marrying George is such a good idea, takes George's place in the wedding.

Katherine Hepburn starred in the original Broadway production and in the 1940 film with Cary Grant and Jimmy Stewart. Grace Kelly, Bing Crosby, and Frank Sinatra starred in the 1956 remake with music called *High Society*. Play and films were all very successful.

Additional Reading

Hamm, Gerald. *The Drama of Philip Barry*. Philadelphia: n.p., 1948.
Roppolo, Joseph. *Philip Barry*. New York: Twayne, 1965.

Thornton Wilder (1897–1975)

Thornton Wilder was born in Madison, Wisconsin. He spent part of his childhood in China, where his father served in the American Consulate. He studied at Oberlin College for two years prior to World War I service in the U.S. Coast Artillery. After World War I, Wilder continued his education at Yale for his bachelor of arts degree and Princeton for a master of arts in 1926. He spent many years as a visiting professor at several American universities, and he received a bouquet of honorary doctorates in his lifetime. During World War II, Wilder served in the intelligence division of the U.S. Army Air Corps.

From the beginning Thorton Wilder was an experimental, expressionistic dramatist. He worked against the prevailing realistic mode of the drama of his time. He was also optimistic as to the future of the world and America. Furthermore, Wilder saw the stage as a pulpit to preach his love of life, good will, and belief in humanity. Wilder was a craftsperson who produced a limited number of highly polished plays. He also wrote seven popular novels. Today, however, Wilder is remembered for *Our Town* (1938), arguably the most popular and best loved American play; *The Skin of Our Teeth* (1942), Wilder's fantastical history of the human race; and two one-act plays that, like *Our Town*, are frequently performed in colleges and schools: *The Happy Journey to Trenton and Camden* (1931), in which four chairs and the audience's imagination allow Wilder to take us along with the Kirby family on a seventy-mile car trip in twenty minutes; and *The Long Christmas Dinner* (1931), in which ninety years of a family history is reenacted around a dining room table.

Wilder's *The Merchant of Yonkers* (1938) was revised as *The Matchmaker* (1954) and reincarnated as the hit musical *Hello Dolly!* (1964).

Our Town (1938)

Our Town is set in Grover's Corners, New Hampshire (based on Peterborough), in 1901, where two families, the Gibbses and the Webbs, live side by side. Teenage George Gibbs and Emily Webb fall in love and marry. Emily dies in childbirth and the audience melts to tears. While her funeral is taking place, Emily, because she died so young and will miss so much, is offered the opportunity to go back to a single day in her life. Her choice is her twelfth birthday. In that day she realizes that living people cannot appreciate the wonders of daily life. The message is that we must stop, look around, and appreciate the goodness of life while we able to do so.

A stage manager narrates the play, serves as Greek chorus, and performs several roles. The set is very simple: two ladders, some tables, and chairs.

In its idealization of early twentieth-century small town, middle-class American life, *Our Town* owes something to Eugene O'Neill's *Ah, Wilderness!* (1933).

The Skin of Our Teeth (1942)

In *The Skin of Our Teeth* Mr. and Mrs. Antrobus and their children, suburbanites living in Excelsior, New Jersey, represent the human family, which will survive all catastrophes and disasters by "the skin of our teeth." An ice age is coming. The family pets are a mammoth and a dinosaur that go outside the house and don't survive. Mr. Antrobus invents useful things to help the family survive as thousands of years roll by. A beauty queen tries to steal Mr. Antrobus away from his wife and fails. The Great Flood is coming and Mr. Antrobus rescues the animals two by two. A terrible war is survived. The drama of life goes on even as *The Skin of Our Teeth* concludes. Written in the darkest hours of World War II, the play says that humankind will endure.

Additional Reading

Castronovo, David. *Thornton Wilder.* New York: Ungar, 1986.
Harrison, Gilbert A. *The Enthusiast: A Life of Thornton Wilder.* New York: Fromm, 1983.

Eliott Nugent (1899–1980)

The last of the American dramatists born in the nineteenth century, Eliot Nugent was born in Dover, Ohio. His father was the playwright and actor J. C. Nugent, with whom Elliott collaborated. Nugent received a bachelor of arts degree from Ohio State University in 1919. He was destined for the stage as both writer and actor. Nugent wrote or collaborated on fifteen plays of which one is outstanding: *The Male Animal* (1940), written with the *New Yorker* humorist-cartoonist James Thurber. Nugent was a mild satirist and a writer of comedy of manners. His general target: suburban, bourgeois American society.

The Male Animal (1940)

Although it is a comedy, *The Male Animal* evidences Nugent's serious concern that America had become so materialist and conformist that individual intellectuals felt isolated and disconnected. A college professor, Tommy Turner, faces a personal and a political problem. With the former, he is worried over the fact that a former boyfriend of his wife is coming back to the college for a visit. In the second situation, Turner's job is jeopardized because as a liberal he read a letter in class written by the anarchist Vanzetti to his daughter before his controversial execution. The campus newspaper editorializes against him. Tommy's wife stays true although the male animals, Tommy and his rival, get into a fight. Fortunately, he is not in trouble with the college administration after all. Academic freedom survives.

Additional Reading

Nugent, Elliott. *Events Leading Up to the Comedy: An Autobiography.* New York: Simon and Schuster, 1965.

Langston Hughes (1902–1967)

Langston Hughes was the leader of the Harlem Renaissance and probably the greatest African American poet. He was born in Mis-

souri but came north for his higher education, studying at Columbia and Lincoln universities. Hughes wrote eight full-length plays
as well as the libretto for Kurt Weill's 1947 opera version of Elmer
Rice's *Street Scene.* Hughes also established African American theater groups in Harlem, Los Angeles, and Chicago.

Hughes's most successful play is *Mulatto* (1935). It is of great
significance in the history of African America theater because it was
the first drama written by an African America to have a long run on
Broadway—373 performances.

Mulatto (1935)

Set in the Old South, *Mulatto* is a tragedy of two gifted young people, brother and sister, of mixed blood who are destroyed by racism.
Arrogant and patriarchal Colonel Thomas Norwood had fathered
several children by his African American housekeeper, Cora Lewis.
Sally and Robert are particularly bright, and so Norwood sends
them to the north for education. When Sally returns home, the
stereotypical, villainous overseer, Talbot, seduces her. Robert will
not be treated as a black; he insists that his father treat him as a white
person. Furious, Colonel Norwood threatens to shoot his son, and
Robert attacks his father and strangles him. When it appears that a
mob will lynch him, Robert kills himself.

Despite the melodramatic nature of the plot, audiences, black
and white, were moved by the deep emotions in the play and troubled by its implication that it is dangerous to mix blood.

Additional Reading

Berry, Faith. *Langston Hughes: Before and Beyond Harlem.* New York: Carol
    Publishing Group, 1992.
Emanuel, James A. *Langston Hughes.* New York: Twayne, 1967.
Hughes, Langston. *Big Sea: An Autobiography.* New York: Hill and Wang,
    1963.

Lillian Hellman (1905–1984)

Lillian Hellman was the most important American woman dramatist of the twentieth century. Deft at ironic detachment, she wrote
powerful, realistic social dramas in the manner of Ibsen. Her social
consciousness commanded great respect. She wrote some fifteen
original plays and adaptations.

Hellman was born in New Orleans, Louisiana. Her Jewish father owned a large shoe store in the city. She went to college in New
York City, studying at New York University and Columbia, and she
received a master of arts degree from Tufts University in 1940.
While working as a publisher's reader and a journalist, she met the
writer Arthur Kober. They were married in 1925 and divorced in
1932. The great love of her life was the detective storywriter
Dashiell Hammett, with whom Hellman shared thirty years of collaborations, battles, and alcoholism.

Hellman endeared herself to American liberals by defying the
House Committee on Un-American Activities in 1952 in refusing to
inform on friends who might have been members of the Communist party in earlier years. She suffered being blacklisted by Hollywood and she battled in court with the writer Mary McCarthy, who
claimed that Hellman lied in her memoirs.

Hellman's first play, *The Children's Hour* (1934), the story of two
schoolteachers accused by a pupil of being lesbians, shocked audiences and made her reputation as a major American playwright.
Her finest work is *The Little Foxes* (1939), about the rapacious Hubbards, a family with questionable values and morals who consider
their actions above reproach. Other major plays include *The Watch
on the Rhine*, (1941) in which an anti-Nazi German in exile in America must kill a Nazi secret agent; *The Searching Wind* (1944), the story
of a diplomat who only sees the consequence of his "diplomacy"
when his son is badly wounded in war; *Another Part of the Forest*
(1946), a melodrama in which Hellman brings back the unlovable
Hubbards; *The Autumn Garden* (1951), a subtle but dense play in

which ten characters at a summer resort reveal their weaknesses and shortcomings in Chekhovian fashion; and *Toys in the Attic* (1960), in which two unmarried sisters wage war with their brother's wife over his soul.

Hellman adapted Jean Anouilh's Joan of Arc play as *The Lark* (1955), and she wrote the brilliant libretto for Leonard Bernstein's operatic musical, *Candide* (1956).

The Children's Hour (1934)

The Children's Hour is a grippingly powerful psychological drama. Mary, an adolescent given to lying, is punished by her teacher, Karen Wright, by losing some privileges. To get even she tells her socially prominent grandmother that Karen, who is engaged to be married shortly, and her friend Martha are lesbians. The horrified grandmother condemns the women without a hearing. Rumors are spread. The two women are faced with ostracism and economic disaster, as the removal of children from the school they run means that it must close. The teachers sue Mary's grandmother for defamation of character but lose the case. Martha commits suicide because she realizes that she actually does have sexual feelings for her friend, although she has never acted on them. Karen's marriage plans are ruined. The "bad seed" has done her evil. But the true villains may be the people of the community who have no sense of justice. In Hellman's world, evil resides in the community as well as in individual people.

Little Foxes (1939)

Set in the post-Civil War South, The *Little Foxes* tells the story of an awful family, the hateful Hubbards. Two brothers, Oscar and Ben, need money for an industrial venture that can make them rich. They approach Regina, their wily sister, with the proposition that if she can get Horace, her sickly husband, to loan them $75,000, they will give her a third interest in a mill they will build. Regina's husband wants no part of a deal with the Hubbards, and anyway he feels Regina and he have enough money. Oscar's weak-willed son, Leo, is sent to steal Horace's bonds. Later Horace discovers the theft, but before he can do anything about it, he suffers an attack and drops his medicine bottle as he collapses. He asks Regina for another bottle, but she refuses to get it and instead cruelly watches him die. Now she has power over her brothers because she can charge them with theft, so they are forced to give her three-fourths interest in the mill. Blackmail is a powerful tool in Hellman's dramas.

Of special interest in the play is the troubled mother-daughter relationship between Regina and Alexandra, a rarity in the patriarchal world of early- and mid-twentieth-century American drama.

The Hubbards are a family without human values. Greed is their sole motivation. Hellman has selected them to show her hatred for predatory capitalism.

The Little Foxes was made into a successful film and an opera.

Toys in the Attic (1960)

Two unmarried sisters, Carrie and Anna, love their weak brother, Julian, and derive their main pleasure from taking care of him. Hellman likes to show that people who seem outwardly good, ready to sacrifice their lives for those they ostensibly love, can destroy the very persons for whom they have affection. Julian marries, and the sisters can't bear to lose him. His wife, Lily, becomes their enemy. He has a scheme to make money illegally that is thwarted. Carrie causes Julian to be beaten and humiliated. Broken in spirit, he will stay close to her. His wife wants him, too. Her need is sexual, and it creates havoc. In the end it is the innocent who suffer the most. Although he plans to start all over again, we know that Julian will live the rest of his life as a failure.

Additional Reading

Falk, Doris V. *Lillian Hellman.* New York: Ungar, 1978.
Rollyson, Carl. *Lillian Hellman: Her Legacy and Her Legend.* New York: St. Martin's, 1988.
Wright, William. *Lillian Hellman: The Image, the Woman.* New York: Simon and Schuster, 1986.

Clifford Odets (1906–1963)

In the 1930s and early 1940s Clifford Odets was considered the successor to Eugene O'Neill as the leading original and profound American dramatist. He struggled to portray the difficulties and problems of American life. His reputation has faded because his work contains a certain 1930s sensibility. American problems and values are not the same now as they were in the pre-World War II Depression. But in his depiction of a family drama, particularly a New York City Jewish family drama, Odets opened the way for Arthur Miller's *Death of a Salesman* (1949). Unlike Miller, however, Odets evidenced a youthful optimism that if midcentury America was not "the best of all possible worlds," then the America of the future could be.

Clifford Odets was born in Philadelphia but grew up in the Bronx, the locale of plays such as *Awake and Sing!* (1935). Although he seemed like the dramatist equivalent to the radical proletarian novelists of the 1930s, Odets came from the lower middle class. He was an actor for many years before he became a playwright. In fact he went from high school to the vaudeville stage and early radio. Odets was briefly a member of the Communist party in 1934. His early successes as a dramatist were with the Group Theatre. The radical *Waiting for Lefty* (1935) made his reputation as a socially conscious playwright. *Awake and Sing!,* an anatomy of a lower-middle-class Jewish family during the Depression, proved that he was a major playwright. *Paradise Lost* (1935) has another lower-middle-class Bronx family, not specifically Jewish this time, in which the males are debilitated by capitalism's exploitation of employees. The audience sees the emptiness of their lives. *Golden Boy* (1937), Odets's finest drama, is the tragedy of an artist in the wrong profession. *Rocket to the Moon* (1938), another middle-class drama, is the story of a dentist who tries to alleviate the pain of his unhappy marriage by taking a lover. *The Big Knife* (1949) savages the destructive culture of Hollywood. *The Country Girl* (1950) is a show business drama about an alcoholic actor, almost down and out, who is given a second chance for stardom. He is saved from failure again by a self-sacrificing wife. *The Flowering Peach* (1954) is a warm-hearted comedy about the biblical Noah.

From 1937 to 1941 Odets was married to Academy Award-winning movie star Luise Rainer. After a divorce, in 1943 he married a sweetheart from earlier days, the actor Betty Grayson. They were divorced in 1951.

Odets wrote several excellent screen plays. His career eventually deteriorated because he was trapped in vacillation between his desire to be a major dramatist and the temptation of big money in Hollywood. In 1955 *The Big Knife* was made into a successful film, as was *The Country Girl* in 1954. With the latter Grace Kelly won her Academy Award.

Waiting for Lefty (1935)

Waiting for Lefty, a pro-labor protest play in one act, made Odets's reputation as a playwright. Various members of a taxi drivers' union act out their reason for a strike. Like a chorus in Greek tragedy, other drivers watch, listen, and wait for the entrance of their leader, Lefty. He never arrives. He has been murdered on the way to the strike meeting. A member shouts his call for a vote, but directs it at the audience. In one of the electric moments in American theater, all shout in unison: "Strike!"

Awake and Sing! (1935)

The title comes from the Hebrew Bible: "Awake and sing, ye that dwell in the dust." The young Odets was sure that the dust-dwellers one day would indeed awake and sing. Using his lower-middle-class Bronx Jewish upbringing, Odets presented the extended Berger family as a typical family of that background, time, and place. They live in a tenement flat. The mother is shrewish and selfish; the father is a work drudge; the daughter, Hennie, is expecting a child and has no husband. The son, Ralph, has more possibilities; recognizing this, his philosophical grandfather has made Ralph the beneficiary of his life insurance policy. Then the grandfather "accidentally" falls off the roof and dies. The family begins to disintegrate because the grandfather has been their linchpin. Ralph will persevere as a socialist organizer, and Hennie is rescued by Moe, a crippled World War I veteran.

Golden Boy (1937)

The drama *Golden Boy* is based on a true-life story of an Italian American young man who was a talented violinist but became a boxer because he couldn't earn a living with his music. Odets calls his hero Joe Bonaparte, a man of Sicilian origin who is torn between his desire for money and boxing fame and his love for music. He has an attitude. The world is against him, and he can take out his anger in the ring. As he fights he worries about his hands. Joe is successful in the ring despite an injury to his hand that ends his violin playing. Then he kills an opponent in the ring, and he hates himself for what he has become, a rapacious killer. Joe and his girlfriend run away in his new car, but they are killed in a crash. The play ends with the scene depicting Joe's parents in mourning. Like a modern Faust, Joe had sold his soul and destroyed his art, his love, and his life.

The Big Knife (1949)

A Hollywood story and a cautionary tale, *The Big Knife* centers on Charlie Castle, a well-known Hollywood star with an inflated ego, who has artistic pretensions. He is an unfaithful husband, his acting degenerates, and he evades reality when he runs from an automobile accident in which he has killed a child. Debilitated by alcoholism, he can no longer face life, so he commits suicide. The play depicted Odets's frustration with, and dislike of, Hollywood.

Additional Reading

Brenman-Gibson, Margaret. *Clifford Odets—American Playwright*. New York: Atheneum, 1981.
Miller, Gabriel. *Clifford Odets.*New York: Continuum, 1989.
Weales, Gerald. *Clifford Odets, Playwright*. London: Methuen, 1985.

Sidney Kingsley (1906–1995)

Kingsley was born Sidney Kirschner in Philadelphia. He studied drama and wrote one-act plays at Cornell. He served in the army during World War II. Kingsley's first play, *Men in White* (1933), a melodrama about a young doctor's difficulty in dedicating himself to medicine, received the Pulitzer Prize. *Dead End* (1935) continued his serious examination of the contemporary scene. Although he wrote nine plays, only *Dead End* and *Detective Story* (1949), his finest achievement, are remembered today. In these plays Kingsley created worlds that seem complete and contained as they illuminate the recent past.

Men in White (1933)

Audiences were captivated by the verisimilitude in Kingsley's portrayal of hospital procedures in *Men in White*. George Ferguson, an intern, is a dedicated physician who is engaged to marry a rich woman, Laura Hudson. She can't understand his idealism, and she wants his total attention. When she learns that George had an affair with a nurse who then dies in an illegal abortion, Laura ends the relationship and George leaves the country to study abroad.

Dead End (1935)

Dead End was Kingsley's response to, and description of, life in the New York City tenement slums during the Depression. Crime is rampant, and violence is random. The opening scene is a shocker with boys in swimsuits or nude jumping off a wharf and swimming in the foul East River. These "Dead End Kids" went on to a movie career of their own.

Tommy is the leader of a street gang. His sister, Drina, is trying to save him from a life of crime or worse. He leads the youths on a raiding expedition in which they steal a watch from a rich boy who lives in a nearby apartment house for the affluent. When the wealthy boy's father tries to retrieve the watch, Tommy stabs him to death. He is sent to prison.

In a parallel plot line, a hardened gangster, Babyface Martin, once a local gang member and now idol of the street boys, sneaks back to the neighborhood to visit his mother. He is wanted for murder. His mother rejects him, and the police shoot him down. The play seemed far beyond realism to its first audiences. It was naturalism—the real thing.

Detective Story (1949)

Police Captain Macleod is a dedicated cop. He rides herd on a crime-ridden, tenderloin district full of drug addicts, petty criminals, and other antisocial individuals. He is brutal with prisoners. Macleod is rigid in his morality, and his marriage is in danger because of his attitude. When he finds out that his wife once had an abortion, he breaks down and causes a suspect to shoot him to death. As in *Men in White,* an abortion not only destroys a fetus but also a relationship.

Kingsley was opposed to fanatical zealousness, regardless of the cause. Such behavior is bound to hurt the cause or the ideals it supports. But the great attraction of *Detective Story* lies in Kingsley's deft portrayal of the maniacs, reporters, pickpockets, thieves, and Irish cops who inhabit the precinct station house.

Additional Reading

Clurman, Harold. *Lies Like Truth.* New York: Grove, 1958.
Miller, Jordan Y. and Winifred L. Frazer. *American Drama Between the Wars.* Boston: Twayne, 1991.

John Patrick (1907–1995)

Born John Patrick Goggan in Louisville, Kentucky, John Patrick served in World War II as an ambulance driver with the British Army in many theaters of operations. He wrote more than twenty plays, only two of which were successful—*The Hasty Heart* (1944), based on his wartime experiences in army hospitals, and *The Tea House of the August Moon* (1953), a comic dramatization of a novel by Vern Sneider about the American occupation of Okinawa after World War II. The play won the Pulitzer Prize. Patrick was also very successful as a screenwriter.

The Hasty Heart (1944)

In an army hospital on the Burma front a fatally ill Scottish soldier, unaware that he is soon going to die, is befriended by his ward mates, who know his condition. The soldier is a dour, cold, suspicious, unlikable person, but his fellow patients are determined to cheer his last days. He warms a bit, but when he finds out the truth about his condition, he thinks that their care is only pity, not real affection. But they persist and he changes. The play is overly sentimental, but Patrick's point is well taken—we need each other.

The Teahouse of the August Moon (1953)

The well-meaning Captain Fisby tries to bring American-style democracy and free enterprise to a village on Okinawa, but there is nothing grown or manufactured there of any real value to the outside world. Sakini, a wily villager, turns a projected schoolhouse into a teahouse that also sells alcoholic drinks. The pompous and out-of-touch Colonel Purdy orders the teahouse destroyed. Just as it is razed, Washington learns of its existence and crows about it as an example of American free enterprise brought to natives. Fortunately for the American officers, Sakini and cohorts have hidden the building materials. The Okinawans rebuild the teahouse just in time for a visit from members of Congress and, of course, the press corps.

Teahouse of the August Moon was made into a 1970 musical, *Lovely Ladies, Kind Gentlemen,* that did not succeed.

William Saroyan (1908–1981)

Born in Fresno, California, to Armenian fruit farmers, William Saroyan had a limited education. His father died when he was three, and he and his siblings spent some time in an orphanage. He did many jobs prior to becoming a writer and establishing his reputation with the short story. He was a grocery clerk, a vineyard worker, and a telegraph operator. From 1942 to 1945 Saroyan was a soldier in the U.S. army. Saroyan had a childlike dream of, and compulsive love for, freedom. As a child of immigrants he embraced and embodied the restlessness and rootlessness in the American character. Saroyan was flamboyantly eccentric. He sought publicity egregiously. He married Carol Marcus in 1943 while in the army, and divorced her in 1949. He remarried her in 1951 and divorced her again in 1952. Saroyan gambled away his earnings. He disliked rules and he took pride in breaking traditional theater techniques.

Saroyan came to the attention of the theater world with *My Heart Is in the Highlands* (1939), produced by the Group Theatre. His most important and successful play is the Pulitzer Prize-winning *The Time of Your Life* (1939). Saroyan turned down the award because he claimed he did not believe in prizes. *The Time of Your Life* was the only play to its day to win both the Pulitzer and the New York Drama Critics Circle award. Mixed receptions greeted his subsequent plays *Love's Old Sweet Song* (1940), the story of a gullible spinster and a con man, and *The Beautiful People*, (1941) a comic fantasy about an unconventional family—the son writes single-word novels and the daughter talks to her mice—living in a run-down San Francisco mansion. Only the one-act play *Hello, Out There* (1942) and *The Time of Your Life* are occasionally revived today.

Saroyan's forte was mood. Ideas came out confused. He did not live up to the promise of his youth. In addition to writing some forty plays and many short stories, Saroyan wrote novels, the best known of which is his first, *The Human Comedy* (1943).

My Heart Is in the Highlands (1939)

My Heart Is in the Highlands is an experimental one-act play in which Jasper MacGregor, an immigrant from Scotland, now in California, tells tall tales, spins yarns, sings, and plays the tune "My Heart Is in the Highlands" for children in the home of a failed poet, Ben Alexander, a man about to lose his humble abode. It's a feel-good, sentimental piece.

The Time of Your life (1939)

The Time of Your life is a great mood piece with fine characters. It is set in Nick's waterfront saloon in San Francisco, something like the New York waterfront bar in Eugene O'Neill's *Anna Christie* and *The*

Iceman Cometh. Both writers knew run-down dives quite well. Joe, a generous older man, helps the clientele to express themselves, find contentment, and feel happy. His young friend Tom, and Kitty, a young prostitute, find love. Joe helps a dancer get a job. A supposedly very old "Indian Fighter," dressed in buckskin and named Kit Carson, tells his improbable yarns. A pinball machine addict plays away his nickels until the crescendo of a jackpot proves that there is always the hope of happiness.

The bonhomie of the bar and the anarchism of the characters produce a charming atmosphere, as if the place were a world unto itself. Saroyan shows his deep affection for the poor, the down and out, the eccentric, and the young.

Hello, Out There (1940)

Hello, Out There is a one-act play about a young couple: the man has been framed on a charge of rape, the woman cleans the cells. Surrounded by filth and fear, they manage to find love for a short while. The man is killed; the girl is hurt. Deceit conquers goodness. Still, the play portrays Saroyan's compassion and love of those on the bottom rung of society's ladder.

Additional Reading

Floan, Howard R. *William Saroyan*. New York: Twayne, 1966.
Lee, Lawrence and Barry Gifford. *Saroyan: A Biography*. Berkeley: Univ. of California Press, 1984.

14

Tennessee Williams

American Master and the World War II Generation

American dramatists born just before, during, and shortly after World War I, and who were of the age for military service in World War II, constitute the stellar cluster of those who have written for the American stage. They made the golden age of American drama: 1945 (Williams's *The Glass Menagerie*) to 1968 (Miller's *The Price*). They included realists, expressionists, idealogues, absurdists, and political activists.

Tennessee Williams was the great romantic of the American drama. He was fascinated with the poignant side of the human condition: the suffering and death of the young, the pains of the defeated, the fading of youth and beauty, self-destruction, the violence in love, the vicissitudes of the gay world, and deep despair. Tennessee Williams was a compassionate human being who understood frustration more than most. He drank too much, used drugs, and had destructive homosexual affairs, but at his best he had the dramatic skills, the poetic language, and the vibrant imagination to shape his visions into great dramas.

Tennessee Williams was born Thomas Lanier Williams in Columbus, Mississippi. Tom began calling himself Tennessee when he was living in New Orleans in 1939, although it may have been used by roommates at college as a nickname for the young man from the South. Williams's parents were an unhappy couple who argued continually and violently. Williams's older sister, Rose, was so terrified by her parents' battles that she became mentally unbalanced. She would later undergo a frontal lobotomy and spend many years in institutions. It was Williams who cared for his sister for much of her life.

Williams's aggressive and heavy-drinking father, Cornelius, was a traveling salesman. His puritanical mother, Edwina, was the only child of an Episcopal minister, Edwin Dakin, who was a major influence on his grandson. Edwina and her children lived with her father in several parishes in Mississippi and Tennessee because she did not want to leave her parents and settle into a permanent family home as long as her husband was on the road selling.

Williams was struck down with diphtheria at the age of five and was barely able to walk for two years. Women—his mother, grandmother, and sister—provided his companionship. When, in 1918, Cornelius got a job as the sales manager of the International Shoe Company in St. Louis, Missouri, he bought a small, dark, and unpleasantly furnished house in the city. Then he brought Edwina, now pregnant with their third child, Walter, and Tom and Rose to St. Louis. As Williams and his brother grew up, they were sheltered from their abusive father under their mother's wing and urged her to leave Cornelius, but as a clergyman's daughter she could not do it.

From the age of eleven, when his mother gave him a typewriter, Williams loved writing. He entered the University of Missouri in 1931 to study journalism. There he became interested in playwriting. But his father, angry that Williams had failed R.O.T.C. (Reserve Officers Training Corps), forced him to withdraw from college to do menial work for the International Shoe Company. Williams got back to college—this time it was Washington University in St. Louis— but he dropped out in 1937. He enrolled in the University of Iowa, where he began writing one-act plays, and graduated in 1938.

After college Williams continued to write short plays, to work with regional theaters, and to hold various jobs. He moved to New Orleans in 1939. The personal and sexual freedom Williams experienced in the Mardi Gras city broke the puritanical hold of his mother and grandparents and the repressive tyranny of his scornful, controlling, patriarchal father. Williams had changed forever. Meanwhile, his one-act plays were being performed regionally and being published. He spent the summer of 1939 at Laguna Beach, California, in the sun, writing scenarios for full-length plays.

Back in St. Louis, recovering from an operation, Williams learned that he had received a playwriting grant from the Rockefeller Foundation and a scholarship to a seminar in playwriting at New York City's New School for Social Research. The course was conducted by the Theatre Guild. There he completed his first full-length drama, *Battle of Angels* (1940), a southern drama featuring a helpless, frightened, and repressed southern belle living in the past, a type based on his mother. The play's production received financial backing, and a major director, Margaret Webster, directed it. A big-name actor, Miriam Hopkins, had the lead role, but the play failed in the Boston tryout and never reached Broadway. Boston was not a good initial venue for a play that stirred religion and sex together.

Undaunted, Williams continued to write. His next play was *The Glass Menagerie* (1945), a dream play in which a young man reflects on the years his mother and sister lived in conflicting fantasies. The play instantly became a monument of the American theater, and the thirty-four-year-old author was immediately recognized as a major dramatist. His next play confirmed everything. The Pulitzer Prize-winning *A Streetcar Named Desire* (1947) has long been recognized as Williams's supreme achievement. It is the story of yet another genteel southern belle who is unprepared for the harsh realities of life.

Summer and Smoke (1948) is less subtle than *A Streetcar Named Desire*. It depicts an ironical relationship in which a sexually repressed southern woman, the daughter of a minister, fights off her sexually aggressive lover, only to lose him just as she begins to open up to a passionate life. *The Rose Tattoo* (1950), a lusty comedy (one of Williams's few humorous plays) affirms life by showing how sexual passion can win out over the power of death.

Camino Real (1953) failed because its complex fantasy was too difficult for the audience to follow. But the next play was Williams's third great drama, the Pulitzer Prize-winning *Cat on a Hot Tin Roof* (1955), in which Williams anatomizes the passions and ambitions of a southern family dominated by a patriarchal father. *Orpheus Descending* (1957) was another unappreciated surrealistic fantasy. Williams's next success was the shocking *Suddenly Last Summer* (1958), a story dealing with pedophilia, cannibalism, and lobotomy. *Sweet Bird of Youth* (1959) is another shocker; this time the subjects are seduction, venereal disease, and castration.

The Night of the Iguana (1962) was Williams's last really successful play. It is a compassionate tale of a defrocked minister, down on his luck and living in a Mexican hotel, who makes his peace with humanity, God, and himself. Although the prolific playwright continued to produce plays, after *The Night of the Iguana* Williams's dramas had little Broadway success until his work was no longer welcome there, except for revivals of his early classics. One exception, *Small Craft Warnings* (1972), a play about losers in a beachfront Southern California bar, found some appreciative audiences.

Movie versions of Williams's major plays were generally starstudded, popular, and successful. Actors such as Marlon Brando, Vivien Leigh, Burt Lancaster, Richard Burton, Elizabeth Taylor, and Anna Magnani gave memorable performances in them.

In his later years Williams spent much of his life in Florida. He died tragically in 1983, choking to death on the plastic top of a medicine bottle he was trying to open with his teeth. There were great expectations for Tennessee Williams. Although in the end he did not live up to those expectations, the power, lyricism, and anguish of his earlier plays have made him an international theater immortal.

The Glass Menagerie (1945)

A tender, poignant mood piece of great beauty, *The Glass Menagerie* depicts a disintegrating family as seen in the memory of Tom Wingfield, the son who finally abandons his impoverished mother and sister because he cannot save them. His mother, Amanda, is a former southern belle living in the past and trying to force her values and pretensions on her children: Tom and his shy, physically handicapped sister, Laura, who lives her life in the world of her glass animal figurines.

A Gentleman Caller—that is, a possible suitor for Laura—is brought to the St. Louis tenement flat, but he is already engaged. The attempt to find financial salvation through a marriage is a debacle. All members of the family are hurt and defeated, and the family bond shatters.

A Streetcar Named Desire (1947)

A Streetcar Named Desire is set in New Orleans. A coarse, rebarbative, insensitive worker, Stanley Kowalski, battles his wife Stella's fragile, self-deluding sister, Blanche DuBois, for Stella's love. Stanley rapes Blanche, another wounded southern belle, and drives her over the edge into insanity. Stella is torn between her feelings of responsibility for her sister and her sexual need for the passionate Stanley. Blanche is taken to a mental asylum as the guilt-ridden Stella is held and stroked by her husband.

Stanley represents raw power riding roughshod over a decaying, effete society. Williams implies that sexuality is the primary force in human relations.

Marlon Brando distinguished himself by playing Stanley in the original Broadway production and in the film version (1951).

Summer and Smoke (1948)

Alma Winemiller, a high-minded daughter of a Mississippi minister, loves her neighbor, Dr. John Buchanan, but she is put off by his aggresive sexuality. She is an idealist, and the handsome doctor is far from ideal. John is attracted to Alma because of her idealism and purity, but he shows his attraction by behaving coarsely. When John's father is killed in an accident caused by John's decadent friends, John, remorseful, changes his ways, but chooses to marry a more earthy woman. Alma has been infected with John's carnality, and she becomes a promiscuous woman.

The Rose Tattoo (1950)

Alvaro, a rough-and-ready truck-driving man similar to Stanley Kowalski, must overcome a rival: Serifina Delle Rose's dead husband. The devout Sicilian American widow has been keeping the husband's funeral urn by her side. Alvaro eventually restores her love of life. The change is symbolized by the disappearance of her rose tattoo, which stood for her consecration to her husband. *The Rose Tattoo* is humorous, lyric, and inspiring. One need not be lonely or despairing if one has the capacity for passion.

Cat on a Hot Tin Roof (1955)

Cat on a Hot Tin Roof is a frank play about sexual ambivalence. Maggie (the cat) is married to Brick, an alcoholic former football star and a hunk of a man who has lost sexual interest in her. Big Daddy, the patriarchal head of the wealthy southern family, has been counting on Brick, his favorite son, and Maggie to produce a grandson. Big Daddy is dying of cancer, and either Brick or his less manly brother, Gooper, will inherit the family fortune. Brick has an attachment to the memory of his dead buddy, Skipper.

Maggie will do anything to win her husband back and to obtain the inheritance for them. She reveals to Brick that she had an affair with Skipper, who proved to be gay. As a result of the affair, Skipper killed himself. Brick realizes that his drinking is related to guilt over his homosexual tendencies. Desperate, Maggie lies that she is pregnant. Now Brick will inherit. She takes charge of her husband, discards all the liquor, and states that they will make the lie true. Then she'll allow him to drink again.

The play has many ironies and ambiguities, like life itself. If Maggie is not to be victimized, she must be a strong woman and take charge of a weak husband, thus saving both her marriage and her wealth. Materialism is a stronger basis of a family structure than most people would like to believe.

The brilliant crafting of the play, the sexual theme, and the strong characterizations have kept the play current and vital.

Suddenly Last Summer (1958)

This play of Williams is not as successful as others in evoking sympathy for deviant or grotesque characters. The world of *Suddenly Last Summer* is infused with the cruelty of raw nature. The devouring of Sebastian, a gay young poet, by a piranha pack of vengeful boys on whom he has preyed, and the lobotomizing of Catherine, the pretty girl he uses as a lure, and who witnessed the cannibalism, was too much for the 1950s audience to bear.

Sweet Bird of Youth (1959)

Sweet Bird of Youth is a Hollywood story, but set in a gulf town where a fading, alcoholic film actor, Alexandre Del Lago (who calls herself Princess Kosmonopolis as a consolation for a career coming to an end), appears with a young boyfriend, Chance Wayne. Wayne hopes to use the actor to further his way in the world. A native of the town, he left some years ago after infecting the daughter of the local political boss with a sexually transmitted disease. The boss is out for revenge.

When Del Lago finds out that she has a chance for a comeback, she dumps Wayne, telling him that all he has going for him is his sexy youth and that the "sweet bird of youth" is fading. Wayne stays in town, waiting for the boss's men to come and castrate him. A twenty-first-century audience would be less shocked than the mid-twentieth-century audience was with Williams's "depravity."

The Night of the Iguana (1962)

William's last hit play, *The Night of the Iguana*, is set in a rundown Mexican hotel in which a group of unsuccessful, maladjusted people tell their stories and try to find resolutions for their difficult lives. A defrocked priest, Shannon, is a tour guide through the individual hell each character reveals. When delirious, Shannon is tied up in a hammock. An iguana tied by a foot to a verandah symbolizes Shannon's plight and the plight of all humans: to be bound up within our psyches and our beastly bodies.

Additional Reading

Boxill, Roger. *Tennessee Williams*. New York: St. Martin's, 1987.

Leverich, Lyle. *Tom: The Unknown Tennessee Williams*. New York: Crown, 1995.

Londré, Felicia H. *Tennessee Williams: Life, Work, Criticism*. Fredericton, N.B.: York, 1989.

Williams, Tennessee. *Tennessee Williams: Memoirs*. Garden City, N.Y.: Doubleday, 1975.

Garson Kanin (1912–99)

Born in Rochester, New York, Garson Kanin achieved his greatest success as a director, but one of his four plays is a perennial favorite in regional and community theater. Set in a Washington, D.C., hotel suite, *Born Yesterday* (1946) is the story of Billie Dawn, a former chorus girl and the beautiful mistress of a loud, uncouth, but very wealthy dealer in junk, Harry Brock, whose business methods are dubious and whose political connections are corrupt. Billie seems not to be bright, but she is merely uneducated. Her gaffes bother Harry, so he employs a handsome, young, radical reporter, Paul, to teach her to speak and act with some class, but Paul also empowers her with knowledge and social consciousness.

The young people grow fond of each other. Billie now sees Brock for the boor he is. They fight and she leaves. But Brock had signed over most of his property to her, and she has evidence of his shady dealings, so she returns and exerts her control over him. She won't turn him in to the authorities, and she'll give him back his property a little at a time as long as he behaves himself. Billie's life will begin again with marriage to Paul.

This delightful political satire, with its challenging role for the actor who plays Billie, unfortunately always appears applicable to the American political scene. The rapacious Brocks are ever with us, ready to undermine democracy in the name of free enterprise.

William Inge (1913–1973)

William Inge achieved wide recognition as a playwright and a screen—and television writer. He was born in Independence, Kansas, and he earned a bachelor of arts degree at the University of Kansas in 1935. In the 1950s he was a leading Broadway playwright, whose dramas were made into excellent films. His best-remembered plays deal with the frustrations and anxieties of life in America's heartland, the Midwest.

Inge's first Broadway play, *Come Back, Little Sheba* (1950), established his reputation as a perceptive social commentator. *Picnic* (1953) won the Pulitzer Prize. *Bus Stop* (1955) charmed New York audiences and became a vehicle for a Marilyn Monroe film. *The Dark at the Top of the Stairs* (1957) reflected Inge's unhappy childhood. Inge's main characters are often unhappy people seemingly out of place in their environments. The world of Inge's drama is a lonely place.

Inge continued to write plays until 1970, but none of the later dramas succeeded. Suffering from alcoholism and other ills, Inge committed suicide in 1973.

His 1950s plays continue to attract and satisfy audiences in repertory theater productions.

Come Back, Little Sheba (1950)

Lola, a kind-hearted, frumpy, middle-aged woman, is married to a recovering alcoholic who did not complete medical school but who is called "Doc." She dreams of her lost puppy, Little Sheba. The dog, which ran away a long time ago, was her only source of affection in her unhappy life. Doc becomes infatuated with an attractive college student boarder and jealous of her boyfriend. He goes on a terrible drinking binge. After hospitalization and full of contrition, Doc returns to Lola to make the best of their lives.

Picnic (1953)

In *Picnic* the women of a family are affected by a sexually attractive outsider named Hal. Their placid lives are turned upside down by the arrival of his powerful life force in the heat of summer's end.

Bus Stop (1955)

A poignant comedy, *Bus Stop* is set in a Kansas bus stop diner where a group of bus passengers wait out a blizzard. A naïve, virginal cowboy named Bo is chasing after a not-too-bright but very sexy nightclub singer, Cherie, who is trying to run away from the pesky young man. In the end he learns to temper his sexual aggression with tenderness and true caring, and thus wins her after all.

The Dark at the Top of the Stairs (1957)

In *The Dark at the Top of the Stairs* a middle-class Oklahoma family in the 1920s is beset by problems and a tragedy. The father sells harnesses, and autos are putting him out of business. The most traumatic event is the suicide of his daughter's date, a Jewish boy who kills himself because an anti-Semite humiliates him. The dark at the top of the stairs is the misery in the human condition. Our minds are unknown lands. Still, decent people feel compassion, and that is the distant glow that warms Inge's plays.

Additional Reading

Shuman, Robert Baird. *William Inge*. Rev. ed. New York: Twayne, 1987.
Voss, Ralph F. *The Life of William Inge: The Strains of Triumph*. Lawrence, Kans.: Univ. of Kansas Press, 1989.

Samuel Taylor (1913–2000)

A writer of elegant and witty drawing-room comedies in the 1950s and 1960s, Samuel Taylor was a master of cocktail-time smart talk and epigrams, and well-made plots in the fashion of Philip Barry. His greatest success was the Cinderella-like comedy *Sabrina Fair* (1953), which has been made into two major films to date. Other hits include *The Happy Time* (1950), *The Pleasure of His Company* (1958), and *Beekman Place* (1964). Taylor's work will be revived from time to time for the skillful way in which he captured a milieu.

Sabrina Fair (1953)

Sabrina, the daughter of the chauffeur of the rich Larrabee family, having returned from Paris, now has many suitors, but her feelings are for one of the Larrrabee sons. The two of them circle about until they come together in love, and it helps that the chauffeur has quietly made a small fortune on the stock market.

William Gibson (1914–)

Born in New York City and educated at City College of New York from 1930 to 1932, Gibson left school to act, play piano in bars, write poetry, and then write plays for regional and university theaters. A production at the University of Kansas in 1947, *A Cry of Players*, caught the attention of critics and agents. It is the story of three days in Shakespeare's life, just prior to his desertion of his wife and children and his departure from Stratford to London and fame. In 1968 the rewritten play had a successful production at Lincoln Center.

Gibson's first Broadway play, *Two for the Seesaw* (1958), the love story of a separated businessman from the Midwest and a brash Bronx girl, was a smash success. A film adaptation followed, and a musical version, *Seesaw* (1973), entertained Broadway audiences a generation later.

The Miracle Worker (1959) is the story of Helen Keller, a woman who from her childhood was blind and deaf and who overcame her grave handicaps through the heroic efforts of her teacher, Annie Sullivan, the "miracle worker." A sequel, *Monday after the Miracle* (1982), was not successful. Gibson adapted Clifford Odets's Depression-era play *Golden Boy* into a musical in 1964. *Golda* (1979) is a biographical drama based on the life of the first woman to be prime minister of Israel, the American-born Golda Meir. *The Butterfingers Angel* (1975) is a popular and frequently produced Christmas pageant. William Gibson has proved himself a skilled theater psychologist and a master of staging.

Two for the Seesaw (1958)

Full of kitchen-sink realism, *Two for the Seesaw* is simultaneously set in a decrepit New York City hotel room in which an Omaha businessman, Jerry Ryan, is licking his wounds while seeking a divorce from his wife, and in the hopelessly messy apartment of Gittel Mosca, a Jewish girl from the Bronx who is not succeeding as a dancer.

Gittel and Jerry have an affair. Gittel helps Jerry regain his emotional balance and recommit to his marriage. Although Gittel, so much the finer human being of the two, is heartbroken when Jerry leaves, both characters learn and grow in their brief relationship. Gibson reminds audiences that a romantic interlude can recharge lives and relationships that have staled with time, familiarity, and daily abrasions. A two-character play, *Two for the Seesaw* remains a favorite community theater vehicle.

The Miracle Worker (1959)

Gibson's most popular play, *The Miracle Worker*, has been a perennial inspiration for people with disabilities and for those who aid them.

An inexperienced teacher of the handicapped, Annie Sullivan, whose blindness was cured in childhood, is confronted with the professional and emotional challenge of a lifetime. The child Helen Keller is a blind, deaf, spoiled animal whose father has given up on her, although her mother has not. In a year's time Anne converts Helen into an educable person who will go on to greatness as a writer. The 1962 film version inspired tens of millions.

Additional Reading

Gibson, William. *A Mass for the Dead.* New York: Atheneum, 1968.
———. *The Seesaw Log: A Chronicle of the Stage Production.* New York: Knopf, 1959.

Arthur Miller (1915–): American Master

Arthur Miller is America's greatest living playwright and, arguably, Western civilization's most notable current dramatist. He embodies the conscience of America in the twentieth century. He has seen and absorbed the terrors, the suffering, and the horrors of the Depression, World War II, the Holocaust, the McCarthy era, the Vietnam War, the implosion of Communism, and the African and Balkan genocides as the century ended. Although Miller never lived in a totalitarian state, he understood the power and the danger of ideologies that denied the value of the individual, and the necessity for individual conscience. Miller never hides his politics in his plays. He is fully committed to liberal social democracy.

Arthur Miller was born in New York City. His father was a Jewish immigrant manufacturer of women's coats. His mother was an American-born housewife and mother of three. He grew to maturity in the Great Depression, so that after graduating from Lincoln High School in Brooklyn, he worked as a stock clerk to earn money for college because the Depression had struck his father's business. Miller studied drama at the University of Michigan, where he was awarded the Avery Hopgood prize for playwriting. He helped earn money for his education by working as a journalist. After graduating with a bachelor of arts degree in 1938, Miller returned to New York City, where for a short period he affiliated himself with the Federal Theater Project, did war work at the Brooklyn Navy Yard, and wrote radio scripts as well as two novels.

As a playwright, Miller is a follower of Ibsen both in dramaturgy and in themes. His mode is realism. He writes thesis plays, challenging an audience to make moral judgments. He indicts bourgeois society for its selfishness while he insists on the collective responsibility of all human beings for each other.

Miller's first Broadway play, *The Man Who Had All the Luck,* failed in 1944, but his next play, *All My Sons* (1947), a play about World War II profiteering, was a success. Miller's greatest drama, arguably the greatest American tragedy, *Death of a Salesman* (1948), won the

Pulitzer Prize and brought Miller to the forefront of American dramatists. Miller is fascinated by the potential capacities of humans. They can be compassionate and cruel, selfish and self-sacrificing, creative and destructive. But always they are unpredictable. And unpredictability is the grist for Miller's characterizations.

The Crucible (1953), ostensibly about the seventeenth-century Salem witch trials, reflected on the threat to freedom and justice during the McCarthy-fabricated, anti-Communist hysteria in the 1950s. It is one of Miller's most frequently produced plays. *A View from the Bridge* (1955; revised 1965), set in the Brooklyn Miller knew well, is his version of a Greek tragedy in which sexual passion leads to disaster. *A Memory of Two Mondays* (1955) is a Depression-era Chekhovian mood piece set in a New York City warehouse.

One of the great film scripts of the 1950s is Miller's *The Misfits* (1959), which he wrote for his second wife, Marilyn Monroe, to whom he was married from 1956 to 1961. His first wife was Mary Slattery, with whom he had two children. Miller's third wife is the photographer Ingeborg Morath, whom he married in 1962 and with whom he has a child.

After the Fall (1964) is partly based on his marriage to Marilyn Monroe and seems to explain the traumas and insecurities that led to her suicide. The powerful play, a study in suffering, also speaks to his Judaism and explains his third and last marriage.

Incident in Vichy (1964) is a philosophical and moving World War II play about the human capacity for nobility and sacrifice in the face of inhumanity. Miller returned to the Brooklyn locale for *The Price* (1968), in which two brothers pay the price of rivalry with concomitant loneliness. This is the play in which Miller finally acknowledges his Jewish background, his own Jewishness, and his debt to Old Testament and Talmudic values.

Miller anatomizes good and evil in *The Creation of the World and Other Business* (1972). The play was not a success, nor was the Depression-era drama *The American Clock* (1980).

The Ride down Mt. Morgan (1991) is a strange play that sadly ad-

vocates a patriarchal and wealthy man's "right" to bigamous relationships, regardless of the pain they bring to women and children.
Yet Miller's fierce commitment to the joy of life shines through and
somewhat redeems the unpleasant drama. *The Last Yankee* (1991) is a
short play about two men from different stations in life who meet in
a hospital while visiting their wives, who are suffering from depression. *Broken Glass* (1995) refers to *Kristallnacht*, the 1938 event in
which German thugs destroyed many of the synagogues in the
country and attacked Jews. A Jewish American wife and her husband, living in Brooklyn, struggle with a marriage that has shattered like glass. *Mr. Peters' Connections* (1998) is set in a bar where
Peters, a retired pilot, fantasizes about his dead brother and other
people in his past life as, in an impressionistic way, he searches for
his identity.

Arthur Miller is an idealist, ever disappointed but still hoping if
not always believing that the human condition can be improved. In
his plays he is a retriever of lost souls. At his best Miller is a poet
whose language flies us beyond reason to the realm of the heart,
where songs of disappointment are always playing.

Arthur Miller is not as prolific a playwright as were Eugene
O'Neill and Tennessee Williams. But his plays have had as much or
perhaps even more impact on the social and political awareness of
Americans than the two other dramatists who stand with him at the
head of American drama.

All My Sons (1947)

All My Sons argues that each person is fully responsible for his or
her actions and for what those actions do to other human beings. An
airplane engine manufacturer during World War II, Joe Keller has
turned out faulty units that resulted in the crash of several planes
and the death of young pilots. During an investigation Keller let his
business partner take the blame. Joe's son Larry is an aviator, and he
has been reported missing and presumed killed in a crash. A letter

to his brother Chris states that Larry knew what his father did and, because he was ashamed that Joe caused the death of his buddies, he decided not to come back from his next combat mission. Joe finally realizes that he not only killed young men serving the country but was also responsible for his own son's death. He knows now that "they were all my sons." Then he kills himself.

Death of a Salesman (1949)

Willy Loman, a garment-industry traveling salesman, is worn out. He can't drive to New England and sell as he once did. He loves his elder son, Biff, who left home some years ago after he found his father in a hotel room with a woman. Willy is fired by his unfeeling boss, even though he is sixty-three and has devoted his life to the company. The father-son relationship is a tortured one. In the end, the now mentally ill Willy commits suicide in order to leave his son twenty thousand dollars from his insurance policy in the hope that he could give his son something of greater worth than his amoral values and his belief in the American dream. *Death of a Salesman* is the great tragedy of the little man, tossed about by the economic forces he thinks he controls but that, in fact, control and ultimately destroy him.

The Crucible (1953)

Set in Salem, Massachusetts, in 1692, *The Crucible* is really a universal story about man's inhumanity to man and the dangers of fanaticism. John Proctor is a farmer who has had an affair with Abigail, the niece of a leading minister in the town. She has been working for Proctor and his wife, Elizabeth. When Elizabeth fires Abigail, the angry girl accuses her of being a witch. The atmosphere at the time is filled with hysteria, and Proctor tries to save his wife by confessing his adultery. But his confession is nullified by Elizabeth's refusal to betray John. In order to save his life he must recant publicly and name other names to provide more victims for the witch hunt. He is tempted. Life is good. But in the end he chooses dignity and death. Evil is religious or political fanaticism. Evil also is the desire of some people to have life and death power over others.

A View from the Bridge (1955; enlarged in 1965)

Eddie Carbone, a Brooklyn longshoreman, seems happily married, but without realizing it himself, he has fallen deeply in love with the young, beautiful niece of his wife who lives with the Carbones. She meets and falls in love with Rodolpho, a young, Italian illegal immigrant. Furiously jealous, Eddie does everything he can to destroy the relationship between the young lovers. Finally, he betrays the boy to the immigration society. It is a death act in the working-class Italian immigrant society of Brooklyn. In revenge, Rodolpho's brother kills Eddie.

The play is operatic. The emotions portrayed by the seemingly simple characters are deep, complex, archetypal, alarming, and larger-than-life.

After the Fall (1964)

After the Fall is Miller's most personal and introspective drama. Quentin, the protagonist, is a lawyer. During the play he seems to talk to the audience, an analyst, or a jury. But he is really judging himself. Quentin is soon to be married a third time. He reveals the impact he has had on his parents, his first wife, and most of all on Maggie, his glamorous second wife with whom he had a difficult marriage because of her fear, insecurity, and instability. Ultimately, she committed suicide. He is with his third wife as they visit a former German concentration camp and struggle to get beyond the nightmare of the Nazi period.

After the Fall plays very powerfully. The audience is fascinated by the intimacy revealed and by the analytic treatment of finely drawn characters who seem to emerge directly from Quentin's mind.

Incident at Vichy (1964)

In Vichy, France, the site of the collaborationist French government after the defeat of France by the Germans in 1940, a group of men have been rounded up to be identified as Jews and sent to a concentration camp, presumably to their deaths. One is a nobleman, Von Berg. A Jewish psychiatrist states that he believes all gentiles harbor some anti-Semitism. Each person has a Jew to hate, even Jews. Men are called into the office of the Nazi commander and are condemned. Von Berg comes out of the office freed with a pass. He is not a Jew. He gives his pass, the means to freedom, to the waiting psychiatrist as an act of faith. The doctor is dismayed. He will be in the Christian aristocrat's debt for the rest of his life.

The Price (1968)

The theme of *The Price* is that all relationships require their participants to pay a price. The cost may be high, even too high, but without relationships there is no love, only loneliness. We are always beholden to others because we need them.

Two brothers, Victor and Walter, who have been estranged because their upbringing and environment have valorized competition, now meet in the midst of the stored furniture from the family home. Growing up, material success was valued as the main achievement, not successful relationships. They believe in the price, not human value. Therefore, they can't love each other.

Fortunately, their wise old uncle, Gregory Solomon, a dealer in secondhand furniture who comes to buy up the junk in their lives, teaches them to go beyond retribution and find the faults within themselves. In any case, the naked truth of the past cannot be recalled. It no longer exists. Solomon is a homespun Jewish philosopher. The play ends with the old man's laughter at the folly of human ego. Gregory Solomon is one of Miller's greatest characters.

Additional Reading

Griffin, Alice. *Understanding Arthur Miller.* Columbia: Univ. of South Carolina Press, 1996.

Hayman, Ronald. *Arthur Miller.* New York: Ungar, 1972.

Miller, Arthur. *Timebends: A Life.* New York: Harper and Row, 1987.

Moss, Leonard. *Arthur Miller.* Boston: Twayne, 1970.

Schlueter, June, and James K. Flanagan. *Arthur Miller.* New York: Ungar, 1987.

Horton Foote (1916–)

Born in Wharton, Texas, Horton Foote studied acting at the Pasadena Playhouse and then moved to New York City to begin his career as a playwright. He wrote a series of engrossing plays about rural Texas, called the *Orphans' Home Cycle.* The complications of family life—coming of age, sorrow, loss, looking for work, losing jobs, rejection in love, the what-might-have-been— intrigued him. As a result his work had a universality that transcended his regionalism and captured the affection of audiences who saw their own daily lives reflected on the stage.

Foote's most successful plays are *The Widow Claire* (1986) and the Pulitzer Prize-winning *Young Man from Atlanta* (1995). His latest play is *The Last of the Thorntons* (2000). His screenplays for *To Kill a Mockingbird* (1962) and *Tender Mercies* (1983) won Oscars. His film *The Trip to Bountiful* (1985) is also highly regarded.

Carson McCullers (1916–1967)

Born in Columbus, Georgia, to Lamar and Marguerite Smith, McCullers left home for New York City at seventeen to study piano at the Julliard School and writing at Columbia University. She married Reed McCullers in 1937. Never strong in health, McCullers was partially paralyzed at twenty-nine, and during the last years of her short life she was confined to a wheelchair. McCullers was a very successful novelist whose main theme was the unhappiness and dislocation of adolescence.

McCullers's one play is an adaptation of her 1945 novel *A Member of the Wedding*. The play version (1950) was a major hit. It is the charming story of a twelve-year-old southern girl who desperately wants to go along on the honeymoon of her beloved brother and his bride. Her disappointment leads to understanding, maturation, and a boyfriend of her own.

In 1963 Edward Albee adapted for the stage McCullers's short novel about a brutal battle of the sexes, *The Ballad of the Sad Café*. It had only a short run on Broadway.

A Member of the Wedding (1950)

Frankie Adams is twelve years old and estranged from her slightly older girlfriends, who have already become interested in boys. She hangs out with her little cousin, John Henry West, and she is looked after by her surrogate mother, the four-times-married African American cook, Berenice Sadie Brown. Frankie's world is Berenice's kitchen, and she strives to break out of her confined space and connect to the wide world.

Frankie's mother is dead. Her soldier brother comes home to marry his hometown sweetheart, and Frankie wants to join them on their honeymoon. Heartbroken when she is told she can't do that, she tries to run away from home. In the end, however, Frankie is reconciled. She turns thirteen and wants to be called Frances. Frankie is an endearing character, and the play is a satisfying excursion in nostalgia.

Additional Reading

Cook, Richard M. *Carson McCullers*. New York: Ungar, 1973.

Graver, Lawrence. *Carson McCullers*. Minneapolis: Univ. of Minnesota Press, 1969.

Savigneau, Josyane. *Carson McCullers: A Life*. Boston: Houghton Mifflin, 2001.

Robert Anderson (1917–)

Born in New York City and educated at Phillips Exeter Academy and then Harvard University, from which he received a bachelor of arts degree in 1939 and a master of arts in 1940, Robert Anderson planned a life in the theater early on. Called to war, he won a Bronze Star serving in the U.S. Navy during World War II. Anderson's first-produced play was *Come Marching Home* (1944).

Anderson's greatest success was *Tea and Sympathy* (1953), the story of a shy student at a private school whose headmaster's sensitive wife helps him to acquire confidence in himself. *Silent Night, Holy Night* (1959) is the story of women deeply hurt by their husbands' infidelities. *You Know I Can't Hear You When the Water Is Running* (1967), a set of four short satires, had a popular reception. *I Never Sang for My Father* (1967) depicts the neediness of a son trying to find some love in his aged, bitter father.

Robert Anderson's plays are about loneliness, a human condition for people of all ages, in and out of marriage. His protagonists tend to be middle-aged. Their lives are disappointing. They have difficulty expressing this disappointment or showing their feelings at all. Men have special difficulties. They need to conform to the manly, stoical ideal projected in the films. Sensuality is a weakness, and they must not evidence sensitivity. Consequently, they leave the women in their lives hungry for sex and affection.

Tea and Sympathy (1953)

Because he is shy, Tom Lee is suspected of being a homosexual by his schoolmates in the boys' school he attends. His father and the schoolmaster make things worse with their interference. The schoolmaster's wife is sensitive and wise enough to realize that the emphasis on masculinity often hides mature men's fear of being gay. Compassionately, she offers sex to Tom, knowing that it will give him confidence in his sexuality.

Additional Reading

Adler, Thomas P. *Robert Anderson*. Boston: Twayne, 1978.

Ossie Davis (1922–)

Born in Cogdell, Georgia, son of a railway construction engineer, Ossie Davis was educated at Howard University from 1935 to 1939 and Columbia University in 1948. In World War II he served overseas in the U.S. Army. He married the actor Ruby Dee in 1948. The couple has had brilliant stage, television, and film careers. Davis has also directed in the theater.

Davis, a busy actor, has only written a few plays, but one of them, *Purlie Victorius* (1961), had a major impact on the New York stage. It is a satire on race relations in which racial prejudice and stereotyping are exposed as viciousness, madness, and folly.

Purlie Victorius (1961)

Young, black Purlie Judson returns to his small town home in the South to restore Big Bethel, now an old barn, to the church it once was. His church is to be an integrated one, and it will symbolize a new freedom for African Americans. With brilliant language, Davis re-creates the stereotypes of the American racial scene: the Uncle

Tom, the mammy, the Confederate-worshipping southern white, the white sheriff, and the plantation. Of course Purlie Judson wins out in the end over the bigots and the sellouts. *Purlie Victorius* has the ring of Swiftian satire. A musical version, *Purlie* (1970), was less well received.

Additional Reading

Davis, Ossie, and Ruby Dee. *With Ossie and Ruby: In This Life Together.* New York: Morrow, 1998.

Arthur Laurents (1918–)

Arthur Laurents was born to middle-class parents in Brooklyn. He studied playwriting at Cornell University. Laurents is best known for two plays, *Home of the Brave* (1945), the story of a World War II Jewish veteran who comes to grips with the anti-Semitism he found in the army; and the more successful *The Time of the Cuckoo* (1952), a play about an American spinster in need of love who has a romantic adventure in Venice. *Invitation to a March* (1960) is about a young woman who tries to go along with the world's values but rejects the world's banalities when she finds true love. Laurents is also a successful librettist with such hit musicals as *West Side Story* (1957) and *Gypsy* (1959).

Laurents's plays are about lonely people afraid of other people, who nevertheless need love, companionship, and approval. His characterization is psychologically strong, and he is successful in creating the appearance that his characters are independent and truly speaking for themselves. Laurents continues to write into the twenty-first century. *Big Potato* (2000) is a dark comedy-drama about the Holocaust.

The Time of the Cuckoo (1952)

Leone Samish, an unmarried American woman, comes to Venice hoping to find romance in the most romantic of Italian cities. Of course, she finds it with an Italian Romeo, Renato, who, alas, proves to be a gigolo and married too. But Leone has had both adventure and the kind of experience she would never have had safely back at home. The play is poignant. Laurents is gentle with Leona and Renato. *The Time of the Cuckoo* was turned into the delightful musical *Do I Hear a Waltz?* in 1965 with music by Richard Rodgers and lyrics by Stephen Sondheim.

Paddy Chayefsky (1923–1981)

Paddy Chayefsky had a successful career writing for stage, television, and film. In all three media his mode was realism. He was born in the Bronx and attended a public high school and then City College of New York. Chayefsky served in the U.S. Army during World War II and received a Purple Heart.

Chayefsky wrote five plays: *Middle of the Night* (1956), a play about a May-December romance that Chayefsky based on his television script of the same name; *The Tenth Man* (1959), a play about exorcism and a young couple involved in the process; *Gideon* (1961), a biblical drama; *The Passion of Josef D.* (1964), a life of Stalin; and *The Latent Homosexual* (1968), a satire of the drive for and cost of success. The last two failed and Chayefsky devoted the rest of his life to writing for film.

The television drama *Marty* (1953) is one of the great television scripts. The film version in 1955 won the Oscar for best picture and best screenplay.

Middle of the Night (1956)

Middle of the Night is a sensitive study of an affair between a wealthy older man, a widowed manufacturer, and his receptionist, thirty years his junior. Her husband is an unpleasant musician. The respective families of the lovers vehemently oppose the relationship. The man's daughter can't stand the thought of her father betraying the memory of her dead mother. Only the daughter's husband can appreciate his father-in-law's feelings. Beleaguered, the receptionist returns to her musician husband for a short while, but then, despite everything, the May-December couple fight the taboos and opt for their own version of happiness.

The Tenth Man (1959)

Nine elderly orthodox Jewish men in a synagogue need a tenth Jewish man to complete their required minyan of ten. They are ready to exorcise the demons debilitating Evelyn, a schizophrenic and the granddaughter of one of the worshippers. Arthur, a young Jewish man passing by, is talked into joining the group. He too is an emotionally troubled person; he is deeply depressed. In the process his demons are exorcised but Evelyn's persevere, and Arthur falls in love with her. He is convinced that he can cure the girl through his devotion, and he proposes marriage. The play has a mythic atmosphere and a fine sense of old world-new world conflict.

Gideon (1961)

Chayefsky's most ambitious play, *Gideon* is a debate between God, who appears on earth as an angel but is really an old man with little regard for humans, and Gideon, a not-too-bright young farmer who must become a military leader to free the Israelites from the domination of the Midianites. Gideon can't believe he has been the one chosen to do this, but the angel performs miracles and Gideon accepts his destiny. He is shown the plan for victory, and he succeeds against great odds. Alas, Gideon comes to think that his success was not due to God, but to human forces. The angel is very disappointed of course. The play is a parable about the egotism of humans, who inevitably believe more in themselves than in God.

Additional Reading

Clum, John M. *Paddy Chayefsky* Boston: Twayne, 1976.

James Baldwin (1924–1987)

Harlem born, James Baldwin was the eldest of nine children and the son of a minister. As a youth, he was a preacher too. After a sojourn in Greenwich Village, he emigrated to Paris in 1948 where he met the African American novelist James Ellison and began his writing career. His novels and polemics are among the mid-twentieth century's outstanding literary achievements. He was a major black spokesperson against racial discrimination. Baldwin maintained residences in New York City and Paris. He died in the south of France.

Two of Baldwin's plays have had an impact. *The Amen Corner* (1955; New York production, 1965) is a play about the trials of a female African American minister. It demonstrates how poor African Americans try to find solace in religion, and it states that the downtrodden need compassion more than the preaching of God's will. The better known *Blues for Mister Charlie* (1964) is based on the lynching of a Mississippi African American previously investigated by Baldwin.

Blues for Mister Charlie (1964)

Richard Henry is a young African American musician, the son of a preacher. He has come back to Mississippi from the North where drugs hurt him and where he was frustrated socially and professionally. At home, spoiling for trouble, he gets into a fight with, and is killed by, a white racist, Lyle Britton, who previously killed an African American man objecting to Britton's attempt to have sex with the man's unwilling wife. Britton is acquitted of Henry's killing by an all-white jury. At the trial, a liberal white southern journalist betrays his values when, although he knows that Britton is guilty, he can't bring himself to testify that Britton's white wife is lying. The journalist represents the white tragedy of racism, and Richard's father, the Reverend Meridian Henry, represents the black tragedy of racism, for he no longer believes that the races can live together in justice and harmony. Rather, racial violence is inevitable. The play is a warning to the racist southern white community of the time that their blues are being written.

Additional Reading

Pratt, Louis. *James Baldwin.* Boston: Twayne, 1978.
Sylvander, Carolyn W. *James Baldwin.* New York: Ungar, 1980.

Charles Gordone (1925–)

In 1970 Charles Gordone became the first African American playwright to win the Pulitzer Prize. The play was *No Place to Be Somebody,* which was also the first Off-Broadway play to win the prize. Gordone was born in Cleveland, Ohio, and was raised in Elkhart, Indiana. He studied at the University of California at Los Angeles and Los Angeles State College, where he received a bachelor of arts degree in drama. Gordone also studied television writing at New York University. Gordone did a tour in the United States Air Force. *No Place to Be Somebody* is Gordone's only commercially successful full-length play. Other Gordone dramas include *A Little More Light Around the Place* (1964), *Baba Chops* (1974), *The Last Chord* (1976), and *Roan Brown and Cherry* (1985).

Gordone has had much success as a director and actor. For Gordone the stage has been a platform to explain his politics, his personal frustrations, and his hope for humankind. He discounted the idea of black playwriting or black theater in favor of a theory of art that supersedes race and ethnicity.

No Place to Be Somebody (1969)

No Place to Be Somebody is an expressionistic play about the difficulties African Americans have in relating to the dominant white culture in which they are immersed. The play is set in Johnny's Bar, where the owner, Johnny Williams, an African American racketeer, vents his anger at white America. Besides being a bar owner, Johnny is an employer of prostitutes: he pimps for a black and a white woman. Johnny is having an affair with a white college girl. His bartender is a white man who wants to be black; that is, he dreams of being a black musician. It is an impossible dream not only because of his race but also because he is a drug addict.

Johnny wants to take on the Mafia and is hoping his pal Sweets Crane will help him when he gets out of prison. But Sweets is tired of life as a criminal and Johnny despairs.

The play's narrator, and surrogate for Gordone, is Gabe, an unemployed actor. He is fair skinned and therefore can't get work as either a black or a white character. Gabe is also a playwright writing a play about Johnny. In the end Johnny asks Gabe to kill him. Gabe does so, thus eliminating the protagonist of the play he is writing and now is unable to conclude.

Frank D. Gilroy (1925–)

Born in the Bronx, Frank D. Gilroy graduated from DeWitt Clinton High School in the Bronx and then served in the U.S. Army during World War II. After the war he went to Dartmouth College and graduated in 1950. He also spent a year at the Yale School of Drama. Although Gilroy has written over fifteen plays, he is best known for two successes: *Who'll Save the Ploughboy?* (1962), the story of a war veteran who has saved his buddy's life in combat and now has to save it again when civilian life has been terrible for him, and the Pulitzer Prize-winning *The Subject Was Roses* (1964). At his best Gilroy shows great skill in writing biting, sardonic dialogue, as his unhappy people deal with the emotional battles that disappointed middle-class people so often face.

The Subject Was Roses (1964)

A naturalistic drama painful to view, *The Subject Was Roses* is the story of a World War II veteran who comes home to the Bronx battlefield in which his parents war. A welcome home party the night before has left father and son badly hung over. The mother attacks the father for what has happened. The sympathy is with the father, whom the young soldier loves. In a few days the twenty-one-year-old veteran, Timmy, moves out of the domestic combat zone. He had once blamed his father for the strife. Upon returning home, he blamed his mother. Leaving, and now more mature, he realizes that blame is the wrong idea. They and he need compassion.

Murray Schisgal (1926–)

Brooklyn born and the son of a tailor, Murray Schisgal quit high school in 1943 to join the U.S. Navy and serve in World War II. After four years of service, he attended the Brooklyn Conservatory of Music and then earned a law degree in 1953 from Brooklyn Law School. After graduation, he practiced law and taught high school English.

Schisgal developed a reputation as an Off-Broadway absurdist playwright in the 1960s. He was grouped with Edward Albee, John Guare, and Arthur Kopit because all satirized middle-class American life in bitingly funny one-act plays such as Schisgal's *The Typists* (1963) and *The Tiger* (1963). In the latter play a postman kidnaps a housewife in order to rape her. The housewife is so impressed with the postman's rhetoric and gentlemanly behavior that she forgets that she has been kidnapped. They fall in love. *The Typists* satirizes office life as two typists, one female, one male, alternately joust and court over the years.

Schisgal's most important full-length play is *Luv* (1963), a satire on the gyrations of modern love. It had a very long run on Broadway—nine hundred performances! *Jimmy Shine* (1968; revised as *An Original Jimmy Shine* in 1981), which portrays the artist's struggle for simple meaning, and *All over Town* (1974), a play about upper-middle-class liberals, have found receptive audiences.

Luv (1963)

A warm, funny play about the emotion of love, *Luv* portrays a classic sexual triangle: husband, wife, and best friend. The three zany characters—Milt, Ellen, and Harry—deserve each other, a fact that gives a delicious and devilish twist to the somewhat predictable plot. They are eccentric, neurotic, depressed, and suicidal. As they change partners in the erotic dance, they illustrate the author's irreverence for the institution of marriage. Schisgal implies that no one is satisfied in it, yet everyone keeps trying.

At the play's opening Milt runs into his old college friend Harry, who is attempting suicide by jumping from a bridge, and he talks him out of it. Milt is unhappy too because he wants to leave his wife, Ellen, and marry another woman. He decides to pass his wife on to Harry. Harry marries Ellen. Milt marries his girlfriend, but soon decides he wants Ellen back and so plans to kill Harry, who, after all, once wanted to kill himself. Milt's plot fails but he and Ellen do get together again. Marriage is a mad world.

Neil Simon (1927–)

Neil Simon is America's Molière. No other American writer of comedy for the stage has ever equaled, let alone exceeded, the string of Broadway hits that Simon has had—not even George S. Kaufman. Simon is without a doubt the most popular playwright ever to write for the American stage. He is the great chronicler and creator of

New York folktales. His success in the American theater was breath-taking in its rapidity and scope. He is the only living American play-wright to both own a Broadway theater (the Eugene O'Neill Theater) and have one named after him.

Marvin Neil Simon was born in the Bronx, New York, on 4 July 1927, the second son of Mamie and Irving Simon. Danny Simon, Neil's older brother, later encouraged Neil to become a comic writer. Little Marvin Neil was nicknamed "Doc" at the age of three because he loved wearing a toy stethoscope, and the name Marvin was soon dropped entirely.

Irving Simon was a salesman in New York's garment industry. The Simons soon moved to Washington Heights in Manhattan, then also a Jewish area. When Irving occasionally left his wife and chil-dren, Mamie supported the family by working in sales at Gimbel's department store in Herald Square.

When Mamie and Irving finally divorced, Neil moved in with relatives in Forest Hills, Queens, New York, where he attended high school. Simon soon transferred to the all-boys DeWitt High School back in the Bronx. Simon graduated from high school in 1943. He was only sixteen and World War II was raging. Working part-time in the garment industry to earn money for college, Simon entered New York University to pursue a degree in engineering under the auspices of the Army Air Corps Reserve program. As part of his mil-itary training he was sent to Biloxi, Mississippi, for basic training and later to Lowery Field in Colorado. Simon took courses at the University of Denver but never received a bachelor's degree.

When the war was over, Simon was discharged in 1946, and he proceeded to New York City to work as a mail clerk in the East Coast offices of Warner Brothers Pictures, where Danny was em-ployed in the publicity department. It was Danny who got him the job. Simon married Joan Baim, a dancer, in 1953, the first of his four wives. Neil and Joan had two children. Joan was only forty when she died of breast cancer in July 1973. Desperately unhappy and lonely, Simon met and married the actor Marsha Mason late in 1973. Their courtship and early marriage were the subjects for Simon's first truly autobiographical play, *Chapter Two* (1977).

During the time of Simon's marriage to Joan Baim, the Simon brothers became a comedy-writing team for the National Broadcasting Company (1956–57) and the Columbia Broadcasting System (1958–59). They worked as partners for several years, writing radio and television shows, including programs starring Phil Silvers, Jackie Gleason, and Red Buttons. When Danny decided to direct television productions in 1956, Neil stayed with CBS to write for the Sid Caesar Show.

At the same time, Neil Simon was trying to find a producer for *Come Blow Your Horn,* a somewhat autobiographical play about two brothers who break away from the confining Jewish home they had grown up in to enjoy bachelor life in a New York City apartment. Finally, in 1961 the play opened on Broadway and was a commercial success. Simon never looked back. His unprecedented string of Broadway hits had begun. His next assignment was writing the book for the musical *Little Me* (1962), a spoof of a femme fatale's memoir. *Barefoot in the Park,* the story of mismatched but loving newlyweds who overcome their contrariness, followed in 1963. It ran for an amazing 1,530 performances on Broadway. Simon became famous. But the comedy that forced doubting critics to catch up with the public's delight with Neil Simon was *The Odd Couple* (1965), in which two divorced men of opposing interests, temperaments, and ideas about neatness wage war in the apartment they share.

Simon next wrote the book for *Sweet Charity* (1966), a musical about a prostitute struggling to find Mr. Right while being continually abused by men. *The Star-Spangled Girl* (1966) has two radical young men alternately attracted to a beautiful but politically conservative girl. The three one-act plays of *Plaza Suite* (1968) take place in a hotel room where a marriage breaks up, old love comes to life again, and a hysterical bride is calmed not by her parents but by the groom's last-minute appearance when he orders his bride to "cool it."

In 1966 Simon once more had a musical and a straight comedy on Broadway. *Promises, Promises* begins with a young executive lending his apartment to his boss to make points and allow the married employer to meet his mistresses. During the course of the play a girl attempts suicide, the young executive saves her, and they fall in love. The show is a musical version of the 1960 film *The Apartment*. The ironically titled *Last of the Red Hot Lovers* (1968) tells of the bumbling of a 1950s man in the sexually permissive 1960s unsuccessfully trying to have affairs.*The Gingerbread Lady* (1970), less successful than the earlier comedies, depicts the travails of an alcoholic woman trying to put together the pieces of her life.

The Prisoner of Second Avenue (1971), a hit again for Simon, shows how the tensions of New York City life can drive a Manhattanite nearly insane. *The Sunshine Boys* (1972) delighted New Yorkers with its tale of two old vaudevillians who hate each other but have a chance to come together one more time for a nostalgic television show. *The Good Doctor* (1973), derived from several of Chekhov's stories, and *God's Favorite* (1974), which modernizes the Book of Job, did not succeed with either critics or audiences.

Paralleling the structure of *Plaza Suite,* and reflecting Simon's move to California, *California Suite* (1976) consists of four one-act plays in which a child must decide which of her divorced parents she wants to live with; a happily married man gets drunk, sleeps with a prostitute, and must explain this to his wife; an English couple tests its relationship as the actor wife is about to attend the Academy Awards ceremony; and a pair of friendly couples find that vacationing together can be hell.

After *Chapter Two* (1977) Simon wrote the book for *They're Playing Our Song* (1979), a small, rather intimate musical about a composer and a lyricist who collaborate and fall in love. At this time Simon was focused on film, writing successful original screenplays and film adaptations of his most successful comedies.

I Ought to Be in Pictures (1980) is a charming play about a young girl from New York City who goes out to Los Angeles supposedly to get into the movies but really to establish a relationship with her screenwriter father who abandoned his family when she was a child. But *Fools* (1981), a play set in Ukraine, reads like a fairy tale. It failed despite an interesting plot.

Simon and Marsha Mason divorced in 1982. Simon's marriage to Diane Lander in 1987 ended in divorce one and one-half years later. They remarried in 1989 and divorced again in 1997. Simon is presently married to the actor Elaine Joyce.

Arguably, Simon's most memorable and profound work is the semiautobiographical trilogy about the young life of the fictional youth Eugene Jerome: *Brighton Beach Memoirs* (1983), the story of a bright Brooklyn boy, Eugene Jerome, growing up in an unhappy household in the Depression; *Biloxi Blues* (1985), in which Eugene is in the army and interested in girls; and *Broadway Bound* (1986), where Eugene begins his writing career, sees his family break up, and comes to understand and love his long-suffering mother.

The Odd Couple (female version) (1985) offers a deliciously funny and "politically correct" rewrite of the 1965 play with an all-women cast. New York critics panned the play, but audiences all over America, in little theaters, regional theaters, and dinner theaters, love it.

Rumors (1988) proved that Simon could write a farce as well as Feydeau. *Lost in Yonkers* (1991), amazingly, was the first Simon play to receive a Pulitzer Prize. It is the World War II story of two Jewish boys whose mother has died and who must adjust to life with a seemingly unloving grandmother. In *Jake's Women* (1992) Simon departs from his usual realism and has his protagonist psychoanalyze himself through the proscenium to the audience. The musical version of *The Good-bye Girl* (1993), for which Simon wrote the book, is the author's only total failure in the musical genre. *Laughter on the Twenty-Third Floor* (1993), the story of a young comedy writer working for a famous television comedian, is as funny as any broadcast Simon ever scripted.

London Suite (1995) is modeled after *Plaza Suite* and *California*

Suite. Simon even reintroduces the Academy Award-nominated actor and her gay husband from *California Suite.* It was Simon's first and only play so far to open Off Broadway, due to the mounting costs of Broadway productions. In 1997 Simon returned to Broadway with the unsuccessful *Proposals* (1997), a play about male-female relationships in the 1950s and the first Simon play that featured major African American characters. *The Dinner Party* (2000) is a farce set in a posh Paris restaurant in which three divorced men unexpectedly come face-to-face with their former wives, while Simon offers an insightful and sometimes funny meditation on marriage. The characters are supposedly French, but their banter sounds like a California group therapy session.

Simon writes about the human experience, its frailties and peculiarities. Like all great writers of comedy, including and especially Shakespeare, he skillfully intertwines comedy, poignancy, and wisdom. He employs wit, gags, and farce with remarkable dexterity. He is a skilled craftsperson and a gentle philosopher. His values are those of the general American public, and although he writes about family, marriage, love, sex, and friendship, he never really disparages them with his mild satire. The values of his early plays are those of middle America in the 1950s. In the twenty-first century those plays have become sociohistorical plays. The later plays changed with their times. Throughout his playwriting career Simon evidenced his affection and respect for women.

In the earlier plays, and a few of the later ones, Simon seems to want to "machine gun" his audience with gags and farcical shticks. He can drive people into paroxysms of laugher with concomitant choking throats, tearing eyes, and flailing arms.

As his comedies evolved, they took on a more serious and introspective edge. As he matured, his plays matured too. Characterization grew in importance, and the role of gags and farce diminished. Continued growth is an admirable trait and a significant accomplishment in a playwriting career now in its fifth decade. Ultimately, Simon philosophizes that life is comic. Perhaps he is closer than is generally realized to the existentialist-absurdist playwrights of the 1960s who depicted the comicality, futility, and idiocy they saw in life with absurdity. Simon returned to his earlier romance with New York in *Forty-Five Seconds from Broadway* (2001).

Come Blow Your Horn (1961)

Quasi-autobiographical and conventionally farcical, *Come Blow Your Horn* is a tale of two brothers, Buddy, the younger, and Alan, the older. The setting is Alan's New York City bachelor pad, and the subject is Buddy's coming into manhood and cutting the umbilical cord with his loving but overprotective Jewish mother and father. The apartment is for freedom and sex, one and the same for young men in the sixties. Alan is jaded with womanizing and shirking work, and Buddy begins to emulate him just as Alan starts to settle down and sound like his father. In the end Buddy has made his escape from the mother who wants to smother him with love and the father who likes to keep a close eye on his sons. Also, the family finally approves of Alan's bride-to-be.

Barefoot in the Park (1963)

A pair of young newlyweds, Corie and Paul, has had a storybook honeymoon in New York's Plaza Hotel and now move into a walk-up apartment at the end of six mountainous flights of stairs. Corie, who is a free spirit, has found the apartment and thinks it has great possibilities, but Paul, who is a lawyer, sees it as inappropriate for an up-and-coming attorney. In fact, the couple is not really compatible in temperament. Corie's mother visits, and a relationship begins between her and the romantic neighbor, Mr. Velasco. Stuffy Paul is shocked. He thinks his marriage is a disaster and is headed for a divorce court. Fortunately, he throws over his inhibitions, gets drunk, and dances barefoot in the park. The couple compromises on attitudes and values and, presumably, lives happily ever after.

The Odd Couple (1965)

Set in the New York City apartment of the slob Oscar Madison, a sportswriter divorced from a woman named Blanche, *The Odd Couple* is a comedy about the difficulties that people who have contrasting personalities and values encounter in trying to live together. Good-natured Oscar invites his friend, Felix Unger, to move in with him. Felix is compulsively neat, fussy, and hypochondriacal, and has separated from his wife the day the play opens. The men are impossibly mismatched and soon get on each other's nerves, to say the least.

A double date that Oscar has arranged with the neighbors, the Pigeon sisters, turns into a disaster, and Oscar throws Felix out but is then racked with guilt. Felix, however, has won over the sisters, who love his sensitive ways, and he decides to move in with them. Oscar is relieved, and both men have changed; Felix is more self-confident, and Oscar begins to clean up his act.

As character types, Oscar and Felix, through the play, the film, and the television series, have become urban folk heroes who humorously symbolize extreme and opposing idiosyncrasies that can never be reconciled.

The Star-Spangled Girl (1966)

Andy Hobart and Norman Cornell (both named for upstate New York colleges) are radicals publishing a magazine titled *Fallout* from their apartment. They are broke, and Andy must fake affection for the landlady to avoid being evicted. The beautiful Sophie Rauschmeyer moves into their building. Norman falls for her, even though she is an ultraconservative woman. Awkward in his wooing, he causes her to lose her job, and she becomes angry with him. Now Sophie needs money too, and she accepts Andy's offer to work on the magazine. Soon Sophie becomes enamored of Andy, and Norman catches them kissing. Hurt, he plans to give up editing *Fall-*

out and move out. Disappointed with Andy's reluctance to commit, Sophie also plans to leave. But Norman changes his mind and goes back to work on the magazine. Andy's feelings for Sophie intensify, and she decides to stay in the radical nest partly because she supports free speech, and partly because her sexual attraction for Andy wins out over her politics. Without much of a plot, the play is, nevertheless, very funny, full of the joys and foibles of youth, and sexually charged. Critics and the author equally were disappointed in the play, but American audiences around the country enjoyed the mild satire on the country's "new" Bohemians.

Last of the Red Hot Lovers (1968)

It is the 1960s and Barney Cashman, the married owner of a fish restaurant and a man who can't seem to get the odor of fish off his hands, is sexually frustrated. He is middle-age and overweight, and the sexual revolution is raging around him in the streets. Life (sex) is passing him by, and so he plans to use his mother's apartment when she is out in the afternoons as a place to seduce women. Each woman turns out to be more than he can handle. A promiscuous woman he meets in the restaurant wants sex right away, and he is too shy not to start with some romancing. A young hippie he picks up in the park gets him high on marijuana before anything can happen. A friend's wife is depressed and bursts into tears. Desperate, Barney phones his wife, Thelma, and asks her to rendezvous with him at her mother-in-law's, but she can't understand what's got into him. "The best laid plans of mice and men . . ." *Last of the Red Hot Lovers* is a small gem of wry humor and social commentary.

The Prisoner of Second Avenue (1971)

In the 1970s Neil Simon was growing less enamored of New York City as shown in his 1970 screenplay *The Out-of-Towners*. This disenchantment can also be seen in *The Prisoner of Second Avenue*. In this play, Mel and Edna Edison live in a typical small Upper East Side apartment, the setting of the play. Mel is a troubled man on the edge. His company is having financial difficulties, and he loses his job. The apartment is burglarized when the Edisons are out. It's summer, it's hot, and the air conditioner is noisy. Mel is at war with a neighbor. Finally, he has a nervous breakdown and becomes hostile to Edna.

Edna gets a job to support them and then calls a family conference, asking for financial help from Mel's brother and sisters for a down payment on a summer camp out of the city that Mel could manage. They are not interested until they see Mel's condition, and then they agree to help. But Mel snaps out of his depression, and the Edisons don't have to leave town. Edna's love and caring brings him through.

The play amused New Yorkers, who could shake heads in empathy with Mel's travails. The play seemed especially topical in the seventies, when the city was in a financial crisis and many New Yorkers had lost their usual confidence.

The Sunshine Boys (1972)

Willie Clark and Al Lewis are old, retired vaudevillians who worked as a comedy team, Lewis and Clark, for years. Now they have drifted apart, although they both speak as if they were still doing comic routines. Willie, angry at Al for retiring, lives in New York City and is still trying to work in show business, even though he can no longer remember lines. An opportunity arises for them to work together again. A television network wants them to revive one of their skits for a nostalgia show. When they meet in Willie's apartment to rehearse, they begin to fight, even though they have not seen or spoken to each other in eleven years. At the studio Willie, who has always resented the way Al poked him in the chest during the routine, loses control of his anger and has a heart attack. In the end they realize their performing days are over and both decide to move into a home for actors in New Jersey. Even Willie can no longer fight old age. His long, stubborn, crotchety refusal to acknowledge the aging process, despite his failing body and mind, is both a source of laughter and admiration.

Chapter Two (1977)

Neil Simon wrote *Chapter Two* to help him deal with the loss of Joan and his marriage to Marsha Mason the same year Joan died. In the play the writer George Schneider has returned from a European trip he undertook to help him get over the death of his wife, Barbara. His brother, Leo, can see that George is still deeply grieving, and his remedy is that George should start dating again.

But George is unable to connect with any of the women he meets. Leo thinks that a friend of a friend, the recently divorced Jennie Malone, could be the right one for George, and he writes down Jennie's phone number on a slip of paper. George, depressed, has no intention of calling, but accidentally he rings her number. They meet and fall in love, but George is plagued with guilt. They marry anyway, but George is difficult and unhappy. He tells Jennie that he is going out to Los Angeles to think things over. She informs him that he has done nothing wrong in seeking happiness again, and that she is glad to be married to the finest man alive. George returns to her and the marriage, and he begins to write a book about this experience. Simon's play says "yes" to the instinct for life that all healthy people have, even after a terrible loss.

Brighton Beach Memoirs (1983)

The Brighton Beach trilogy is the story of the growth from boyhood to manhood of Eugene Jerome and the disintegration of the marriage of his parents, Kate and Jack Jerome. The first play, *Brighton Beach Memoirs,* is set in the Jerome's three-bedroom house in Brooklyn in the year 1937. The play shares some of the evocation of the

Depression era and the intensity of crowded living in Clifford Odets's Jewish Bronx dramas.

The Jerome house is packed with extended family, including Eugene's older brother, Stanley, Kate's sister, Blanche, and her children, and Kate's socialist father. The Jeromes are lower-middle-class Jews. Jack, a worn-out garment industry worker, has relatives living in Poland, and he wonders if he can put them up in the small house if they can escape the Germans should war come.

Eugene is in his early teens, a would-be writer, and a very randy boy. He is the family gofer, always being sent to the store. Eugene is turned on by baseball and his cousin Nora's legs, which he studies under the dining table while she takes no notice of him. As a bright, optimistic youth, Eugene is a clever and witty observer of his family, whose ups and downs he narrates to the audience. He learns much from his older brother and understands Stanley's humiliation at having gambled away money needed by the family for its basic needs. And he comprehends the suffering of his Aunt Blanche, who must live in her older sister's house and survive through family charity. The great beauty of *Brighton Beach Memoirs* is the vivid characterizations and the evocation of New York City life in the late 1930s.

Biloxi Blues (1985)

A conventional military comedy about basic training, a young recruit trying to lose his virginity, and a soldier finding a nice girl to fall in love with, *Biloxi Blues* has Eugene Jerome doing his military service in a company that includes a closet gay man who is one of the most compassionate recruits; a hard but fair company sergeant; and another Jewish soldier, Arnold Epstein, who is embittered by the anti-Semitism he is subjected to. Eugene's relationship with a prostitute is treated with feeling and not made a subject for gags and farce, and his romance with a pretty and virtuous local schoolgirl at a USO dance is a touching sequence in this character-based play.

Broadway Bound (1986)

World War II is over and Eugene has returned to the family home in Brooklyn, where he and his brother, Stanley, sell a comedy sketch to a radio program. They learn the painful truth that comedy stemming from the observation of family foibles hurts the models in the family. *Broadway Bound* is the most serious play in the Brighton Beach trilogy. Jack, the wise, caring, and generous father in *Brighton Beach Memoirs*, now has a mistress and leaves his wife. The boys are furious. Stanley vents his anger but Eugene squelches it. The socialist grandfather cruelly rejects his daughter Blanche, because after having been a poor, widowed mother of two, living partially on charity, she marries a man with some money. Kate, the mother, is unhappy, and her compulsive need to keep the house in order and orchestrate the family doings has made her seem a cold and nagging person, so that Jack's infidelity and departure can be understood, if not condoned.

The most poignant and moving episode in *Broadway Bound* is that in which Kate is talked into revealing the most romantic moment of her life—its very high point—when as a young girl she danced one night with George Raft, a famous movie star of her youth. Eugene takes the George Raft part, and in an oedipal moment they dance lightly and happily—the same age for once in their life together. Kate emerges as the most interesting and complex character in the trilogy as Simon tempers her hardness at last.

In this time of great interest in autobiography, direct or fictionalized, it appears the Brighton Beech trilogy will be remembered as Neil Simon's finest achievement.

Lost in Yonkers (1991)

Perhaps Neil Simon's darkest and most disturbing play, *Lost in Yonkers* is set in 1942 in a Yonkers apartment over the Kurnitz family's candy store. Grandmother Kurnitz is a German Jewish widow who has raised four children, including Eddie, a widower, who has been forced to leave his two adolescent sons with his mother while he struggles for a living on the road. Grandmother Kurnitz is a tyrant who has dominated all her children except for Louie, a gangster, who stands up to her until he goes off to serve in World War II. His sister, Bella, is slightly retarded, and her mother has mistreated her since early childhood. She tries to escape through a possible marriage, but her boyfriend is not strong enough to face his disapproving parents. Eddie returns and reclaims his sons, who feel that they have survived a kind of battle experience or a concentration camp. Through *Lost in Yonkers*, Simon reveals that the tyranny in a home, even a Jewish one, can be a microcosm of the tyranny in German-occupied Europe during World War II.

Jake's Women (1992)

Most of *Jake's Women* takes place in Jake's head. He is a fifty-three-year-old married writer who loves his art because it allows him to control characters in the way he can't control the women in his life, although he'd like to. In his fantasies he calls up women from his present and his past and gives them lines, but they sometimes rebel against his control to the point of coming onto the stage unbidden by his mind, upbraiding him for the bad choices he has made in his life.

Jake's women include his dead wife, Julie, brought to "life" in his creative fantasies, who wants to see and talk to her daughter, Molly, as she is now, a college student; his sister, Karen; his analyst, Edith; and Maggie, his current wife who is actually present (but this is a play of course) at the beginning, when she leaves Jake, and at the end when she is about to return to him.

The most poignant moment in the play is when Jake brings his dead wife together with their daughter and listens to their joyous reunion while standing in the shadows of the stage. One is reminded of dead Emily's desire to have one day of her life with her mother again in Thornton Wilder's *Our Town*, although in *Jake's*

Women it is the dead mother who wants a brief reunion with her living daughter. In the end Jake must of course stop rewriting his life in his mind and return to reality. *Jake's Women* is experimental and postmodern in its incorporation of the audience in the theatrical space, and in its disregard of the prevailing mode of stage realism. In its fascinating complexity, *Jake's Women* is one of Simon's most interesting and thought-provoking plays. And yet it is very funny too.

Additional Reading

Johnson, Robert K. *Neil Simon.* Boston: Twayne, 1983.

Konas, Gary, ed. *Neil Simon: A Casebook.* New York: Garland, 1997.

McGovern, Edythe M. *Neil Simon: A Critical Study.* New York: Ungar, 1979.

Simon, Neil. *Rewrites: A Memoir.* New York: Simon and Schuster, 1996.

———. *The Play Goes On: A Memoir.* New York: Simon and Schuster, 1999.

15
...

Edward Albee and the Post–World War II Playwrights

American Dramatists Not Old Enough
for Service in World War II

The period after the end of World War II brought existentialism, absurdism, political radicalism and activism, African American and feminist themes, and postmodern experimentalism to the American stage. Starting in the 1950s, the most innovative movement in mid-century American drama was the theater of the absurd, in which American dramatists, following European innovators such as Samuel Beckett, contemplated the absurdities of human existence. They demonstrated them by abandoning theatrical realism and logical dialogue, characterization, and situation. Thus, they reflected the universal absurd. In 1961 the critic Martin Esslin named the work of the Albert Camus-influenced existentialist-absurdist dramatists "The Theatre of the Absurd." The international movement endured from the 1950s to the 1970s and its values reverberate in the contemporary plays of such American dramatists as Sam Shepard and Suzan-Lori Parks.

Near the head of the parade that included Samuel Beckett, Eugène Ionesco, Jean Genet, Arthur Adamov, Fernando Arrabal, Harold Pinter, and Tom Stoppard, seemingly destined for the stature of American master, was Edward Albee. Albee, despite having written nearly thirty-five plays, has not lived up to early critical opinion and has lost some of his audience, but he remains a contender. He continues to write, and there is still time.

Edward Albee (1928–)

Edward Albee was born in Washington, D.C., to a single mother named Louise Harvey, who named him Edward. His father is unknown. Two weeks after Edward was born, he was given up for adoption. Although Albee learned at age six that he was adopted, he did not find out the name of his birth mother until 1989, after his adopting mother died and he went through her papers.

Albee was adopted by Reed A. Albee, the wealthy son of E. F. Albee (the founder of the Keith-Albee Vaudeville Circuit) and Frances Cotter Albee, who had been a department store salesperson and model. She was his father's third wife. Later on, when Mrs. Albee discovered that Edward was gay, she became hostile to her son. Mother and son were estranged for much of the rest of her life. Frances Albee, a tall, commanding women, is the model for several of Albee's domineering female characters, including Mommy in *The Sand Box* (1960) and *The American Dream* (1961), as well as A in *Three Tall Women* (1991). Albee's favorite relative was his maternal grandmother, the model for Grandma in *The Sand Box* and *The American Dream*. Only Grandma Cotter gave him the attention and the affection he desperately needed as a child.

Clearly, despite the luxuries of his surroundings, his childhood was unhappy. His mother was a busy socialite and his father was remote. Perhaps the child was always aware that he was not "to the manner born" and felt himself to be an outsider. That unhappiness may have led to his savaging American family life and the appearance of misogyny in his dramas.

Albee grew up in a mansion in Larchmont, New York, an affluent suburb of New York City. He saw Broadway plays and met theater people early in his life. As a child of the rich, he was sent to a
boarding school at eleven and then to a prep school in which the
sensitive youth, on the receiving end of physical abuse, continued
to see himself as an "other." A "tour of duty" in a military academy
was one of his parents' mistakes. Finally, Edward was enrolled in
the Choate School, where his teachers were more responsive to his
needs and where a literary bent was spotted and encouraged. At
Choate, Albee began to write plays, fiction, and poetry.

After graduation Albee matriculated at Trinity College of Hartford, Connecticut, but bored, he only lasted three semesters. His disappointed parents became more and more critical of him. He was so
alienated from his mother that he did not see her again for the next
seventeen years. He met his father only by accident. Albee had a
trust fund from his paternal grandmother, so he moved to Greenwich Village, the center of artistic and gay life in New York City in
the mid-twentieth century. This exodus from the land of plenty was
his act of defiance and emancipation. In New York Albee worked at
a series of white-collar jobs to supplement his income while serving
a writer's apprenticeship, writing some poetry but primarily plays
and novels that found neither producers nor publishers.

As a theater-goer, he saw the great first Broadway productions
of Tennessee Williams's and Arthur Miller's early plays, but he was
most taken by the Off-Broadway and the European avant-garde
dramatists Samuel Beckett, Eugène Ionesco, and Jean Genet, the
playwrights who introduced the theater of the absurd to the theatrical world. Now the Broadway theater seemed more absurd to Albee
than the experimental plays he was seeing. In his enthusiasm for the
new mode Albee, in three weeks, wrote *The Zoo Story* (1959), first
produced in Germany and in German. It was on the same bill with
Beckett's *Krapp's Last Tape,* and it was very successful. Along with
Beckett's play, it was next produced Off Broadway in 1960. Now
young Albee was linked with the great Samuel Beckett.

The Zoo Story is a one-act drama about the death wish in the young. Short Albee plays poured forth. *The Sand Box* and *Fam and Yam* were produced in America the same year as *The Zoo Story. The Death of Bessie Smith* opened in Berlin in 1960 and moved to New York the next year.

In *The Sand Box* Albee savages Mommy and Daddy while dotty Grandma proves the sanest in the family. *Fam and Yam* presents a dialogue between an established playwright and a neophyte angry at the commercial theater. *The Death of Bessie Smith* depicts the racism that led to the famous blues singer's death. *The American Dream* (1961) builds on *The Sand Box* as Mommy, Daddy, and Grandma reappear. Other short plays include *Box* (1968), *Quotations from Chairman Mao Tse-Tung* (1968), *Listening* (1976 on BBC Radio; 1977 in Hartford), and *Counting the Ways* (1976 in London; 1977 in Hartford).

Albee's masterpiece, *Who's Afraid of Virginia Woolf?* is, in a certain sense, a continuation of the adventures of Mommy and Daddy in *The American Dream.* The 1962 drama about the profanity-filled, near-mortal combat between a middle-aged college professor and his wife propelled Albee to the forefront of the younger American dramatists. The play won many awards but not the Pulitzer Prize, which it should have won. The pusillanimous administering board for the prize, afraid of controversy over the play's rough language and sexual scenes, overruled the recommendation of the jurors and decreed that no Pulitzer would be awarded in drama for the year. The 1966 film version starring Richard Burton and Elizabeth Taylor was also a great critical and box office success.

Albee then sidetracked into a series of less-than-successful adaptations, including *The Ballad of the Sad Café* (1963), based on Carson McCullers's novella; *Malcolm* (1966), based on James Purdy's novel; *Everything in the Garden* (1968), based on Giles Cooper's play; and *Lolita* (1981), based on Vladimir Nabokov's novel. Two musicals Albee wrote lyrics for did not do well: *Bartleby* (1961), based on Herman Melville's story; and *Breakfast at Tiffany's* (1966), based on Truman Capote's story.

Tiny Alice (1964), the story of a religious man seeking martyr-dom, befuddled critics and audiences. *A Delicate Balance* (1966) is an intellectual treatise on familial relationships that won the Pulitzer Prize. A 1996 revival was a smash hit. *All Over* (1971), a story of an unhappy family quarreling at the deathbed of the father, was un-successful. *Seascape* (1975) won Albee his second Pulitzer Prize. In this pleasant fantasy play, a middle-aged couple on a beach en-counter two human-sized amphibious lizards with which they in-teract. *Listening* began as a 1976 BBC radio play that eventually arrived Off Broadway in 1993. The play is set in an insane asylum where a catatonic girl, a cook, and a therapist interact.

Albee lived with several talented partners, including the play-wright Terrence McNally. In midcareer, drinking began to affect his life and work negatively. Undoubtedly, alcoholism marred Albee's middle years. Albee also was plagued by personal attacks by some homophobic critics.

But Albee never stopped writing plays. *Counting the Ways* (1976) reminds the audience of Elizabeth Barrett Browning and Robert Browning as He and She discourse on life. *The Lady from Dubuque* (1980) interweaves the relationship between three subur-ban couples as death is confronted. *Finding the Sun* (1983) is a melan-choly play about couples on a beach in the process of breaking up. *The Man Who Had Three Arms* (1984) tells the allegorical story of a freak—symbolizing celebrity-hood—who loses his following when he sheds his extra arm. In *Marriage Play* (1987) a middle-aged subur-ban couple, married for thirty years, face the trauma of breaking up. *The Lorca Play* (1992) is a rambling, biographical sketch of the great twentieth-century Spanish playwright and poet, Federico García Lorca. *Fragments* (1993) is an experimental play about loneliness.

Three Tall Women premiered in Vienna in 1991 and had its New York opening in 1994. It is the story of a dying old woman who con-fronts her middle-aged and young self. It gave Albee his third Pulitzer Prize and did much to restore his reputation as a leading American playwright. *The Play about the Baby* (1998; rewritten 2000) is another drama about troubled parents and a child who may or may not exist. In 2002, *The Goat, or Who Is Sylvia?* a naturalistic drama of infidelity, is scheduled to open on Broadway.

Edward Albee is a serious, intelligent writer, a poet of alienation, attempting to delineate and address the existential questions that inform contemporary philosophy. He does so by plunging through the superficialities of American life and rummaging among the moral assumptions, vain pretensions, self-destructiveness, and dangerous illusions that litter the landscape of the American psyche.

Albee is a master of characterization. He has the ability to incorporate the prejudices, values, inner feelings, outlooks, and politics of his characters through the dialogue he places in their mouths. At its best, the power of his stage speeches engenders rapt attention in his audiences, forcing them to work hard to capture subtext and connotation, as well as to feel the impact of iterative, structuring metaphor.

Finally, Albee has faint hope for meaningful human encounters and for the efficacy of even attempting communication. Still, the collective human patient is still alive, and that, after all, is something.

The Zoo Story (1959)

Set on a park bench in New York City's Central Park, *The Zoo Story* depicts a confrontation between a middle-class man, Peter, a husband, a father, and a publishing executive, and Jerry, a poorly dressed, compulsive, and seemingly disturbed young man who wants to talk with Peter.

There is a dispute as to who has rights to the bench. Peter is angry that his afternoon reading and relaxation have been disturbed by the intruder, who insists on telling the story of a confrontation with his landlady's vicious dog. Peter does not want to listen, let alone understand. Jerry forces a fight and shoves a knife into Peter's hand. Then Jerry impales himself on the knife so he can find peace. At last the pathetic Jerry has made a significant contact with another human being.

The Sand Box (1960)

Mommy and Daddy drag Grandma out to the beach—the sand-box—and callously dump her there. When she finally has a chance to speak, she soliloquizes about the shabby treatment her daughter and her son-in-law have given her. She has been treated like a house pet, sleeping on an army blanket under the stove. Finally the dying woman meets a gentle and kind young man who does calisthenics, and who is really the Angel of Death. In *The Sandbox* Albee condemns the indifference and even cruelty of middle-class, middle-aged people to their elderly parents.

The American Dream (1961)

In *The American Dream* Albee rakes the American woman while caricaturing the American family, especially the American mother. Mommy emasculates Daddy. The couple are sterile as well as venal and inhuman. They have no names because bourgeois American society is homogenous. Mommy adopts a child but is dissatisfied with her "purchase" because the boy shows independence, so she mutilates him piece by piece until he is dead. The young man from *The Sandbox* appears as the identical twin of the dead son, who has escaped Mommy. Grandma stands for the old, uncorrupted values of American society, but she is waiting for a van and movers to pick her up and take her to a nursing home.

The Death of Bessie Smith (1961)

The Death of Bessie Smith uses a unit set in which the downstage setting is the admissions room of a hospital, while on a ramp upstage scenes related to Bessie Smith's death are performed. The blues singer, who does not appear in the one-act drama, bleeds to death in a car outside a whites-only hospital in the South while her companion, Jack, tries to get her into another hospital. At the second hospital the play deals with the effect of the arrival of the corpse on several characters: a politically liberal intern, a bigoted white nurse who enjoys listening to blues music, her segregationist father, and a handsome African American orderly with rebellious tendencies. In *The Death of Bessie Smith* Albee points out the waste that racism causes and how all Americans are affected by it.

Who's Afraid of Virginia Woolf? (1962)

George and Martha (like the Washingtons), a childless couple, have a strange and rocky marriage that includes fighting and pretending that they have a son. George is a quiet intellectual holding the rank of associate professor of history in a small New England college. Martha, the daughter of the college's president, is a loud, foulmouthed, and sexually frustrated woman. She despises George because he has not been as successful in his career as her father has been. Under the influence of alcohol, the couple set out to destroy each other.

At two A.M. George and Martha return home drunk from a party for new faculty. A young couple, Nick, a new biology teacher, and his wife, Honey, accompany them for a nightcap. Between two and five A.M. a sadomasochistic orgy of psychological pain takes place as the three acts—"Fun and Games," "*Walpurgisnacht*," and "Exorcism"—proceed. As the conflict escalates, George ventures into forbidden territory and "kills off" their son.

In the end an incantation by George ends the inter- and intra-couple warring. The wounded look to their wounds. *Who's Afraid of Virginia Woolf?* is a shocking portrayal of an American marriage, but at the same time it is a very funny play, for the audience sees the supposedly placid and genteel life in the ivory tower as yet another human zoo.

Tiny Alice (1964)

Miss Alice is the richest woman in the world. She lives in a mansion that has a model of the mansion in it, so one can perhaps think of Alice the woman as different from Tiny Alice, who lives in the "Wonderland" within the model.

The wealthy Alice wills a huge fortune to the Catholic Church. She wants Julian, a lay brother, to come to her and receive the gift. Julian is a man who would have become a priest except for his inability to reconcile his conception of God with the anthropological figure humans have created. He has spent years in a mental institution. Julian's superior sets him to the task of securing the gift, but Julian finds himself enmeshed in the very controversy of his life: sorting out the difference between religious ecstasy and sexual hysteria. Alice turns out not to be an old woman but a beautiful young one. Julian is seduced, and the price is his soul. Julian and Alice marry, but she abandons him. He is shot by a lawyer, and he dies in the pose of a crucified martyr. Alice may be God, or perhaps it is sexual passion that is divine. For Julian, Alice has been enough of a deity for him.

Tiny Alice is a powerful, ambitious, and somewhat confusing but always challenging drama. It is theater of the absurd without the comedy. As an existential writer Albee seems to say: existence over essence, or choose life; God lies in that direction.

A Delicate Balance (1966)

A Delicate Balance is a play about finding and maintaining a balance between caring for others and individual survival. A comfortably situated middle-aged couple, Agnes and Tobias, is visited by the wife's alcoholic younger sister, Claire, their daughter Julia, who is breaking up with her fourth husband, the husband's best friend, Harry, and his wife, Edna. The latter have arrived full of fright over the sudden loss of meaning in their lives. They spend the night and depart to get their things and move in with Tobias and Agnes.

Agnes fears for her sanity, but Tobias is sure she is sane. They must decide if they are willing to let their friends stay with them, and they make a generous and moral decision to do so, although in the end it is not necessary. Here, Albee reveals how humans are always teetering on a psychological razor's edge. Menace is always lurking outside the door, and survival and sanity are the stakes people play for.

Seascape (1975)

Nancy and Charlie, middle-aged and prosperous, are vacationing at the seashore. They love the water, and the idea of living in the sea like fish is intriguing. They review their married life with some acrimony, as boredom has set in like a disease. While Nancy and Charlie are on the beach, two humanoid amphibian creatures appear from the sea. They, Sarah and Leslie, are also middle-aged, and they seem to be the alter egos of Nancy and Charlie, as the humans would be if they were sea creatures. The two couples interact in a variety of ways, sometimes friendly and sometimes hostile. They have much in common, and Albee is implying that evolution could have happened differently yet with similar results. Most of all, the two couples share their understanding of the mortality of all living things. They part in recognition of the miracle of existence.

Seascape is an allegorical fantasy that has a lyricism and an optimism that make the play delightful to experience.

Three Tall Women (1991)

Three Tall Women may come to rank second only to Who's Afraid of Virginia Woolf? as Albee's greatest work. In the play an unlikable, once rich, ninety-two-year-old woman is dealing with her middle-aged secretary and chief caregiver, identified only as A, and a young female attorney called B. But A becomes the old woman in her middle age and B, the woman when young. A relives important moments in her life while taking care of her real-time business and needs. A is bitter about her husband, who cheated on her, but then she married him for his money, and she was fonder of her horses than she was of her husband and son.

A has a stroke at the end of the first act. As act 2 opens A is in bed, or rather a dummy is, while A enters and encounters her younger selves. Her prodigal son comes onstage and stands as a silent witness as his mother rages at him and announces that she can never forgive him. In the third act A is dying. She cannot convince herself that her son ever loved her. She has never been happy, but the dying moment may be the best time of her life, for it will bring an end to her existence.

A (for Albee?) is modeled after Albee's mother, who died in 1989 at the age of ninety-two. Albee began to write the play in 1990, and it may have been the instrument of Albee's final peacemaking with Frances Albee for her various rejections of him and refusal to come to terms with his sexual orientation. In the end the Tall Woman simply dies.

Three Tall Women is a Picasso-like total portrait of a woman's life, seen from every perspective and direction—the three ages of a woman. But it is a son's play, a song of a hurt son. It moves many men deeply. For different reasons, such as the frequency with which sons disappoint mothers, it moves many women too. The power is elemental: a story of life and death.

Additional Reading

Amacher, Richard E. *Edward Albee.* Rev. ed. Boston: Twayne, 1982.

Bigsbee, C. W. E. *Edward Albee.* Englewood Cliffs, N.J.: Prentice-Hall, 1975.

Cohn, Ruby. *Edward Albee.* Minneapolis: Univ. of Minnesota Press, 1969.

Gussow, Mel. *Edward Albee: A Singular Journey: A Biography.* New York: Simon and Schuster, 1999.

McCarthy, Gerald. *Edward Albee*. New York: St. Martin's, 1987.

Paolucci, Anne. *From Tension to Tonic: The Plays of Edward Albee*. Carbondale, Ill.: Southern Illinois Univ. Press, 1972.

Roudané, Matthew C. *Understanding Edward Albee*. Columbia: Univ. of South Carolina Press, 1987.

Howard Sackler (1929–1982)

Howard Sackler was born in New York City. He received his higher education at Brooklyn College, then worked as a screenwriter, a director, and a playwright for several regional theaters.

Howard Sackler's *The Great White Hope* (1967) won the Pulitzer Prize. It is the story of the first African American heavyweight boxing champion, Jack Johnson, the predecessor to Joe Louis and Mohammed Ali. Johnson is called Jefferson in this blank verse drama. The American public hates him because he beats whites, is arrogant, and has a relationship with a white woman. Johnson is persecuted, exiled, and humiliated. His girlfriend is driven to suicide. Strong as he is, neither he nor any other individual alone can overcome the prejudice and hostility of the majority. The boxing ring is a powerful metaphor for black-white hostility. In the end Johnson gives up and gives in, but not until he has smashed up his final white challenger, The Great White Hope.

The role of Jack Jefferson is a challenging role for an African American actor, because Jack Johnson the pugilist was larger than life.

Bruce Jay Friedman (1930–)

Born in the Bronx, Bruce Jay Friedman graduated from DeWitt Clinton High School and the University of Missouri, receiving a bachelor's degree in journalism in 1951. Friedman then served two years in the U.S. Air Force. Better known as a novelist, Bruce Jay Friedman has written six plays, the most successful being the zany comedy

Scuba Duba (1967). The play is the wildly funny story of Harold Wonder, a thirty-five-year-old man whose wife, Jean, has run off with an African American man named Foxtrot. Wonder carries around a scythe as a security blanket. Clearly in psychological trouble, Wonder seeks help from his Jewish mother and his psychiatrist. A theater of the absurd potpourri of characters inundate the stage. Jean brings her lover home. Harold leaves to go off with women, determined to see if he is ready for a new life in a world of sexual freedom.

Lorraine Hansberry (1930–1965)

Lorraine Hansberry was the first African American woman to have a Broadway production. In her short life she only completed two plays, but her work brought a new energy, direction, and commitment to the American theater. *A Raisin in the Sun* (1959) was in the forefront of civil rights liberalism, because it demanded that the middle-class audience "see" the experience of the African American family and recognize it as being little different from that of the poor white American family, except for the handicaps of prejudice.

The play has grown in popularity over the years until it is now a cherished work of Americana, presenting the proud story of the African American family, with its strengths and its weaknesses. It exists on a sociological plane with Eugene O'Neill's story of the Irish American family, *Long Day's Journey into Night,* and Arthur Miller's somewhat disguised tale of the Jewish American family, *Death of a Salesman.*

Lorraine Hansberry was born in Chicago to affluent parents active in African American political and cultural life. She was the youngest of four children. Her father had made a considerable amount of money in real estate, and he devoted years to a successful law case against housing discrimination that went all the way to the Supreme Court.

Even though her parents could have sent Hansberry to private schools, and although from the age of eight Hansberry lived in a white neighborhood, as a matter of principle she was sent to segregated public schools, graduating from Englewood High School in 1948. Meanwhile, Hansberry's father died in 1945 in Mexico, where he was arranging to move his family, as he no longer felt free in the United States.

Hansberry went on to spend two years at the University of Wisconsin at Madison, where among her courses she studied drama and stage design. She also attended classes at the Art Institute of Chicago before moving to New York City in 1950. There she worked at various jobs while serving her apprenticeship as a writer. One job was as a waitress in a restaurant owned by the family of the songwriter and music publisher Robert Nemiroff, whom she married in 1953 and divorced in 1964.

Hansberry worked on *A Raisin in the Sun* for more than two years. She took her title from the famous long poem "Harlem" by Langston Hughes, in which the poet asks, "What happens to a dream deferred, / Does it dry up like a raisin in the sun, / . . . or / Does it explode?" The play depicts the members of a beleaguered but courageous African American family demanding their right to live where they wish, while preserving the dignity passed on to them by many generations of hardworking people. It was originally directed by Lloyd Richards, America's outstanding African American stage director. From the opening night, *A Raisin in the Sun* was recognized as an American classic. The play was made into a film (1961) and a successful musical, *Raisin* (1973).

The Sign in Sidney Brustein's Window (1964) attacks liberal white intellectuals who are too involved in abstract theories and too timid to plunge into the practical world of involvement. A few months after the play opened, Lorraine Hansberry died of cancer on 12 January 1965. The loss to American drama was incalculable.

A Raisin in the Sun (1959)

A Raisin in the Sun is a celebration of African American hope in the future and belief in the ultimate, if long delayed, justice implicit in the documents of American democracy. It also reflects the determination of African Americans to be seen by the white majority as real people, sharing universal values and dreams.

The Younger family, living in a crowded Chicago tenement, is led by Lena, a strong, matriarchal figure. Her husband, a laborer, has died, leaving a ten-thousand-dollar insurance policy with Lena as the beneficiary. Her son, Walter Lee, a disgruntled chauffeur with a wife who works as a cleaner and is pregnant with their second child, wants to invest the money in a liquor store along with a shady partner. Lena uses some of the money to put a down payment on a house that happens to be in a white neighborhood. The rest she gives to Walter with the instructions that he put it in the bank, with half of it going for her daughter's medical school education.

Walter Lee is naïve, and he gives all of the money to the grifter, who runs off with it. The family is stunned by his foolishness and then horrified that Walter is willing to take a bribe from a white neighborhood organization anxious to keep the African American family out of the neighborhood. In the end Walter comes to his senses and refuses the bribe. The family will work to meet the payments, and they will move into their first home, hoping that they will eventually find acceptance by their neighbors and peace. They are marching toward the American dream.

A Raisin in the Sun shows Hansberry's deep understanding of and affection for the African American family. But the play goes beyond its ethnic boundary. It is really about the American family, black, white, or immigrant. All share the American dream of holding together, owning a home, maintaining dignity, obtaining quality education for the children, and rising economically.

The Sign in Sidney Brustein's Window (1964)

Sidney Brustein is a liberal intellectual married to an actor, and his marriage is troubled. Brustein has remained outside of the political process. He is drawn into supporting a reform candidate in a city election, and he puts a campaign sign in his window. The candidate wins, but Brustein learns that supporting good causes does not insure that the committed are above corruption. The successful candidate sells out, friends disappoint, an African American proves to be bigoted, and a gay playwright uses sex to get his way. All humans are imperfect. A fully moral life is hard to attain. In the end Brustein overcomes his disillusion and despair to rededicate himself to fight for what is good and right in society.

The Sign in Sidney Brustein's Window is overwritten, but Hansberry's ability to write dialogue, her keen observation of Greenwich Village life, and her commitment to democracy save the play. As a modern morality play, it retains its currency.

Additional Reading

Carter, Steven. *Hansberry's Drama: Commitment amid Complexity.* Urbana, Ill.: Univ. of Illinois Press, 1991.
Cheney, Anne. *Lorraine Hansberry.* Boston: Twayne, 1984.

A. R. Gurney (1930–)

Albert Ramsdell Gurney Jr. was born in Buffalo, New York, the son of wealthy socialites whose life revolved around the insurance and real estate businesses, the Episcopal Church, and exclusive schools and clubs. Gurney went on to become America's leading playwright dedicated to portraying, examining, and gently criticizing the mores of his class—wealthy white society. He has written nearly forty plays so far.

Gurney studied at St. Paul's Preparatory School in New Hampshire and Williams College in Massachusetts, where he received a bachelor of arts degree in English literature in 1952. After graduation, as the Korean War raged, he served as an officer in the United States Navy until 1955. Under the G.I. Bill Gurney entered Yale Drama School from which he received a bachelor of fine arts degree in 1958. In 1957 Gurney married Mary Forman Goodyear. The couple has four children. After a short stint of prep school teaching, Gurney commenced teaching literature at the Massachusetts Institute of Technology, where, during a twenty-five-year career, he obtained the rank of full professor. Writing was his part-time occupation for many years.

Most of Gurney's early plays are one-acts. His first New York production was a one-act play titled *The David Show* (1968), an unsuccessful political satire on 1960s values. Gurney's first full-length New York success was *Scenes from American Life* (1970; revised 1988), in which Gurney, now fully at home in subject and medium, depicts in harsh sketches the slow fall of the selfish upper class from the Depression years to the immediate future. In the early 1970s Gurney began to win drama awards.

Based on a John Cheever story, *Children* was first produced in London in 1974 and was followed by a New York production in 1976. The story of a conflicted middle-class American family struggling through a Fourth of July weekend received mixed reviews, but further productions attracted major stars to the lead roles. The 1976 play *Who Killed Richard Cory?* in which a middle-aged lawyer breaks away from his constricted background was a limited success. Determined to make the theater his main career, Gurney moved his family to New York City. The move increased Gurney's production and sharpened his work. Eventually, however, New York became too distracting, and the family moved to a Connecticut farm.

The Middle Ages (Los Angeles, 1977; New York, 1982) presents a power struggle in a wealthy family where a hard, unbending father attempts to control a son trying to live his own life. It is set in the paneled trophy room of an exclusive men's club. *The Dining Room* (1982) was a major success. It became a favorite with regional companies. Recalling Thornton Wilder's *The Long Christmas Dinner,* the play shows a white family declining over three generations as six actors come and go in various roles, although the room remains unchanged. *What I Did Last Summer* (1983) is a coming-of-age drama of a young boy's 1945 vacation at a resort near Buffalo. Gurney went to Henry James's story *The Aspen Papers* for the plot of *The Golden Age* (1984), in which an elderly socialite living with her divorced, alcoholic daughter has her life upset by a young scholar researching a deceased writer.

The *Perfect Party* (1986), a comedy of manners, has a white professor, Tony, compulsively striving and failing to host a perfect party. The event is an allegory for the American need to find perfection in life. *Sweet Sue* (1986) pictures a May-December affair between an older woman and a young man. *Another Antigone* (1988) also found a large audience in regional and repertory theaters as well as Off Broadway. It is the story of a conflict between a patrician college professor and a strident female Jewish student. The antagonists are separated by a cultural as well as a generational gulf. Here Gurney also explores modern anti-Semitism.

The Cocktail Hour (1988), a funny play about the consternation of two white, upstate New York parents who are unhappy that their son has written a negatively revealing autobiographical play that exposes family secrets, was a major New York success. *Love Letters* (1989) continues to attract well-known actors around the country to participate in the two-character play that requires only a table and two chairs for a setting in which a man and a woman read the moving letters they have written to each other in the course of their lifetimes.

The Snow Ball (1991) is based on Gurney's 1985 novel of the same name. In it a final Snow Ball in Buffalo, New York, is the setting for recollections of past decades and the sad statement that neither love nor talent can overcome class difference. In *The Old Boy*

(1991) a politician worries that his career may be jeopardized by the news that the pal he roomed with in prep school has died of AIDS. Gurney's favorite play, *Later Life* (1993), is a moving play about second chances in love. The very popular *Sylvia* (1995) is a comedy about changing roles in a marriage endangered by a midlife crisis and the arrival of a dog. *Overtime* (1996) is based on *The Merchant of Venice*. It attacks cultural stereotypes by deconstructing the typical. *Labor Day* (1998) is a comedy set on a Connecticut farm where an unsuccessful, middle-aged playwright is continually interrupted by family problems as he tries to deal with an aggressive director.

Far East (1999) is a Gurney masterpiece about military life in occupied Japan during the Korean War. *Ancestral Voices* (1999) is a short, elegiac play depicting the decline of an affluent extended white family in Buffalo, New York, from 1935 to 1942. As in Tennessee Williams's *The Glass Menagerie,* the play is narrated by the son.

Two one-acts, *Darlene* and *The Guest Lecturer* (1999), are very different from each other. The former is the story of an exhausted marriage. A suburban couple finds a sexually provocative letter under the windshield wiper of the car. Jim is appalled, but Angela is titillated. She wishes that her husband had written it, but, alas, he is no longer interested in sex. *The Guest Lecturer* finds a regional theater nearly broke. All that can be afforded is a lecture on drama. Pandemonium ensues. Gurney's latest play, *Human Events* (2001), depicts the frustration of an academic writer and is set in the Victorian period.

The prolific A. R. Gurney has also written novels, short stories, screenplays, and television plays.

Love Letters (1989)

A wealthy, staid, conservative lawyer, Andrew Makepeace Ladd III, and his corespondent, Melissa Gardner, a struggling artist, were friends, then lovers. Now, after they have broken up and gone their separate ways, they continue as pen pals, reading their letters aloud. The letters reveal a bittersweet and sometimes frustrating relationship. The correspondents have a sense of humor, and they remain spiritually close. The audience has the pleasure of filling in what is felt but left unsaid.

Sylvia (1995)

A comedy about the pressures of city life and midlife disappointment, *Sylvia* is set in a Manhattan apartment where Greg, a middle-aged man, depressed by his disappearing interest in his work, is having his midlife crisis. A dog, Sylvia—played by a young woman—comes into his life. They have a happy relationship. Kate, Greg's wife, a woman whose career as a teacher is blossoming with the children gone, tries to be the voice of reason, but she finds Sylvia to be her rival for Greg's affection. Psychoanalysis is called for, and the trio eventually recovers equilibrium.

Far East (1999)

In occupied Japan in the mid-1950s, young Navy Lieutenant Junior Grade Sparky Watts, an Officer Candidate School graduate, is seeking adventure in the Far East. He is a Princeton University alumnus and the son of a wealthy socialite Milwaukee family. Watts is upright, loyal, and decent, but somewhat naïve. Captain James Anderson, his commanding officer, a Naval Academy graduate and World War II combat aviator, at first dislikes this privileged, ingenuous young man, but he eventually grows fond of Watts, who reminds him of his younger self and of his son from a previous marriage, a naval aviator who died in Korean combat.

Watts immediately falls in love with a Japanese woman and plans to marry her. Anderson's wife, Julia, who is both sexually and maternally interested in Watts, informs his influential family that miscegenation is about to take place, and it pulls strings to have Watts returned to the States. Watts is torn between his passion and his devotion to his family. In the end he leaves Japan, promising to return to his love but knowing he will not. Captain Anderson is angry with his wife because of her interference, and she is tired of being second in his affections to the navy. Their marriage is over.

Gurney's characterization and dialogue are just about perfect in *Far East*. His ability to depict the time and place is remarkable. The antecedent echoes in the play, Puccini's *Madam Butterfly* and James Jones's *From Here to Eternity*, only further enrich *Far East*.

Adrienne Kennedy (1931–)

Like August Wilson, Adrienne Kennedy was born in Pittsburgh. Her parents were Cornell Wallace Hawkins, a social worker, and Etta Haugabook Hawkins, a schoolteacher. The family moved to Cleveland in 1935. Kennedy attended the unsegregated Cleveland elementary and secondary schools, and then went on to the segregated Ohio State University, where she endured racial bigotry. She married Joseph Kennedy a few weeks after graduation. They had two children and were divorced in 1966. Her college majors were social work and education, not drama or theater. She studied creative writing at Columbia University from 1954 to 1956.

Kennedy began her playwriting career when she was twenty-two and pregnant. In the early 1960s she and Joseph Kennedy traveled to Africa and then to Italy. Upon returning to America her husband obtained a teaching job at Hunter College, and they settled in New York City, where Kennedy joined Edward Albee's playwriting workshop at Circle in the Square. She continued to write experimental drama, and in 1995 the New York Public Theater produced a Kennedy series of seven plays.

Adrienne Kennedy's best-known works are four one-act plays: *Funnyhouse of a Negro* (1964), which presents African American experiences as if America were a crazy amusement park feature; *The Owl Answers* (1965), about a biracial female school teacher driven mad by literary and historical figures of the English world; *A Rat's*

Mass (1970), an expressionistic drama filled with terror, horror, incest, and madness; and the three-scene surrealistic drama *A Movie Star Has to Star in Black and White* (1976). Kennedy is strongly influenced by the themes, techniques, and anarchy of the theater of the absurd. She is an original writer who has rejected realism, instead employing ritual, expressionism, and surrealism in her wildly imaginative work that has inspired younger playwrights such as George C. Wolfe and Suzan-Lori Parks.

A Movie Star Has to Star in Black and White (1976)

Clara is an African American young woman who wants to be a writer. Her brother, Wally, is in a hospital, comatose after an automobile accident. He will live, but will be brain damaged and paralyzed. Throughout the play, Clara converses with the actors in famous American movies such as *Now Voyager, Viva Zapata,* and *A Place in the Sun.* Her hallucinatory conversations stem from her unhappiness. The settings for scenes and segments include the deck of an ocean liner in a movie, the lobby of a hospital, Clara's brother's room, and an old bedroom of Clara's. During the play, which is taking place in Clara's mind, she confesses her problems and unhappiness to the movie stars. Her husband, Eddie, has changed since he came home from Korea; she has lost a child and is pregnant again but bleeding. As the play ends she is talking to her silent brother, who is lying in his hospital bed.

Clara is a woman suffering terribly from the pain that comes with living and with loss. Her escape is to construct a giant montage of her parents' younger lives, her brother's service in Europe in World War II, her collapsing relationship with Eddie, her possible miscarriage, and the movies she has enjoyed.

Additional Reading

Kennedy, Adrienne. *People Who Led to My Plays.* New York: Knopf, 1986.

Lonnie Elder III (1931–1996)

Lonnie Elder III was deeply concerned with the trials of the African American family. Born in Americus, Georgia, but educated in the North, Lonnie Elder III studied at Trenton State College in New Jersey and the Yale School of Drama. He is best known for the powerful play *Ceremonies in Dark Old Men* (1965), the play for which he received a Pulitzer nomination. Reminiscent of Lorraine Hansberry's *A Raisin in the Sun*, it is the story of a Harlem family trying to escape poverty and despair.

Elder's more recent drama, *Splendid Mummer* (1988), is a successful biographical play about the internationally famous nineteenth-century African American actor, Ira Aldrich. Elder had a parallel career as a film and television writer.

Ceremonies in Dark Old Men (1965; Revised 1969)

Elder portrays the moral dilemma of an African American ex-vaudeville dancer, Russell Parker, who has an unprofitable barbershop in Harlem. His grown sons, Theopolis and Bobby, won't accept menial jobs, because Parker has passed on his unwillingness to work hard for little pay to his sons. He has depended on the money his now-deceased wife earned. Now Parker's daughter, Adele, works to support the men in the family.

Unwilling to work for others, Parker lets himself be dragged into the underworld of Harlem. Theo thinks that only illegal activities can save the family. He has fallen under the sway of a Harlem revolutionary leader who wants to drive white businesses from Harlem. The barbershop becomes a front for illegal gambling and liquor selling. Instead of saving the family, illegal activities and deceit destroys it as Bobby is killed in a robbery attempt. Theo and Adele will find other ways of surviving. Parker is exposed as the vain and selfish man he is.

Jack Gelber (1932–)

Born in Chicago, the son of a Rumanian immigrant, Jack Gelber attended John Marshall High School and the University of Illinois, receiving a bachelor's degree in journalism in 1953. He moved to New York City in 1955 and married Carol Westenberg in 1957. Then he began to write. His first play, *The Connection*, was produced by Julian Beck and directed by Judith Malina for the Living Theater in 1959. The play depicts the lives of drug addicts past and present as they await the arrival of their "connection" with the next fix.

None of Gelber's succeeding ten or more plays has had much success. They include *The Apple* (1961), a play about the chaos of contemporary existence; *Square in the Eye* (1965), which shows the quarrels of married life; *The Cuban Thing* (1968), which depicts the effect of the Cuban Revolution on the middle class in Havana; *Sleep* (1972), which tells of scientists who create dreams in dreamers who create other dreamers dreaming; *Jack Gelber's New Play: Rehearsal* (1976), which discusses the author's playwriting aesthetic; *Starters* (1980); *Big Shot* (1988); and *Magic Valley* (1990). Gelber has also been a successful director.

The world of Gelber's drama is a fragmented one. There is security and peace for no one. Respite comes through drugs and sleep. Conflict pervades society and the closest of human relationships.

The Connection (1959)

The Connection is a play in which a play is being filmed as heroin addicts await their fix. Characters are types that move in and out of the drama's frame. Actors, the film crew, the producer, the playwright, Sister Salvation (who tries to save addicts), and others are folded into the action as they argue about the script and try to impose order and reality on the lives of the addicts who refuse to cooperate. The play is an existential assemblage of disorder and suffering through which the casts—the actors in Gelber's play and the performers in the film—seek to improvise an existence in the face of meaninglessness.

Herb Gardner (1934–)

Born in Brooklyn and educated at the High School of Performing Arts and several colleges, Herb Gardner is a cartoonist as well as a playwright. He is best known for the smash hit comedy *A Thousand Clowns* (1962), although he has been quite successful writing for television. Among Gardner's other plays are *The Goodbye People* (1968), about an unsuccessful Coney Island vendor trying to make a comeback with a hotdog stand; *Thieves* (1974), about New York City apartment-building life on a hot June night; *I'm Not Rappaport* (1985), in which a sharp-minded old Jewish radical fights for his independence; and *Conversations with My Father* (1992), a moving play about a son coming to understand his father's life and the Jewish immigrant experience.

Gardner's world is funny and sad—the essence of Jewish humor. The human condition of urban man and woman is one requiring either laughter or escape for survival. Gags and skits can help us face the existential void and get through the night.

A Thousand Clowns (1962)

A television writer, Murray, living a chaotic life, hates the kind of work he is doing. Writing for inane programs such as the series about Chucky the Chipmunk is destroying him. Still, he needs the job, but unfortunately he is fired. Now he faces the loss of his son, Nick, to the Child Welfare Bureau. Sandra, the welfare worker on his case, falls in love with him, and his luck begins to turn. Chucky's ratings drop, and the show's star is sure that the loss is due to Murray's absence. He is rehired. Now he and Sandra can have a happy life with Nick. The play is a feel-good work interlaced with humor and a delightful zaniness.

Imamu Amiri Baraka (1934–)

Amiri Baraka is best known today as a poet and an African American activist. For nearly forty years he has been a radical spokesperson for economic, social, and political equality for America's black community. He assumed this role early in the African American Civil Rights and Black Power movements of the 1960s. He led the first charge of the cultural brigade in the war against racism with his first and greatest play, *Dutchman* (1964), a drama of racial conflict. *Dutchman, The Toilet* (1964), and *The Slave* (1964), all one-act plays, are the most famous and important of Baraka's two dozen dramas.

Imamu Amiri Baraka was born LeRoi Jones in Newark, New Jersey. He attended Rutgers for a year and then transferred to Howard University where he received a bachelor of arts degree in English in 1954. Baraka served in the U.S. Air Force from 1954 to 1957. In New York City he became a part of the vibrant Greenwich Village Beat world led by Allen Ginsberg. But in 1967, fed up with what he saw as ineffectual intellectualism and determined to find a new and active role for himself in the long historical struggle of black America, LeRoi Jones became a Black Muslim minister and changed his name to Imamu Amiri Baraka.

Baraka has also had a distinguished career as a college professor. He continues to reside in and serve his community in Newark. Baraka has married twice and has nine children, including two stepdaughters.

The Toilet (1964) is the story of a teenage African American youth who leads his gang in the slaying of a white person he secretly cares for. *The Slave* (1964) is the story of an African American leader who explains to his white ex-wife that he is resigned to leading his people to the forthcoming Armageddon, whether or not he thinks his cause is right. Both plays are one-act dramas.

Dutchman (1964)

A one-act drama, *Dutchman* is based on the legend of the Flying Dutchman, a sea captain who, because he blasphemed God, was doomed to sail the seas forever. Richard Wagner's operatic version differs. He has the Dutchman searching for a woman who will love him faithfully and thus raise the curse. For Wagner the woman brings redemption. In Baraka the woman is the Dutchman, and she brings death.

Baraka's sea is the underground maze of the New York City subway system, and the ship is a train. Clay, a young, middle-class, integrated African American intellectual, is on his way uptown to a party when he is seemingly picked up by a beautiful but clearly disturbed blonde woman named Lulu, who, after having aroused Clay's sexual interest, taunts him for his bourgeois values and his denial of his African American heritage. This stirs up Clay's inherent antagonism for the dominant culture, and it provokes him to rage—just what Lulu wants. Seemingly justified, she kills Clay and gets ready for the next black victim.

Baraka sees white society as a trap for African Americans. He despairs of racial peace and understanding, because he believes white America is irrevocably racist. *Dutchman*, with its fusion of symbolism and realism, is Baraka's masterpiece.

Additional Reading

Baraka, Amiri. *The Autobiography of LeRoi Jones/Amiri Baraka.* New York: Freundlich Books, 1984.

Benston, Kimberly W. *Baraka: The Renegade and the Mask.* New Haven: Yale Univ. Press, 1976.

Woodward, Komozi. *A Nation Within a Nation: Amiri Baraka and Black Power Politics.* Chapel Hill, N.C.: Univ. of North Carolina Press, 1999.

Joseph A. Walker (1935–)

Born in Washington, D.C., and educated at Howard University, where he received a bachelor of arts degree in philosophy in 1956, Joseph A. Walker did military service in the U.S. Air Force as an officer. Later he attended Catholic University of America, where he obtained a master of fine arts degree in 1970. He has taught at Yale University, City College of New York, and Howard University.

Author of ten plays, Walker is best known for *The River Niger* (1976), a play that depicts the frustration of the African American male. Walker's work is ideological. He uses broad-brushed characters to point out the conflicts between black and white America. His plays seem both timeless and timely.

The River Niger (1976)

Less pessimistic than much of Walker's work, *The River Niger* celebrates the strong bond that can exist between a black father and his son. Middle-aged Johnny Williams adores his son, Jeff, who is in the air force. Williams works as a house painter, although he is really a poet, whose poem "The River Niger" says to African Americans that they must never forget their African heritage.

Williams, unsuccessful in life, eases his frustration with alcohol. When Jeff returns home, Williams learns that his son hated military life and has been dismissed from the service. Jeff is now determined to eschew family and societal ties in order to pursue his own desires. He returns to a gang to which he previously belonged. The gang is betrayed by a traitorous member, and Williams, trying to save Jeff and his friends, has a gun fight with the traitor. Dying, Williams shows his love for his son by taking on himself the guilt of the gang. Now the young men have an opportunity to rebuild their lives. Williams and his wife represent the strength of the African American community in face of the pitfalls that await young black men in the dangerous urban world of their time.

Ed Bullins (1935–)

The prolific author of nearly forty plays, Ed Bullins is best known for three plays: *The Electronic Nigger* (1968), a comedy in which stereotypes battle each other in the language of racial politics; *Goin' a Buffalo* (1968), in which petty criminals prey upon each other; and *The Taking of Miss Janie* (1975), a play about the underlying hatred that prevents any relief from racial hatred.

Bullins was born in Philadelphia, where he attended public schools and the William Penn Business Institute. He receive further higher education at Los Angeles City College, San Francisco State College, and elsewhere. He served in the U.S. Navy from 1952 to 1955. Bullins moved to New York City in 1967 to work in Off-Broadway theater. At one time Ed Bullins was the minister for culture of the Black Panthers. Now he resides in California.

Bullins chose to write about the problems of the African American community and its individual unit—the family—as it sails on a seething urban ocean of violence, corruption, and suffering. By using agitprop, his plays combine surrealism with naturalism, although at the same time he stokes up a black nationalistic consciousness in his audience. Bullins's work is marred, however, by anti-Semitism and his fascination with sexual violence.

Goin' a Buffalo (1968)

On a surrealistic set that contrasts with the realism of the drama, a group of Los Angeles African Americans on the fringe of respectable society want to move to an easier environment for their activities: prostitution, drug dealing, and hustling. Buffalo, New York, seems the perfect place for them. Curt, a twenty-nine-year-old African American man who is their leader, considers himself to be outside of society, and so he justifies his activities as the natural thing to do when there is no place for him in the white world. Curt has a big drug deal set up that will provide enough money for his pals, his wife, Pandora—a nightclub singer exploited by her African American boss—and him to migrate east to Buffalo. Their plans, however, are foiled by the treason of his friend Art, who treats Curt the way Curt treats the world. After betraying Curt, Art uses drugs and violence to force Pandora and the white prostitute Mamma Too Tight to go with him to Buffalo, where the women will have to work as prostitutes for him.

Here, Bullins reveals how African Americans are victims of a society in which money rules. They have no choice but to live outside of the law, and to survive by obtaining money any way they can. He deplores it when individuals in the underclass are as vicious to each other as the world is to them.

The Taking of Miss Janie (1975)

As *The Taking of Miss Janie* opens, Janie, a white girl, is "taken"—that is, raped, by Monty, her African American friend. He has been waiting for years for the opportunity to assault her. Through a flashback we learn that they met at school a decade before, in the turmoil of the 1960s. They and their schoolmates come under the influence of a Black Nationalist fiercely opposed to integration. Black-white friendships are difficult, and the chances of their enduring through racial positioning are small.

One African American woman in the play is so depressed that she is an easy sexual mark for anyone. Monty's former wife becomes a lesbian after two marriages. Bullins's characters can foresee no change in their lives. They seek solace and escape in religious sects, drug addiction, and even suicide. Finally, Monty beats a Zionist Jew to death for pointing out his hypocrisy. Then he takes Janie to bed, this time with Janie resigned to her fate as white sex object. The Monty-Janie relationship symbolizes Bullins's view of black-white destiny at the time he wrote the play.

Mart Crowley (1935–1991)

Mart Crowley's *The Boys in the Band* (1968) was one of the first commercially and critically successful plays to show gay culture and life in a fully sympathetic light without making it seem either tragic or campy. It engaged all audiences, both with the stage and with the film version. Crowley was born in Vicksburg, Mississippi. He received his bachelor of arts degree from Catholic University of America, in Washington, D.C., in 1957. He worked as a television executive and wrote only three plays before his early death.

The Boys in the Band is set in a New York City duplex apartment where Michael—who also is present in Crowley's two other plays, *Remote Asylum* (1968) and *A Breeze from the Gulf* (1973)—hosts a birthday party. A group of gay men attend. Some appear very masculine, such as Hank, although at the other extreme there is Emory, who is hysterically effeminate. There is an African American gay and a twenty-dollars-a-time hustler.

Alan, a supposedly straight college friend of Michael, appears, and the party begins a neurotic game of self-exposing that humiliates all present. Michael reveals his anxiety and suffering. All of the men, even Alan, are insecure in one way or another, and they deal with their insecurities with flashing wit and wry humor. Crowley shows the range of gay relationships. His depiction of a gay world of unhappy—even neurotic—homosexuals making the best of their lives now seems somewhat condescending, but in 1968 it represented a courageous appeal for tolerance, acceptance, and understanding. The play was justly applauded.

Rochelle Owens (1936–)

Rochelle Owens was born in Brooklyn. She graduated from Lafayette High School in 1953 and worked at various jobs in New York City while she learned her craft as a playwright. In 1962 Owens married the poet and scholar George Economou, her second husband. Eventually the couple moved to Norman, Oklahoma, where Economou taught at the University of Oklahoma. Owens has won many awards for her drama and has been a writer-in-residence or visiting lecturer at several universities.

Rochelle Owens's play *Futz* (1965; revised 1968), the first of more than a dozen plays, shocked Off-Broadway audiences with its aberrational sex, satire, parody, wild humor, and understanding of the unconscious mind. With *Futz* Owens became the first lady of the American theater of the absurd. In *Futz* an orgy between Cyrus Futz, Amanda—the pig he loves—and the lustful Majorie infuriates the puritanical community, even though the sexual participants hurt no one. Murder ensues; Cyrus Futz and even poor Amanda are killed. With this play, Owens created an original theater of the grotesque.

Homo (1966), *Belch* (1968), and *The Karl Marx Play* (1973, with music by Galt MacDermot) are further examples of Owens's experimentation and moralistic attack on societal repression. *Chuck's Hunch* (1981), the story of a self-pitying male artist, aligned Owens with feminism and the women's movement. Class and culture conflict in her plays, and powerful visual and verbal images charge her work with original poetry.

Alfred Uhry (1936–)

The only triple-crown-winning playwright—the Tony, the Oscar, and the Pulitzer—Alfred Uhry began playwriting late. Although he worked in the theater as a successful lyricist, his first nonmusical effort, *Driving Miss Daisy* (1987), the story of an elderly, wealthy, southern Jewish woman and her African American chauffeur, won the Pulitzer Prize for drama, an amazing accomplishment. Uhry also wrote the successful screenplay for *Driving Miss Daisy*.

Uhry was born in Atlanta, Georgia, and graduated from Brown University in 1958. His second nonmusical drama, *The Last Night of Ballyhoo* (1997), a play about an Atlanta Jewish family in the 1930s that is more concerned with social position than with the menace of Hitler in Europe, was also received with great acclaim. Uhry's latest work is *Parade,* a musical about the lynching of Leo Frank, an innocent Jewish man, in Georgia in 1914.

Driving Miss Daisy (1987)

The action of *Driving Miss Daisy* takes place over twenty-five years. Miss Daisy is a seventy-two-year-old widow when the play opens. Her forty-year-old son, Boolie (a successful Jewish businessman), hires Hoke, an African American chauffeur, age sixty, for her. At first Miss Daisy is annoyed with her son because she feels that the chauffeur will intrude into her life. The play depicts the growing friendship and mutual dependency between the Jewish matriarch and the poor African American driver as both advance into old, old age. Both people maintain their dignity and integrity to the end, despite changing social and economic times. *Driving Miss Daisy* is a minor masterpiece of finely crafted and understated drama.

Kenneth H. Brown (1936–)

The author of seven plays, Kenneth H. Brown is best known for *The Brig* (1963), produced while he was resident playwright with the Living Theatre in New York City. Brown was born in Brooklyn and has had little education beyond high school. Nevertheless, Brown has been a resident playwright at Yale University and Hunter College and a visiting lecturer elsewhere. He served in the U.S. Marine Corps from 1954 to 1957. For a time he was confined in a military prison, a brig, and that experience was the basis for his devastating play, whose theme, man's inhumanity to man, is informed by Antonin Artaud's theater of cruelty. Human beings can only be freed from their ferocity by understanding that there is a reservoir of hatred, cruelty, and violence in their subconscious minds that must be contained.

The Brig, an antimilitary drama, is set in a Marine base brig, Camp Fuji, in the Pacific. The action follows a group of prisoners through its daily routine, as defined in the *Marine Corps Manual*'s guidelines, in respect to the behavior of prisoners. Their lives are a living hell. They are beaten and verbally abused, but the worst cruelty is their humiliation. They are reduced to numbers. The cruelty inflicted on the men is without justification. *The Brig* is a fierce indictment of military justice and the military way of life.

Jean-Claude Van Itallie (1936–)

Jean-Claude Van Itallie's first play, *War* (1963), a short drama about two men who come to personify human conflict, caught the attention of those drama critics of the 1960s who were fascinated by the extraordinary vitality of the Off-Broadway and Off-Off-Broadway movements of those turbulent days. At that time Van Itallie was playwright-in-residence with the Open Theatre in New York City and very much influenced by Ionesco and the theater of the absurd.

Van Itallie was born in Brussels, Belgium. He was brought to the United States in 1940, educated at Great Neck High School on Long Island, Deerfield Academy in Massachusetts, and Harvard University, receiving his bachelor of arts degree in 1958. In 1952 Van Itallie became a United States citizen.

Van Itallie, a poetic dramatist, is a master of the short play, which is akin to the short story, with Chekhov serving as a model. Some two dozen of his original plays have been produced. *American Hurrah* (1966) offers a triptych of three one-act plays—*Interview, TV,* and *Motel*—assaying violence in American society.

The Serpent (1968), perhaps Van Itallie's most ambitious work, deals with the central biblical story of temptation in the Garden of Eden, which he treats as a parable for the fall of humanity and the archetypal introduction of murder into the human community.

Lanford Wilson (1937–)

Lanford Wilson is a popular playwright whose success has been connected to his work with New York City's Circle Repertory Company, which he cofounded in 1969. Wilson was born in Lebanon, Missouri. After graduating from Ozark High School, he attended Southwest Missouri State College in Springfield, San Diego State College, and the University of Chicago. Wilson has authored more than thirty plays.

Wilson's first Off-Broadway plays, all one-act dramas, portrayed the clash between traditional American values and the demands of contemporary life. The plays attracted the attention of experimental and regional theaters. Five of Wilson's later full-length plays moved him into the mainstream of American theater. First came *The Hot l Baltimore* (1973), in which life in a once elegant but now rundown Baltimore hotel full of interesting characters is depicted; next Wilson wrote *The Mound Builders* (1975), in which the past battles the present on an archeological dig; finally came the Tally family trilogy: *Fifth of July* (1978), in which a gay couple is bravely presented, and in which a paralyzed Vietnam veteran sets out to sell the old Tally house and break with the past; *Tally's Folly* (1979), which portrays the wooing of Aunt Sally by a New York Jewish businessman; and *Tally and Son* (1981, revised 1985 and 1986), in which back in World War II Aunt Sally Tally's father and grandfather wage their war over the family business. The Tally trilogy has the atmosphere and sometimes the nostalgic poignancy of Chekhov's *The Cherry Orchard* and *Uncle Vanya*. Wilson is a master of dialogue and a sharp observer of character. Like Chekhov, Wilson is deeply concerned with how the fabric of society is created and sustained. He also knows it is constantly changing.

Later plays by Wilson, such as *Angels Fall* (1982) and *Burn This* (1988), did not find large audiences.

The Hot l Baltimore (1973)

The condition of the old hotel, about to be torn down, is indicated by the neon sign outside with its "e" out. No one is interested in replacing it. The hotel guests and hang-abouts include petty thieves, prostitutes, and indigents. Bill, the night clerk, a good listener, watches over on the cast-off inhabitants. One prostitute, The Girl, is only nineteen but is full of romantic nostalgia for the old railway days of the hotel. Bill adores her because she is essentially an innocent. She wants to help young Paul who is searching for his grandfather, who may have lived in the hotel. Jackie and Jamie, sister and brother, are passing through on their way to Utah, where a few acres of land are waiting for them to farm. The Girl knows the area and realizes they have been tricked and are doomed to fail. In fact all are doomed to fail and disappear, including the hotel, which will be torn down in thirty days. Only The Girl is sentimental and wants to fight to save the old hotel.

The setting and the sympathy of *The Hot l Baltimore* are reminiscent of Saroyan's *The Time of Your Life* and O'Neill's *Hughie.*

Arthur Kopit (1937–)

Although he has written some twenty-five plays, four expressionistic works—*Oh Dad, Poor Dad, Mamma's Hung You in the Closet and I'm Feelin' So Sad* (1960), *Indians* (1968), *Wings* (1978), and *End of the World* (1984)—made Arthur Kopit's reputation as a dramatist in the 1960s through the early 1980s. Kopit was born in New York City. He graduated from Lawrence High School in 1955 and Harvard University in 1959. He has taught playwriting at several American colleges and universities, including Wesleyan University, Yale University, and City College of New York.

Oh, Dad, Poor Dad, Mamma's Hung You in the Closet and I'm Feeling So Sad is a play about the emasculation of the American male. The symbols in *Indians* represent the near annihilation of the American

Indian by white America. In *Wings* a woman recovers from a stroke as Kopit plots the landscape of a chaotic mind. *End of the World*, a painful comedy, features a playwright writing a play about the dangers of nuclear proliferation in which a playwright writes a play about the dangers of nuclear proliferation. Above all, Kopit is a social commentator and a political satirist who foregrounds the absurdities in contemporary American life through pointed exaggeration.

Indians (1968)

Kopit reverses the early film cliché in *Indians:* the Indians are good and the whites are bad. The Indians have dignity and the whites are grotesque. Buffalo Bill Cody's famous Wild West Show is the setting for the play. Cody gallops onstage with a prop horse, and the audience is informed of how many buffalo he killed. We learn of the treachery of governments in Washington. The great Chief Joseph is reduced to repeating his famous speech of resignation and surrender as a showpiece. Throughout the play Buffalo Bill, in fringed jacket and white goatee, stomps about, ineffectual, not bright, well meaning, sure he is doing right with his show and never quite aware of his role in a genocide.

Tina Howe (1937–)

Much of Tina Howe's work has dealt with the grotesque. She pays homage to the nihilism of Beckett, Ionesco, and Albee, but in her finest work she resorts to conventional realism to create a jewel of contemporary feminist drama: *Painting Churches* (1983).

Tina Howe was born in New York City. She graduated from Sarah Lawrence College with a bachelor of arts degree in 1959. She also studied at Chicago Teachers College from 1963 to 1964. Howe is married and has two children.

Howe's subject is the intricacies of modern culture in regard to rituals, relationships, art, and behavior. Although Howe has written fifteen plays, only *Painting Churches* and *Coastal Disturbances* (1987), a play in which a young woman photographer is involved in a love triangle, have had considerable success. *One Shoe Off* (1993), Howe's latest play, depicts New York artistic sophisticates battling ennui upstate. Howe especially likes to write about artists and the making of art. Comedy is her forte.

Painting Churches (1983)

The title *Painting Churches* is a pun: Margaret (Mags) Church, a young portrait painter, returns home to visit her elderly Boston Brahmin parents in order to paint the couple before they retire from Boston to spend the rest of their lives on Cape Cod, in what was their summer place. Gardiner Church is a Pulitzer Prize-winning poet, once a friend of Robert Frost and Ezra Pound. But now he is nearly senile, unable to write poetry, and struggling unsuccessfully to write criticism. Mags has had a long history of conflict with her mother, but she has loved her gentle father deeply. Now she thinks her mother is abusing her father, but in the course of painting the portrait of the couple she comes to understand the sacrifice her mother is making by becoming nurse and caretaker to the once great and famous Gardiner Church.

The play is also about how parents come to appreciate the abilities of an artistic child. Lastly, *Painting Churches* is about the decline of the upper-class, New England, white family, once the foundation of American culture and society.

John Guare (1938–)

John Guare mixes farce and high drama in his portrayal of the decline and fall of the contemporary American family. He was born in New York City and received his primary and secondary education at Joan of Arc Elementary School and St. John's Preparatory School in the city. Guare studied at Georgetown University from 1956 to 1960, receiving his bachelor of arts degree in 1960. Yale School of Drama awarded him a master of fine arts degree in 1963. Guare served in the U.S. Air Force Reserve. He married Adele Chatfield-Taylor in 1981.

Two of Guare's approximately thirty original plays have had a significant effect on the American stage: *The House of Blue Leaves* (1971), the absurdist farce about the American family home as a mental institution; and *Six Degrees of Separation* (1990), a realistic drama about a poor, gay, clever African American boy who cons his way into an upper-class white home in New York City.

In 2000 Guare's 1982 play *Lydie Breeze* had a successful revival in New York. It is the story of a Civil War nurse, Lydie, who sees how humans change radically over time. *Chaucer in Rome* (2001), a titillating dark comedy of modern life, was received with respect and interest.

The House of Blue Leaves (1971)

In *The House of Blue Leaves*, contemporary American family life is depicted in a zany situation. A would-be songwriter has an insane but gentle wife. He wants to escape New York for Hollywood, but he can't get away because of the pope, a deaf starlet, a mad bomber, and three nuns. Desperate, he murders his wife, and then the world has neither place nor tolerance for his imagination.

Six Degrees of Separation (1990)

Paul is a young, intelligent, self-educated, gay, homeless, New York City African American. By claiming to be Sidney Poitier's son and the school friend of the son of the Kittredges, a wealthy white couple living in an expensive condo off Central Park, he gets accepted and supported by the Kittredges and their friends. His story is that he was mugged in the park and his wallet was stolen, but he is actually separated from them by race, class, sexual orientation, and money.

Eventually, the wealthy whites realized they have been conned. What Paul really wanted was a caring foster family and some affection. Alas, the Kittredges could give him some money and temporary shelter but not parental love. Among other things, *Six Degrees of Separation* indicts Park Avenue liberalism.

Charles Fuller (1939–)

Through his best-known play, *A Soldier's Play* (1982), and the screenplay *A Soldier's Story,* which he wrote for it, Charles Fuller showed the American public that white middle-class values do not necessarily serve African Americans in their struggle for equality.

Charles Fuller was born in Philadelphia and was educated at two local colleges, Villanova from 1956 to 1958, and La Salle from 1965 to 1967. In between he served in the U.S. Army from 1959 to 1962 in Korea and Japan. He is married and has two children.

Of Fuller's fifteen plays, two (besides *A Soldier's Play*) have had a significant impact: *The Brownsville Raid* (1975), the dramatization of the 1906 raid and subsequent railroading and scapegoating of justifiably enraged African American soldiers who had fought valiantly beside Theodore Roosevelt in the Spanish-American war; and *Zooman and the Sign* (1980), which is about a father's search for an alienated fifteen-year-old drug-runner who has stabbed the man's twelve-year-old daughter to death.

Fuller has chosen as a central theme in his drama the internalized effect that racism has had on African Americans. It has led them to despair and self-destruction through their realization that they have little control over their lives and the lives of those they love and want to protect.

A Soldier's Play (1982)

A Soldier's Play could have been the story of any group of African American soldiers in the days of the segregated army. The year is 1944 and an African American sergeant named Vernon Waters has been murdered on a Louisiana military base. Of course, the Ku Klux Klan is suspected. Captain Richard Davenport, an African American military lawyer, conducts the investigation. It is learned that in order to get the attention and respect of white officers, Vernon treated the African American soldiers under his command with brutality and cruelty, lest any of them might do something to justify racism. The petty tyrant even goes to the extent of hounding one of his soldiers to death. He did these terrible things even though he hated his white officers. Soon it appears that one of his men probably murdered him.

Davenport realizes how dangerous it is to let a disturbed non-commissioned officer, seething with racial self-hatred, shame, disgust, and a belief in black inferiority because African Americans are not allowed to command white troops, have authority over African American soldiers. He warns the white officers, who treat the murder as symptomatic of violence in African American units, that for the good of the service they must get used to the idea that one day African Americans will give orders to white *and* black troops.

Israel Horovitz (1939–)

The author of more than fifty plays, Israel Horovitz sets out to map the human condition in America in what may be called modern morality plays. Horovitz was born in Wakefield, Massachusetts. He studied at the Royal Academy of Dramatic Arts in London from 1961 to 1963 and later received a master of arts degree in English from Columbia University. He has taught English and theater at City College of New York and Brandeis University. Horovitz has been married three times and has six children.

Horovitz is best known for one play, *The Indian Wants the Bronx* (1968), a violent drama reminiscent of Albee's *The Zoo Story*. The Indian in the play is not a Native American trying to reclaim ancestral land in the Bronx. He is Gupta, a Hindu gentleman who can't speak English and who is waiting late at night for a bus in Manhattan to take him to the Bronx where his son lives. Because he has only his son's phone number, he needs help from strangers, but he is trapped and terrorized by two bored young white hoods, Joey and Murph.

Gupta's "crime" is that he is an "other." Because he is different and vulnerable, he is game for the sharks of the city. They leave him on the street, beaten, sobbing, and holding a telephone severed from its box. Horovitz thus indicts man's inhumanity to man, the innate and mindless cruelty in people, and the xenophobic hatreds that are the curse of urban life.

Terrence McNally (1939–)

Terrence McNally, a social satirist, is recognized as one of America's leading playwrights. His dramatic work shows his wide range of interests, his humor, and his continual growth. Of NcNally's nearly forty produced full-length and one-act plays, eight stand out: *The Ritz* (1973; revised 1975), an outrageously funny play about a beleaguered garbage-collecting contractor from Cleveland hiding out from murderous relatives in a Manhattan gay bathhouse; *The Lisbon Traviata* (1985), a play full of pathos as well as comedy about AIDS and gay men who adore the great divas of opera and live for their performances; *It's Only a Play* (1985), a very clever farce about the critical reception to a Broadway opening; *Frankie and Johnny in the Claire de Lune* (1987), a realistic yet charming character study and a moving love story about a middle-aged, working-class couple finally learning to trust each other; *Lips Together, Teeth Apart* (1991), a play probing homophobia in a Fire Island house once owned by a man who has died of AIDS; *Love! Valour! Compassion!* (1994), which delineates the gains and the fears of middle-class gay life in the 1990s; *A Perfect Ganesh* (1993), where Hindu religious vitality and the intervention of the elephant god Ganesh move American visitors to peace, understanding, and forgiveness; and *Master Class* (1995), in which the late prima donna Maria Callas holds a master class and reviews the great moments of her career.

McNally also wrote the book for the successful Broadway musical *Kiss of the Spider Woman* (1990), based on the novel by Manuel Puig.

Terrence McNally was born in St. Petersburg, Florida, and grew up in Corpus Christi, Texas. His parents were affluent, and he had a happy childhood. His father, Hubert McNally, and his mother, the former Dorothy Rapp, had come from New York City. McNally early on was exposed to opera, classical music, and theater. He attended a parochial school, where opera became a passion and where he began to write plays. Next he studied at Columbia University, where he received a bachelor of arts degree in English in 1960. From 1961 to 1962 McNally worked as a tutor to the teenage sons of John Steinbeck, accompanying the Steinbeck family on a tour of the world. McNally lived with Edward Albee for several years in the 1960s. Today, Terrence McNally is the most significant voice of understanding, reconciliation, and compassion in the American theater.

Frankie and Johnny in the Claire de Lune (1987)

Two middle-aged people, Frankie, a wary, jaded waitress, and Johnny, a volatile short-order cook, share with the audience the intimacy of their up-and-down courtship in and about the sofa bed in Frankie's New York City one-room, walk-up flat. The play begins with their first lovemaking. Will it merely be a one-night stand? As background to their idyll and their lovemaking, while the audience roots for the success of their relationship, they hear Bach's *Goldberg Variations* at first, and later, as it becomes clear that they really do care for each other and will stay together, Debussy's *Claire de Lune* washes over their tryst. The play is both sentimental and wonderfully satisfying.

Lips Together, Teeth Apart (1991)

The play takes place on Fire Island where there is a gay summer community. The house was owned by a gay man with AIDS who committed suicide, and inherited by his sister, a woman who never approved of her brother's lifestyle. She is staying in the house with her husband and another heterosexual couple. The foursome cannot accept or become a part of the gay community in which they are staying. One of the husbands, John, has learned that he is dying of cancer, and he shares the same disgust, disappointment, fear, and sense of mortality that a gay sufferer with AIDS feels. McNally is pointing out that regardless of sexuality, all thinking and feeling humans share pain, the loss of desire, and the aging process. Homophobia is indicative of a poverty of spirit. Compassion is the defining human characteristic. To have it, and also to love and have courage, always signifies the exemplary human being.

Love! Valour! Compassion! (1994)

Love! Valour! Compassion! continues the sympathetic portrayal of middle-class gay life in American drama begun with Mart Crowley's *The Boys in the Band* and continued with Lanford Wilson's *Fifth of July*. Eight gay New York City men spend three summer holiday weekends in the 1970s in a country house owned by Gregory, an aging dancer and choreographer. Six are middle-aged. They have done well financially. They are well educated and are either artists or lovers of the arts. One couple, Arthur and Perry, seems almost straight, but their relationship is threatened by Arthur's desire for blind Bobby, the young lover of Gregory, who in turn hurts Gregory by having sex with Ramon, a dancer who spends most of his time in the nude. Arthur also desires Ramon, who was brought to the party by John Jeckyll, a troublemaker. The men dance with each other, enjoy classical music together, and turn each other on with erotic memories.

But in fact, all the men are part of a community, and they not only share love, but in the end they are mutually supportive. The play has humor, but AIDS casts its shadow because two of the men are ill with it. Also, almost all the men are driven by desire, what McNally sees as the true life force, and thus their physical state takes on too great a significance in their lives. In the end all the men go into the lake in the nude. Exposed to each other and to the world, they are merely part of common humanity.

Additional Reading

Zinman, Toby Silverman, ed. *Terrence McNally: A Casebook*. New York: Garland, 1997.

Jason Miller (1939–2001)

Born in Long Island City, New York, Jason Miller graduated from Scranton University, in Pennsylvania, with a bachelor of arts degree in 1961. He also spent a year at Catholic University of America in Washington, D.C. He is best known for his Pulitzer Prize-winning play, *The Champion Season* (1972). The naturalistic, well-made play discloses the dark and ugly underside of success.

Twenty years after the season of their success, four star high school basketball players are having a reunion with their retired coach, a man who taught them Vince Lombardi's lesson: that winning "isn't everything—it's the only thing," and not merely in sports but also in life.

The setting is the coach's living room. A fifth player, Martin, has not returned. He was the one selected by the coach, a bigot, to break the ribs of an opposing African American player so as to insure the team's famous victory. Martin is clearly not proud of what he did. None of the former players is happy, though they have achieved degrees of success. They have betrayed each other and will continue to do so. The cult of winning at all costs has made them dishonorable and exploitive of the weaknesses of others. The coach senses disunity, and he wants them to stick together in the glory of the champion season. The play is a microcosm of and a satire on the ethos and materialistic values of 1950s America.

David Rabe (1940–)

David Rabe returned from the Vietnam War to shock the American theater-going public with his powerful, disturbing expressionist war plays: *Sticks and Bones* (1969), *The Basic Training of Pavlo Hummel* (1971), *The Orphan* (1973), and *Streamers* (1977). Of Rabe's subsequent plays only *Hurlyburly* (1984; revised 1988), a Hollywood parable, has had an impact. The recent *The Dog Problem* (2001), a satire on the value of life, has revived Rabe's career.

Rabe was born in Dubuque, Iowa. After schooling in Dubuque Catholic schools, he received a bachelor of arts degree in English from Lorcas College in Dubuque in 1962. He attended Villanova University in Philadelphia from 1963 to 1964, working on a master of arts degree. He left the university for full-time writing, but in 1965 he was drafted into the army for the war in Vietnam. He spent two years in the army, most of it in Vietnam. His experiences in the military became the basis for the main body of his work as a playwright.

After his discharge Rabe returned to Villanova to finish his master of arts degree. There he began to write drama and teach writing. Rabe married Elizabeth Pan, a laboratory technician, in 1969. They had one son. After his divorce from Elizabeth, Rabe married the actor Jill Clayburgh in 1979.

It took an avant-garde producing organization, the New York Shakespeare Festival Public Theatre, directed by the legendary Joseph Papp, to appreciate Rabe's genius and to bring his vision to the American public. Rabe's plays anatomize the death wish in the American male character and the American penchant for self-delusion.

Sticks and Bones (1969)

Sticks and Bones begins with a slice of Americana, using the famous television icons Ozzie and Harriet and their two sons, David and Rick. The effect of the Vietnam War on a typical American family is essentially what *Sticks and Bones* is about. David becomes a soldier and goes off to the war. When he returns, he is blind and mentally disturbed. He carries on a conversation with an imaginary Vietnamese girl about the horrors he has seen. The family is fragmented. Ozzie is deeply depressed. Harriet tries to reach out to David and is beaten off with his cane. A hearty priest gets the same treatment. The family talks David into suicide and Rick provides the razor, helping his brother slash his wrists. The sardonic last action is Rick's preparing to take the last family photo. What a price America paid for its Vietnam adventure!

The Basic Training of Pavlo Hummel (1971)

The Basic Training of Pavlo Hummel is about the soldier's preparation for war. Pavlo is a simpleminded young man who is trained to be a killer. He dies in a fight but, ironically, not in battle, but in a fight over a prostitute. A fellow soldier throws a grenade at him. The play takes place in the soldier's mind as he is dying. Hummel is baffled and confused. He represents the indecision and bewilderment of American society in the Vietnam period, a society in a state of chaos.

The Orphan (1973)

The Orphan is highly symbolic and dense in imagery. Rabe presents the Vietnam experience in the guise of Aeschylus's *Oresteia* trilogy.

The story of Agamemnon's return from the Trojan War blends into a return from the Vietnam War. Both wars are immoral. Two actors play Clytemnestra. The dress is modern. Orestes sings rock, and even the god Apollo has a number. Violence at home is represented by the Charles Manson family and abroad by the My Lai atrocity. All want to rationalize their part in the violence and murder of the times. The narrative thread disappears, and *The Orphan* is the least successful of *Rabe's* Vietnam War plays.

Streamers (1977)

Streamers is a play about the fact that the Vietnam War debacle and its harm to the fabric of American society was not only a result of political deception but also of the moral failure of individuals who became accomplices in the creation of a great evil. The title is the word for failed parachutes, which instead of holding chutists up let them fall to their deaths.

In the play, set in an army barracks early in the war, a group of soldiers, who, like most, know nothing of why they are being sent to fight, reveal their inner selves under the tension of the impending danger. Roger, an African American ghetto youth, is about to re-place one violent environment for another. Richie, a gay man, comes from a wealthy background but is insecure because his sexu-ality makes him vulnerable from a source other than the enemy: the American Army. Martin can't adjust to army life and is ready for suicide. Billy is an intellectual and an idealist who provides the point of view of the play.

Carlyle, a psychotic African American soldier from a different unit who seems to be the macho soldier type, makes a pass at Richie. The men in the unit know they must get rid of Carlyle to save them-selves, but they fail. All the men in the play are falling apart. Carlyle eventually goes berserk and kills Billy and another soldier. The sol-diers have inflicted wounds and death only on themselves.

Hurlyburly (1984; revised 1988)

Hurlyburly's title comes from *Macbeth's* opening scene when the three witches ask when they shall meet again, and they answer "When the hurlyburly's done / When the battle's lost and won." The battle lost and won in Rabe's *Hurlyburly* is the Vietnam War. But another battle goes on interminably: the aggression of American men on women.

Hurlyburly is a Hollywood story of a group of desperately self-indulgent men, cut off from their wives by divorce or separation, who exploit each other and satisfy their infantile needs for gratification by abusing women and commodifying them for homosocial exchange. They are totally hostile to woman and devoid of morality. The new barracks is the Hollywood apartment. With savage humor Rabe depicts his male characters, Eddie, Mickey, Phil, and Arty, as full of frustrated rage, indulging in a male fantasy of uncontrolled power play and lust. All women and men in the play are dehumanized by the repulsive patriarchy of these sexual savages. The play is a slashing indictment of the American male, as is much of Rabe's work.

Additional Reading

Zinman, Toby Silverman, ed. *David Rabe: A Casebook*. New York: Garland, 1991.

Luis Valdez (1940–)

Luis Valdez is the leading Chicano playwright. Almost all of his work has been in Spanish, but *Zoot Suit* (1978), a play in English about the effect of racism on a 1942 murder case and on the Mexican American community, reached mainstream American theater with a Broadway production.

Valdez was born in Delano, California, the son of poor farmworkers, and attended San Jose State University. He is married and has three children. Valdez founded the El Teatro Campesino in 1965 to dramatize the problems and treatment of California's agricultural workers. It is the best known of more than one hundred Chicano and Latino theater companies in America.

Valdez wrote and directed the films *Zoot Suit* (1982) and *La Bamba* (1987).

Charles Ludlam (1943–1987)

Born in Floral Park, New York, Charles Ludlam was an actor and a director as well as a playwright. He received a bachelor of arts degree in drama from Hofstra University, in Hempstead, New York, in 1965. He has served on the faculty of, or has lectured at, many American universities. Ludlam is best known for his role as founding director of the Ridiculous Theatrical Company. He wrote some thirty comedies for the company before dying of AIDS. His themes are as serious as Molière's: lust, greed, hypocrisy, and sycophancy; his techniques for dramatizing those themes are farce, parody, satire, melodrama, obscenity, scatology, and outrageously funny characterizations.

Favorite Ludlam plays include *Big Hotel* (1967), *Bluebeard* (1970), *Camille: A Tear Jerker* (1973), *A Christmas Carol* (1979), *Secret Lives of the Sexists* (1982), *Exquisite Torture* (1982), and *The Mystery of Irma Vep* (1984).

The Mystery of Irma Vep (1984)

The name Irma Vep is an anagram for vampire. We know what she does, and *The Mystery of Irma Vep* is a satire of Gothic horror stories. Lord Edward has just married Lady Enid. The servants of the great house, Jane and Nicodemus, are still loyal to Irma Vep, the first mistress of the manor. A mummy cavorts, Nicodemus turns into a werewolf, a monster terrorizes the stage, and Irma's ghost materializes. As was his custom, Ludlam played several roles in his plays. Irma was one of his most famous female impersonations. The world was a sadder place when Ludlam left the stage.

Sam Shepard (1943–)

Sam Shepard has had two parallel careers. He is the author of scores of plays, and he is a successful actor. When he was nineteen he went to New York City to be an actor. In two years he was acclaimed as one of the young, promising, new American playwrights. And Shepard has proved to be very American. He has studied and portrayed various regional dialects; the rhythms and the imagery of American speech; and the values, expectations, and dreams of all classes. Shepard is interested in cowboys, the West, old movies, film noir, slang, science fiction, American history and geography, the environment, rock music, the drug culture, astrology, sexual passion, family relations, horses, racing, and the seemingly inherent violence in Americans.

Shepard's power as a writer is visceral. Shepard's plays seem to emerge from intuition. He has absorbed America. He has an instinctive connection to the American psyche and seems almost a part of the American landscape, merging with what is most desolate and most spiritually impoverished in it. In that respect he is the Tennessee Williams of the West.

Born Samuel Shepard Rogers in Fort Sheridan, Illinois, in an army hospital while his father was serving in the U.S. Army Air Force overseas in World War II, Shepard did not meet his father until he was five years old. His mother moved him all over the United States until they eventually settled down on an avocado ranch in Duarte, California. Shepard's father was violent and alcoholic, and the family suffered. Shepard graduated from Duarte High School in 1960. He studied at Mount San Antonio Junior College in Walnut, California, from 1960 to 1961. Shepard left home to escape his father's brutal ways, and thus freedom became a constant goal and an all-important requirement of his life. This need for, indeed worship of, freedom carried over into the seeming anarchy in Shepard's writing. He is not confined by stylistic fashion, slavish realism, textbook plots, nor the conventions of the well-made play. Sam Shepard continues to break new artistic ground.

Shepard married O-Lan Johnson Dark in 1969. They had one child. After their divorce Shepard began a relationship with the actor Jessica Lange. They have two children.

Shepard's star began its rapid assent with short plays Off-Off-Broadway: *Cowboys* (1964), *The Rock Garden* (1964), *Icarus's Mother* (1965), *Up to Thursday* (1965), *Dog* (1965), *Rocking Chair* (1965), *4-H Club* (1965), and *Red Cross* (1966). Then came Shepard's first full-length play, *La Turista* (1967), a study of contrasting Mexican and American values. Shepard continued to write one-act plays throughout his career, but it is his full-length dramas that have made him a major American playwright: *Operation Sidewinder* (1970), about a computer gone mad; *Mad Dog Blues* (1971), in which mythic characters in a fantasy energize the audience with their confrontations; *The Tooth of Crime* (1972), a rock music play; *Geography of a Horse Dreamer* (1974), in which a gifted handicapper is kidnapped for his knowledge of horses; *Angel City* (1976), a satire about the movie industry; *The Curse of the Starving Class* (1976), in which a family is victimized by gangsters; *Buried Child* (1978), the story of a decaying rural family; *True West* (1980), a murderous conflict of brother against brother; *Fool for Love* (1983), a sexual duel between siblings; and *States of Shock* (1991), a play about the trauma and the loss of war. *Buried Child* won the Pulitzer Prize for drama.

Shepard's latest plays include *Simpatico* (1993); *Far North* (1993); *Eyes for Consuela* (1998), *The Late Henry Moss* (2000) and *When the World Was Green (a Chef's Fable)* (2000), cowritten with Joseph Chaikin.

La Turista (1967)

The two acts of *La Turista* are similar. Act 1 is set in a Mexican hotel room, and act 2 is set in an American hotel room. The time of act 2 seems to precede act 1. In both acts Kent, the husband, is ill, and Salem, the wife, sends for a doctor. Kent and Salem are cigarette brand names. La Turista is Spanish for both tourist and the diarrhea that reputedly discomfits all American tourists visiting Mexico. The illness in the Mexican hotel room is sleeping sickness; in the American hotel room it is La Turista. The doctor is a witch doctor, and his cure includes the ritual killing of chickens. Shepard uses the play to attack stereotypes and to intimate that Americans prefer sleep to facing reality. As is often the case in Shepard, the deep meaning of the play is left to individual interpretation.

Operation Sidewinder (1970)

A state-of-the-art supercomputer, shaped like a sidewinder snake and developed by the U.S. Air Force, is set loose by the inventor to roam the desert. It learns and programs itself, and begins attacking passing tourists. Members of an anti-Air Force conspiracy capture the computer. They take it to a hideout and incorporate it in a ritual where a third world war is predicted. Eventually the body of the computer becomes a tourniquet for shooting up while a UFO takes the best people away from the doomed planet Earth.

The Tooth of Crime (1972)

Tooth of Crime is the story of Hoss, an aging rock musician. Hoss, the protagonist, must engage in epic battle with Crow, a younger rival to his power. Hoss lives in his castle like an ancient king, and he is surrounded by his supporters. He enjoys the company of a beautiful consort. But Hoss must fight desperately to hold onto his leadership. Hoss and Crow duel with hand microphones. When the referee judges that Crow has won by a TKO (technical knockout), Hoss kills him. Fully defeated, Hoss then kills himself. The archetypal male struggle for supremacy goes on.

Angel City (1976)

A group of hopeful people sit and wait in a Hollywood office. They want to impress a movie mogul with a scenario for a disaster film. Shepard sees the creative artist as a perennial victim to the greed of those in the business of art. Also, the movie-going public is fully desensitized and jaded. Outside the world is burning and society is crumbling, but all the public wants is to be distracted by sensationalism. The cry in the film obscures the real cry in the street.

Buried Child (1978)

After years away from Illinois and his grandparents, Vince returns to their farmhouse with his girlfriend, Shelly, to show her his family. He learns that his alcoholic grandfather, Dodge, now dying, once murdered and buried an unwanted child on the farm. Dodge sits in front of a television set and drinks. Vince's grandmother, Halie, is in mourning for another offspring, their son, Ansel. Vince's father, Tilden, is insane, while Vince's uncle is a brutal cripple. Homecoming can be a horror. The buried child in the field symbolizes the deep, dark truth of the family. Thus Vince and Shelly learn that a family heritage is not necessarily love and caring but may be incest and murder.

True West (1980)

In a California suburban house two brothers meet. One of them, Austin, is a liberal, successful Hollywood screenwriter. Lee, his older brother, is a derelict and a thief. He dislikes his successful brother and in a fit of rivalry decides to write a Western film script.

Lee is able to con a producer into backing the project, but he can't produce a written script, and so he forces Austin to work for him while he goes through the neighborhood stealing. Lee is always a menace, and the audience waits for an explosion. Austin is a prisoner in the house until he fights to leave. The house is demolished in the struggle of brothers, one good, one evil. The play ends as good and evil move out into the world to continue their fratricidal conflict. The brothers are two sides of the same coin. America is beaten up in the struggle of good and bad sons.

Fool for Love (1983)

In a cheap motel room near the Mojave desert, a violence-prone rodeo cowboy, Eddie, and his half sister, May, a short-order cook, meet again. They have been lovers, and she has fled from him. Their relationship is a love-hate one, and in a way, *Fool for Love* is a dance of love and hate. He has been searching for her because he wants her back. Their father's spirit sits in judgment, and he reveals his own emotional traumas and past sexual passions. A rejected lover of Eddie shoots up the hotel room. Violence is in the air, and love is without sentimentality. It is always as tentative and fragile as a flower in the desert. May's unsuspecting date provides a little comic relief. For Shepard, the American male is either a menace or an innocent.

Additional Reading

King, Kimberly, ed. *Sam Shepard: A Casebook.* New York: Garland, 1988.
Oumano, Ellen. *Sam Shepard.* New York: St. Martin's, 1986.
Shewey, Don. *Sam Shepard.* New York: Dell, 1985.
Wade, Leslie A. *Sam Shepard and the American Theatre.* Westport, Conn.: Praeger, 1997.

16
...

August Wilson and the New Dramatists
Post–World War II Generations Sure of Themselves

The American playwrights who were born in 1945 and later constitute a vastly talented and highly variegated group of playwrights,
the most notable of whom are two major American writers: August
Wilson and David Mamet.

August Wilson (1945–)

August Wilson set out to write a cycle of plays, one for each decade
of the twentieth century, set in Pittsburgh, depicting the African
American experience, the saga of a people who have been under
constant pressure from captivity in Africa to the present moment.
Wilson understands that pressure. He does not show the actual cruelties and injustices of a social system that has maintained that pressure. His subject is the psychological result of the pressure. Besides
being powerful and profound dramas, Wilson's plays are historical
and social documents. Later in the twenty-first century August
Wilson's dramatic realism will rank with the plays of Eugene
O'Neill, Tennessee Williams, and Arthur Miller as the great dramas
of the entire American experience.

August Wilson was born Frederick August Kittel and named

after his German-born father, a baker. His mother, Daisy Wilson Kittel, and her six children—Freddie was the fourth of six—lived in a two-room flat in the Hill District, the African American section of Pittsburgh. His stepfather was David Bedford, a man Wilson did not get along well with. And Wilson saw little of his birth father. Daisy Wilson Kittel worked as a cleaner to support her children.

Although Wilson could read at the age of four, he had trouble in school, especially at Central Catholic High School, where as the only African American student he was subject to racial harassment. Later, in Gladstone High School, a public school, his experiences were similar, and so he left school at fifteen without a diploma. Wilson began a regimen of serious reading of such authors as Langston Hughes, Richard Wright, and Ralph Ellison. In 1962 Wilson enlisted in the army but returned to civilian life after one year. At eighteen he began working menial jobs.

In 1965 the senior Frederick August Kittel died. The younger Frederick August Kittel, wanting to be on his own, moved out of his mother's flat into an apartment of his own, purchased a typewriter, decided he was going to be a writer, and changed his name to August Wilson. Following the lead of Amiri Amamu Baraka in Newark, Wilson and his friend Rob Penny in 1968 founded an African American theater company in Pittsburgh: Black Horizons Theater. Under the influence of the African American Civil Rights movement, Wilson had become a black nationalist, disavowing the culture of his birth father. But Wilson never became a hater. There are no stereotypical villains in his work, white or black, only human beings.

Wilson's drama is pervasively informed by music because Wilson believes music reflects the energy and vitality of African Americans. The blues is poetry and reflects the great epic of the black diaspora that includes the Middle Passage from Africa, the centuries of slavery, and the massive, early-twentieth-century trek from the agrarian South to the cities of the industrialized North. Note the titles of three of Wilson's major plays: *Ma Rainey's Black*

Bottom (1984), set in 1927, which depicts the problems of African American musicians in the Jazz Age; *The Piano Lesson* (1987; revised 1990), the Pulitzer Prize-winning play in which ghosts and people battle for possession of an historic piano in 1937; and *Seven Guitars* (1995), set in 1948, in which the gun and the guitar struggle for the life and the soul of a musician.

But Wilson is also a great storyteller. He loves to have his characters relate their experiences, or their family myths and traditions. Wilson has incorporated the role of West African griot into the sound box of his techniques.

Wilson married Brenda Burton, a Muslim, in 1969, the year his stepfather, David Bedford, died. The Wilsons had one child, but the marriage ended in divorce in 1972, partly because Wilson found his wife's religious practices problematic. Wilson moved to St. Paul, Minnesota, in 1978, and there he wrote his first major play, *Jitney* (1980; revised 1996, 1998), the story of gypsy taxi drivers in the Pittsburgh of the 1970s.

Wilson married Judy Oliver, a social worker, in 1981. In 1982 Wilson met the distinguished African American director Lloyd Richards, and one of modern American theater's greatest artistic collaborations commenced. In 1984 Richards directed *Ma Rainey's Black Bottom* at the Yale Repertory Theater and on Broadway.

Wilson's other plays in the Pittsburgh Cycle are *Fences* (1985), the Pulitzer Prize-winning drama set in 1957, in which the changing younger generation realizes its debt to the past; *Joe Turner's Come and Gone* (1986), set in 1911, when African Americans are just beginning to feel and express freedom; *Two Trains Running* (1990), set in 1969, when the patrons of a local restaurant must struggle with a future of disruption and change; and *King Hedley II* (2000), set in the 1980s, in which a murderer released from prison tries to turn his life around.

In 1990 Wilson's second marriage came to an end after nine years. He then moved to Seattle. In 1994 Wilson married Costanza Romero, the costume designer for *The Piano Lesson,* and they have two children. August Wilson became widely known by the general American public in 1995, when *The Piano Lesson* was produced on CBS's popular Hallmark Hall of Fame series. Wilson's most recent productions have been revisions of *Jitney* and *King Hedley II* (2001).

Jitney (1980; revised 1996, 1998)

A play set in a gypsy cab office located in a building doomed by coming urban renewal, *Jitney* foregrounds the story of Becker, the owner of the service that is needed to provide transportation for minorities in racially divided Pittsburgh, and his son, Booster. The latter is shortly to be released from prison. Becker is not elated over the event because his son was convicted of the murder of his white girlfriend, who falsely accused him of rape to protect herself from her father's wrath. The judge assigned Booster the death penalty, which led to the death of Booster's mother, who died before the death sentence had been commuted to twenty years in prison. The father-son controversy is bitter, and Becker dies in an industrial accident before the two men can express the love they really have for each other. The pervasive atmosphere of community in the play is so adroitly created and so powerful that the audience is completely drawn into Wilson's world.

Ma Rainey's Black Bottom (1984)

Set outside of Pittsburgh, *Ma Rainey's Black Bottom* portrays the plight of African American blues musicians in the 1920s, when the real-life Ma Rainey was the leading female blues singer. Ma Rainey and her backups come into the white-owned recording studio where she is scheduled to record several popular songs. The white promoters don't like her demanding ways, as she is determined to control the recording session. Her integrity as an artist and as a strong African American woman will not be compromised. Meanwhile her musicians wait in the band room, quarrel with each other, and one is stabbed to death. Thus, regardless of their great talent, the African Americans lose power to the whites because of their violence against each other.

Fences (1985)

Fences is a family play. Troy Maxson, a garbageman, is in conflict with his son, Cory. Troy is bitter because he had great baseball talent, but he could not play major-league ball because he was an African American. He refused to let his son take a college football scholarship because he is sure that there is no future for African Americans in professional sports. Troy's wife, Rose, tries to talk him out of his position, pointing out the success of Jackie Robinson. But Troy needs to believe in a lack of opportunity. His bitterness leads him to infidelity, which threatens the family.

Joe Turner's Come and Gone (1986)

Seven years before the play *Joe Turner's Come and Gone* begins, Herald Loomis was falsely convicted of a crime in Tennessee and had to work on a chain gang. While he was in jail, his wife left their daughter with her mother. Loomis takes the child to Pittsburgh, looking for his wife. Slowly, Loomis comes to realize that his spirit, seemingly broken by ill treatment on the chain gang, can recover if he wills it. He can overcome and survive as other African Americans have.

The Piano Lesson (1987; revised 1990)

A valuable old piano is the center of controversy in a family. Almost one hundred years before, a member of the Charles family, a slave to the Sutters, was ordered to carve decorations on the piano. But two members of the African American family had been traded for the piano. Consequently, the carver sculpted on the instrument a memorial to the family and to the slave experience. His grandson stole the piano, and now that man's granddaughter, Berniece, owns it. Her father was killed by the Sutters to avenge the theft. Berniece and her brother fight over the piano. He wants to sell it. She treasures it. Finally, they come to realize that the instrument is their heritage and must not be sold or lost.

Two Trains Running (1990)

Memphis Lee battles with white city officials in Pittsburgh over the value of his home as it is being devoured by urban renewal. Lee is frustrated and feeling defeated, but a mentally retarded handyman shows him and the community that African Americans don't have to be victims if they have the determination not to be. Every day, for nine years, the handyman has demanded the ham a butcher promised in payment for work done. He won't accept a chicken instead of his due. He stands up for his rights and wins out. Inspired, Memphis Lee is liberated from his debilitating defeatism.

Seven Guitars (1995)

Seven Guitars, a murder mystery, is set in the backyard of a rooming house in Pittsburgh. Floyd Barton has been in jail on a false vagrancy charge. He is a blues musician, and that gives him status. He has cut a hit record but is not getting much money out of it because of the contract he made with the producer, and so he has to pawn his best guitar for the money to pay for the down payment on his mother's headstone.

Floyd just can't stay out of trouble. Rules are not made for him, and often circumstances betray him. He doesn't redeem the pawned guitar in time and he loses it. Floyd robs a finance company and ostensibly has the money he needs, but Hedley, a poultry slaughterer, is Floyd's sexual rival. He cuts Floyd's throat as easily as he kills chickens. A fine musician is dead at thirty-five, but his music will endure.

King Hedley II (2000)

King Hedley has been released from prison after serving a seven-year sentence for having killed the man who scarred his face. He and his friend, Mister, want to open a video store. The money will come from peddling stolen appliances. King Hedley's wife is pregnant. They have no money but he has hope, symbolized by his planting of a garden. His mother wants forgiveness from him for having abandoned him as a child. All are struggling, and the odds against the survival of the poor predict disaster.

Additional Reading

Bogumil, Mary L. *Understanding August Wilson.* Columbia: Univ. of South Carolina Press, 1999.

Elkins, Marilyn, ed. *August Wilson: A Casebook.* New York: Garland, 1994.

Pereira, Kim. *August Wilson and the African-American Odyssey.* Urbana, Ill.: Univ. of Illinois Press, 1995.

Shannon, Sandra G. *The Dramatic Vision of August Wilson.* Washington, D.C.: Howard Univ. Press, 1995.

Woolfe, Peter. *August Wilson.* New York: Twayne, 1999.

Miguel Piñero (1946–1988)

Miguel Piñero began his career as a playwright while serving a term for armed robbery in Sing Sing Prison. After his release, he achieved recognition and success as a playwright and poet but still found it difficult to keep out of legal trouble. Piñero is best known for his prison tragicomedy *Short Eyes* (1974), the story of the murder of a reputed child molester by his fellow prisoners.

Piñero was born in Gurabo, in east central Puerto Rico, and

came to the Lower East Side of Manhattan with his mother and stepfather when he was five. Four years later Adelina Piñero was abandoned by her second husband. She and her many children, including Miguel, the oldest, were forced to live on the streets until they could obtain welfare. Piñero was a streetwise, tough, petty criminal and gang leader, a failure in school, and in and out of correctional institutions until he discovered his writing ability in Sing Sing. But success was hard to live with, and although he returned to live on the Lower East Side, he was no longer at home anywhere. Drug addiction was the worst of his many difficulties.

Piñero married Lovette Rameize in 1977. The couple divorced in 1979. Piñero adopted a son. Piñero's other plays include *Eulogy for a Small Time Thief* (1977), a tragedy in which a father who goes to an apartment to buy sex finds that his teenage daughter is the prostitute; *The Sun Always Shines for the Cool* (1978), in which pimps battle for control of a territory; and *A Midnight Moon at the Greasy Spoon* (1981), an atmosphere play like Saroyan's *The Time of Your Life,* set in a Times Square luncheonette in which characters off the street assemble.

Short Eyes (1974)

The title of the play refers to prisoner slang for a child molester. *Short Eyes* is set in a cell block dayroom of a New York prison. It contains men awaiting trial for various crimes or transfers to other prisons. The group is interracial. They are horsing around, playing cards, cracking jokes, and sizing up the younger prisoners as potential homosexual prey. A mentally disturbed man is pushed into the room. He has been charged with raping a child. Child molesting is the one crime that even the most hardened criminal cannot tolerate. The man is terrified out of his wits. A wise and more compassionate prisoner tries to protect the man after he "confesses" his crime to him in his disturbed manner, but the other prisoners seize the opportunity to vent their pent-up anger, frustration, self-hatred, and violence on the helpless man, who must endure humiliation, torture, and murder. Ironically, the prisoners finally learn that the man they killed was innocent. This slice-of-life, authentic drama is reminiscent of the prison plays of Jean Genet and Brendan Behan.

Albert Innaurato (1947–)

Albert Innaurato is best known for *Gemini* (1977), a play about Italian American family life in south Philadelphia. Innaurato was born in south Philadelphia. After parochial schooling he attended Temple University for two years and then transferred to the California Institute of Arts in Los Angeles, where he obtained a bachelor's degree in fine arts. He received a master of fine arts from the Yale School of Drama. At Yale he wrote plays and made the contacts that led him to the New York theater.

Innaurato first attracted critical attention with the one-act play *The Transfiguration of Benno Blimpie* (1977), the story of a man eating himself to death. Next came *Ulysses in Traction* (1977), about the power of the rehearsal to drown out the world.

Innaurato's more recent dramas have had little success. Still, Innaurato has so much skill with characterization that his next play may indeed return him to critical and popular favor.

Gemini (1977)

An Italian American family in south Philadelphia is celebrating the twenty-first birthday of Francis Geniniani. It is June 1973. Fran is a very intelligent and sensitive Harvard University graduate who lives in a working-class neighborhood where few children go on to college. He is ashamed of his family and his neighborhood. One Jewish neighbor's son is an overweight character in another of Innaurato's works.

To Fran's chagrin two affluent college friends, Judy and Randy Hastings, brother and sister, come to surprise him. Fran has personal problems too. He and Judy have made love, but Fran, unsure of his sexual identity, thinks he may really be in love with Randy. But Judy and Randy are both in love with Fran. The problems don't quite get resolved, but the portraits of family and friends as well as the festive atmosphere of the play made *Gemini* a hit with Off-Broadway, Broadway, and regional audiences.

Marsha Norman (1947–)

'Night, Mother (1982), a gripping two-actor play about a suicide, earned Norman a Pulitzer Prize and her national reputation. The feminist writer emerged along with several other new playwrights from the Actors Theatre of Louisville, Kentucky, where her first play, *Getting Out* (1977), a successful drama about prison life for a woman, was performed. The imaginative play, with its naturalistic dialogue, has two actors playing the protagonist before, during, and after prison.

Marsha Norman was born in Louisville to an insurance salesman, Billie Williams, and his wife, Bertha. Marsha Williams, the oldest of four siblings, was brought up in a middle-class neighborhood, and she went to public schools despite the fact that her parents were fundamentalist Methodists. She graduated from Durret High School and then enrolled in Agnes Scott College in Decatur, Georgia, where she received a bachelor of arts degree in philosophy in 1969. Returning to Louisville, she married her former high school English teacher, Michael Norman. In 1971 Marsha Norman received a master of arts in education from the University of Louisville, which prepared her for work teaching disturbed adolescents at Kentucky Central State Hospital.

Soon Norman was writing full-time and publishing articles and reviews in the *Louisville Times*. The Normans divorced in 1974. Using her former experience in the state hospital, Norman began work on *Getting Out*. She was encouraged by Jon Jory, the artistic director of the Actors Theatre of Louisville.

In 1978 Norman married a successful Louisville businessman, Dan C. Byck Jr., who became a New York producer when '*Night, Mother* opened on Broadway in 1983 after its initial success with the American Repertory Company in Cambridge, Massachusetts. Marsha and Dan were divorced in 1986, and Norman married Tim Dykma in 1987.

Norman has continued to write plays and adaptations, but without duplicating her earlier successes. Her latest work is *Trudy Blue* (1995), about a woman novelist's desperate need to get away from her stifling environment. Norman published a novel, *The Fortune Teller,* in 1987.

'*Night, Mother* (1982)

Norman is especially interested in mother-daughter relations. In this ninety-minute drama without an intermission, a middle-aged daughter, Jessie, believes that her life has been a total failure. It is empty of meaning, and she has not succeeded in relationships. She is unattractive physically. Her husband left her. She has epileptic seizures. She just can't fix the problems of her life. Jessie informs her elderly mother, Thelma, that she intends to commit suicide, and she goes about making preparations, including ways for her mother to deal with her death and get by afterward. At first her mother does not believe her. When, however, her mother realizes that her daughter is absolutely serious, she desperately tries to talk her out of suicide, and fails.

Additional Reading

Brown, Linda Ginter, ed. *Marsha Norman: A Casebook.* New York: Garland, 1996.

David Mamet (1947–)

Unquestionably a major American dramatist, David Mamet is the dramatic poet of the inexpressive, the dishonest, and the selfish American. His characters speak torrents of inanities and profanities, spout locker-room language, stammer and step on each other's sentences, and seem to dredge words up from a swamp of thought. Mamet has a great ear for the linguistic styles of subcultures. A Mamet play can be an exercise in frustration for an audience struggling to keep up with and comprehend the machine-gun dialogue. Yet that dialogue is as much a work of art as is Samuel Beckett's cryptic runs or Tennessee Williams's syrupy southernisms.

David Mamet was born in Flossmoor, Illinois (near Chicago), the son of Bernard and Lenore Silver Mamet. His father was a labor lawyer, and his strong, sometimes difficult mother was a teacher as well as a homemaker. He grew up on the Jewish South Side of Chicago. Mamet's childhood was not idyllic. His parents fought each other with barbed words, and David and his sister joined in. Finally, his parents were divorced when he was eleven. His mother's second marriage embittered Mamet.

While Mamet was in high school and living with his father, he involved himself as an actor and stagehand with the Hull House Theater. Mamet continued his education at Goddard College in Plainfield, Vermont, where he received a bachelor of arts degree in literature in 1969. In his junior year Mamet went to New York City to study acting at Sanford Meisner's Neighborhood Playhouse, but he was not invited to return for a second year of instruction.

Mamet first earned his living as a drama teacher, working for a year at Marlboro College in Marlboro, Vermont, from 1970 to 1971. He then returned to Goddard to teach and write. There he began work on two short plays that would make him famous: *Duck Variations* (1972), in which two old Jewish men exercise and confirm their friendship; and *Sexual Perversity in Chicago* (1974), a shockingly frank play about young singles in the war of the sexes that is full of crude, salacious, but authentic profanity and obscenity. These plays were later performed together successfully Off-Off-Broadway. Mamet's next major play, *American Buffalo* (1975), the story of three small-time thieves who plan to rob a coin collector, premiered at the Goodman Theatre in Chicago. It opened on Broadway in 1977.

Now Mamet had the prerequisites for success, on and Off Broadway, for him to earn his living as a dramatist. He moved to New York City. The two-actor comedy *A Life in the Theatre* (1977), in which an older and a younger actor relate to each other through a smorgasbord of mediocre plays, was Mamet's next success. It remains a favorite of regional and community theaters. The same year *The Water Engine: An American Fable,* a play about the 1930s and an inventor who designs a car engine that runs on water, only to have it stolen by dishonest industrialists, was not successful.

Glengarry Glen Ross (1983) won the Pulitzer Prize. It is the story of disreputable salesmen in a shady, fly-by-night real estate office selling worthless Florida building lots. *Speed-the-Plow* (1987) satirizes Hollywood. *Oleanna* (1992) depicts a conflict between an angry undergraduate woman and her professor. *The Cryptogram* (1995) is a somewhat autobiographical drama about a ten-year-old boy who turns to violence as his parents separate. In *The Old Neighborhood* (1997), a play without the Mamet bite, a divorced, middle-aged man returns to his old neighborhood to reconnect with the past. *Lakeboat* (2001) is Mamet's latest drama.

David Mamet has authored over forty long plays, short plays, and adaptations. He also is a very successful screenplay writer. Mamet married the American actor Lindsay Crouse in 1976. They had two children and then divorced in 1990. Mamet married the British actor Rebecca Pidgeon in 1991. They have one child and live in rural Vermont. In recent years Mamet has become more interested in his Jewish background and heritage.

David Mamet's major plays all have heft and a cutting edge. He is a moralist who is concerned with good and evil, and is fascinated by the improbability of true communication. He sees humans as primarily predators. Like Beckett and Pinter, he expects his audience to fill out the dialogue, read between the lines, and think. Mamet wants to believe in the power of love and the existence of compassion in the human heart, but, simultaneously, he is a prophet who cries out "corruption," "hypocrisy," "betrayal," "venality," and "avarice" when and where he sees it. And he sees it everywhere.

American Buffalo (1975)

In *American Buffalo* Mamet presents a bleak vision of American life as it satirizes capitalism. In a junk shop Don, the owner, his friend Teach, and Bobby, a young junkie and Don's gofer, plot to rob a customer of his valuable coin collection because he bought a Buffalo nickel for the large amount of ninety dollars. Teach was not supposed to be in on the job, but he worms his way in. However, the inarticulate thieves cannot agree, and they begin to fight among themselves until Teach wrecks the shop. The play's dialogue is both powerful and explicit.

Glengarry Glen Ross (1983)

Mamet's most successful play takes place in a Chinese restaurant and at a real estate office. A salesman, Levene, attempts to bribe the office manager into giving him better leads for possible sales of worthless Florida land. Then a salesman tries to get another, who is less sure of his selling ability, to steal leads from the office. Next we see a salesman swindling a helpless, hapless customer, who returns in tears in the second act to beg for his money back. The best leads have been stolen. A detective investigates, and the sales force rats on each other, trying to incriminate the competition. Mamet savagely satirizes predatory American business and sales practices.

Speed-the-Plow (1987)

Bobby Gould is a young movie executive whose job is to approve scripts for production. Charlie Fox is another executive. They flatter, manipulate, and con each other shamelessly. They have worked together before. Gould has to decide between "The Bridge," a script that seems both spiritual and pretentious but is written by an established author, and the script that Fox is pushing. It is a common variety "buddy flick," but the deal involves the chance to steal a famous actor from another studio to do the part. The difficulty is that Fox only has a twenty-four-hour option on the script. As Gould is not interested in "art" but in box office receipts, Fox is confident of closing the deal.

Then an attractive, temporary secretary, Karen, someone not even on the bottom rung of the Hollywood ladder, enters the equation and tries to become part of the promotion of "The Bridge" in order to rise in the studio hierarchy. Gould finds himself attracted to her and asks her to take the script home, read it, and come back to discuss it that evening. She is wise to Hollywood ways but wants to get ahead, so she is willing to have sex with him if it will help her career. Gould thinks Karen genuinely cares for him. She tries to sell the script by reading spiritual, literary passages. Fox seems stymied until he gets Karen to confess that she slept with Gould in order to get into the action. In the end she is tossed out, still a temp.

Women in Mamet's Hollywood are sexual prey, but they knowingly use sex as bait. It's all a game, with power, money, and sex the chips savagely used and played for. The play's title reads like a wish that God will bring an enterprise to quick success. It is also a sexual pun.

Oleanna (1992)

Oleanna, a two-actor play, is set in a college professor's office. The professor, John, is only partly interested in his students. He has tenure and a new house on his mind. An undergraduate student, Carol, who seems not too bright, can't understand his course. John tries to help her when she comes to his office, but she takes his expressions of sympathy as sexual harassment, and she reports him to the tenure committee. There is little foundation to Carol's charge, and she has been put up to mischief by radical feminists, but Bob is insensitive to Carol's perspective. In the end his career and life are in shambles, and he is ready to do violence to Carol. The play invariably causes loud arguments in the audience after the final curtain. The title is ironic, as Oleanna was the name of an eighteenth-century utopia. Mamet shows his audiences that American colleges are not utopias.

Additional Reading

Bigsby, C. W. E. *David Mamet*. New York: Methuen, 1985.
Carroll, Dennis. *David Mamet*. New York: St. Martin's, 1987.
Kane, Leslie, ed. *David Mamet: A Casebook*. New York: Garland, 1992.

Ntozake Shange (1948–)

Ntozake Shange's *For Colored Girls Who Have Considered Suicide/ When the Rainbow Is Enuf* (1975) is a glorious potpourri of poetry, dance, humor, tragedy, and betrayal. In set dramatic pieces Shange depicts the anguish of African American women and the desperate need for black sisterhood as they struggle for recognition as individual human beings in the African American community in which patriarchal values pervade. To be black and a woman is to be doubly oppressed. But the problems that Shange's women face—seduction, date rape, spousal abuse, and the condescension of men—are seemingly universal and timeless.

Ntozake Shange was born in Trenton, New Jersey, into an upper- middle-class family. She received a bachelor of arts degree from Barnard College in New York City and a master of arts from the University of California, Los Angeles, in 1973. Shange took the Xhosa African name in 1971. She has been married twice and has a child. Shange is a distinguished poet who has taught at several American colleges and universities. Although Shange has written more than fifteen original plays and adaptations, only *For Colored Girls* has achieve popular success.

Additional Reading

Lester, Neal A. *Ntozake Shange: A Critical Study of the Plays.* New York: Garland, 1995.

Christopher Durang (1949–)

The author of nearly thirty plays and a successful actor, Christopher Durang is best known for three works: first, his satire *A History of the American Film* (1976, with music by Mel Marvin), in which Durang uses the format of a musical revue to parody and expose the clichés of Hollywood; second, his satire on Catholic education, *Sister Mary Ignatius Explains It All* (1979); and third, *Beyond Therapy* (1981), a story of thirty-something Manhattan singles and their psychiatrists. The latter two plays are favorites in regional, college, and community theaters.

Christopher Durang was born in Montclair, New Jersey, and educated in Catholic parochial schools until he attended Harvard University, from which he received a bachelor of arts degree in English in 1971. He then went on to the Yale School of Drama, from which he received a master of fine arts in playwriting in 1976.

Durang is an absurdist-satirist who targets institutions of American society that to him need deflating and exposure, such as the movie industry, the theater industry, parochial education, the psychiatric industry, male-female relations, and American courtship.

Sister Mary Ignatius Explains It All (1979)

This long, absurdist, one-act play savagely satirizes the most repressive aspects of Catholic education as personified by Sister Mary Ignatius of Our Lady of Perpetual Sorrows School, whose actions are absurdly irrational and whose values are life-denying. Sister Mary Ignatius is a tyrant, and her students are terrified of her. She sees sin everywhere. While she is lecturing, four previous students who dislike her come in. They are people who have had problems in their lives. The class is disturbed as they denounce the nun, but she restores her law and order by shooting them.

Beyond Therapy (1981)

In *Beyond Therapy* two neurotic singles, one a male lawyer who is bisexual, the other a female journalist, look to their psychiatrists for help, only to find them more disturbed than they are. Durang has little respect for the psychiatric profession. The two patients have met through a personal ad, and the woman wants to get married. Like boxers, the pair are coached in the courtship by their therapists. The lawyer's therapist is a woman who carries around a Snoopy toy. The journalist's therapist seduces his female patients. Happily, in the end both people drop their therapists and work on the relationship themselves, with the possibility that they may marry after all.

Wendy Wasserstein (1950–)

Wendy Wasserstein is the leading female American dramatist today. She and such writers as Marsha Norman and Beth Henley are the products of the women's movement of the 1970s. When young, they faced a rapidly changing American society that left them somewhat confused and stressed, unsure how to proceed and where they were going, but determined to succeed on their artistic merits. And they have.

Wasserstein was born in Brooklyn to Morris W. Wasserstein, a well-off manufacturer, and Lola Schleifer Wasserstein, an intelligent homemaker interested in the theater. Wendy was the youngest of four children. Her parents had come to America as child immigrants in the 1920s, just as the great Jewish migration from Eastern Europe came to an end. The family moved to the affluent Upper East Side of New York City when Wasserstein was a child. She attended the Calhoun School, a private institution. Later, at Mount Holyoke College, she majored in history and received a bachelor of arts degree in 1971. While at college she began to contemplate a playwriting career after a summer course in playwriting at Smith College.

Back in New York City Wasserstein studied creative writing at the City College of New York under Joseph Heller and Israel Horovitz, receiving a master of arts degree in 1973. The prestigious Off-Broadway Playwrights Horizon company produced her first play, *Any Woman Can't*, in 1973. She was only twenty-three. Still feeling the need for training, Wasserstein enrolled in the Yale School of Drama and received a master of fine arts in 1976.

Uncommon Women and Others (1975), a funny and compassionate play about the reunion of six graduates of Mount Holyoke College who have gone very separate ways six years after graduation, caused Wasserstein to be recognized as a significant new voice in American theater. *Isn't It Romantic* (1981; revised 1983), the story of the fading friendship between a pair of long-term college friends, one Jewish and one affluent white Protestant, also succeeded.

Wasserstein's finest works to date are *The Heidi Chronicles* (1988), the Pulitzer Prize-winning humorous epic story of the maturation of a bright young Jewish woman of the 1960s; and *The Sisters Rosensweig* (1992), in which three middle-aged Jewish sisters soul-search.

Wasserstein's most recent plays are the unsuccessful *An Ameri-*

can Daughter (1997), in which a woman nominated to be surgeon general of the United States is attacked because she has committed a seemingly minor legal and moral transgression; and *Old Money* (2000), a comedy-drama that is an antitribute to the rich of New York City from 1902 to the middle of the twenty-first century, and in which the old robber barons are contrasted with the new cyber bores and their descendants in Sci-Fi Land. In *Old Money* the actors play three generations of characters alternately, while, in the manner of Tom Stoppard's *Arcadia*, the labyrinthine plot crosscuts between historical periods. The play somehow manages to be both confusing and cliché laden at the same time.

But at her best Wendy Wasserstein creates delicate and delicious portraits of female baby boomers. There is a subtle but serious ideological statement behind her work: Jewish women are strong because they are triply "others," striving to overcome cultural bias, the patriarchal shackles of their ancient religion, and the general impediments American women as a whole have historically experienced. In a wider sense, Wasserstein's most significant contribution is that she has learned to include wry humor as well as profound insight in her depiction of the contemporary life of American women.

The Heidi Chronicles (1988)

As the title implies, *The Heidi Chronicles* takes place over a number of years (from 1965 to 1989) as a group of friends mature and change. In a sense the play is the history of the women's movement incorporated into one woman's life. The purpose of the play is to have the audience reexamine the rebellions of the 1960s, the consolidations of the 1970s, and the surrenders of the 1980s through the eyes and the experiences of Heidi, who at first is a rebellious college student, then a single mother, and finally a hardworking, career art historian, Dr. Heidi Holland, working to create a canon of female art and artists. There are two men in her life, but one is gay and the other is self-absorbed. Heidi adopts a girl child, and Heidi will go through her life as a successful independent person and a role model for future young women.

The Sisters Rosensweig (1992)

Like Chekhov's *Three Sisters, The Sisters Rosensweig* is about three unfulfilled sisters coming together for an occasion and contemplating their lives. In this instance the sisters are Jewish Americans, and the occasion is Sara Goode's fifty-fourth birthday. The year is 1991. The play is set in her expensively and tastefully furnished London residence. The action takes place over a weekend. Sara is a successful expatriate banking executive with a Hong Kong bank. She is divorced and living with a seventeen-year-old daughter who is in love with a young Lithuanian activist worried about the effect the fall of the Soviet Union will have on his country. Sara has had a hysterectomy. She is comfortable with her Jewish background because it is way back in the background. Her current boyfriend is a stiff and somewhat anti-Semitic Englishman.

Uninvited, but with an introduction, Mervyn, a furrier from the Bronx, arrives. He is changing over from animal furs to synthetics. A widower, he instantly falls for Sara and begins to court her. She is put off at first by his accent and his brash "ethnicity," because he reminds her constantly of her background. Eventually, he wins Sara.

Sara's sisters arrive. Pfeni Rosensweig is a globe-wandering travel writer with a bisexual boyfriend who also has a boyfriend. Gorgeous Titlebaum is the funniest of the sisters and the most authentic. Gorgeous is a Newton, Massachusetts, homemaker and mother who has a call-in radio advice program. She is hoping for a television hook-up.

In the end the three sisters and the one daughter go on with their lives. Typical of Wasserstein's major characters, they have all experienced some degree of self-definition. The daughter will go off to Lithuania with her young man. Sara, however, is clearly headed for a return to her Jewish roots.

Additional Reading

Barnett, Claudia, ed. *Wendy Wasserstein: A Casebook.* New York: Garland, 1999.
Ciociola, Gail. *Wendy Wasserstein: Dramatizing Women, Their Choices and Their Boundaries.* Jefferson, N.C.: McFarland, 1998.

Beth Henley (1952–)

Beth Henley took up playwriting as a cause, as she believed that there were few good roles in contemporary theater for southern women. Henley was born in Jackson, Mississippi, the daughter of Charles Boyce Henley, a successful lawyer and Mississippi state politician, and Elizabeth Josephine Becker Henley, an ardent community theater actor. After public schools, Henley enrolled in Southern Methodist University, where she studied drama. She received a bachelor of fine arts degree in 1974. Henley intended to pursue a career in acting. She studied further at the University of Illinois at Urbana and then moved to Los Angeles to live with the actor and director Stephen Tobolowsky and to try to get into films.

Unsuccessful, Henley turned to writing. The result was *Crimes of the Heart* (1979), a southern Gothic tale of three sisters and their loves that won the Pulitzer Prize. The play was first produced by the Actor's Theatre of Louisville and then in New York City. Henley's subsequent plays, about southern women who have odd lives and bizarre adventures, have not succeed as well as *Crimes of the Heart.* Henley lives in California and has a child.

Henley's plays are full of death and dying. Murder and suicide frequently occur. Characters are eccentric, to say the least, but they are usually sympathetic. Sentimentality is rare, and sex is funny. The southern dialect is poetically and prettily rendered. Erskine Caldwell, William Faulkner, Flannery O'Connor, and Eudora Welty seem somehow lurking behind it all.

The Miss Firecracker Contest (1980) tells the story of a zany southern community celebrating the Fourth of July. *The Wake of Jamey Foster* (1982) has a nonmourning Mississippi widow finding a new love. *The Debutante Ball* (1985) shows a mother trying to reestablish her pregnant teenage daughter's reputation through her debut. *The Lucky Spot* (1987) erotically depicts a Louisiana village Depression-era scene. *Abundance* (1989), less humorous than most Henley plays, shows men and mail-order brides in Wyoming at the end of the nineteenth century.

Henley's most recent plays are *Control Freaks* (1992) and *Impossible Marriage* (1998).

Crimes of the Heart (1979)

It's a manic day in the life of the three quirky, small-town Mississippi McGrath sisters. As in Chekhov's *Three Sisters,* the women have come together for a special reason: the impending death of their grandfather. Also, Babe has just shot her husband, whose looks she didn't like. On the other hand, he caught her with a fifteen-year-old lover. Her sister, Lenny, thirty-plus and single, is mourning the death of her horse who was struck by lightning. Meg, a honky-tonk nightclub singer, tries to get Babe the best lawyer in town, but, alas, the best lawyer is the man she shot. The bumbling new lawyer Babe engages falls for her. In the end the sisters are close, happy, and feeding on a birthday cake.

The Miss Firecracker Contest (1980)

Carnelle Scott looks for status and respect in beauty contests. The Miss Firecracker contest is held on the Fourth of July in a Mississippi town. She has previously won the Miss Hot Tamale contest partly by sleeping around. The play's pacing is frantic. A cousin has come from a mental institution where he was sent for assault. An aunt has died after a monkey-gland implant caused her to grow long hair over her whole body. The local seamstress spent her childhood making clothes for bullfrogs. Carnelle loses the contest, but the play ends with all characters full of affection for each other and with the stage lit up with firecrackers.

Ted Talley (1952–)

Best known for *Terra Nova* (1977), the tragic story of Robert Scott's fatal race to the South Pole, Ted Talley was born in Winston-Salem, North Carolina, and was educated at Yale University, where he received a bachelor of arts degree in 1974 and and master of fine arts degree in 1977. He and his wife, Melinda, have one child.

In *Terra Nova* Talley discourses on the nature, vanity, and sometimes folly of heroism. He also is interested in the idea that nations need heroes, even those who lead their followers to disaster and death. Tally further reflects on the great need some people have for fame, to the extent that they are willing to risk their lives and the lives of their followers for it. The better-prepared Amundsen beats Scott to the Pole and survives. Scott has all the attributes of a tragic hero: a good and heroic person who becomes a victim of hubris and fate.

George C. Wolfe (1954–)

Wolfe was born in Frankfort, Kentucky. His father wrote for army newspapers during World War II and later clerked at Kentucky State University. His mother earned a doctorate from Miami University and taught. Wolfe received a bachelor of arts degree from Pomona College in Claremont, California, and a master of fine arts in playwriting and musical theater from New York University. In 1993 Wolfe became the artistic director of the New York Shakespeare Festival, arguably the most important producing organization Off Broadway. His intelligence and bold gift for satire, his musical knowledge and sensitivity, and his overall command of stage skills make him a major force in the American theater in the twenty-first century.

Wolfe's first professional play, *Paradise!* (1985), a satire on Western colonialism, was produced by Playwrights Horizons. Wolfe's second play, *The Colored Museum* (1986), a satire on racial stereotypes and contemporary African American life, immediately established him as a significant American playwright. *Spunk* (1989) is based on three stories by Zora Neale Hurston in which life's passions are explored. Wolfe's musical, *Jelly's Last Jam* (1991), depicting the career of the great jazz composer Jelly Roll Morton, was a Broadway sensation because it went beyond the norms of musicals to present an insightful and critical biography of an artist. Wolfe also directed Tony Kushner's *Angels in America* in 1993.

The Colored Museum (1986)

As if cued by Albee and the theater of the absurd, *The Colored Museum* is absurdly and savagely funny. The play depicts contemporary African American life in eleven satirical vignettes, each called an exhibit. One vignette has a stewardess on a slave ship escorting passengers on a fast-forward trip through the saga of the African American. Another, in the manner of Jonathan Swift's "A Modest Proposal," has an "Aunt Jemima" type singing a blues song about whipping up a "batch of Negroes." African Americans are satirized for dressing stylishly but not thinking deeply. The concern of African Americans for hairstyle is portrayed as a tension marker for assimilation. Earlier African American dramatists and their plays are parodied. Wolfe is saying that for African Americans to survive in America, they need not only to understand and appreciate their heritage, but also to be able to endure the trials white Americans and African Americans themselves create.

Harvey Fierstein (1954–)

In 1981 Harvey Fierstein's *Torch Song Trilogy* made history in the history of gay theater. It is a celebratory and sentimental portrayal of gay life that was fully accepted and enjoyed by the middle-class Broadway audience. The trilogy is an achievement and a liberation.

Harvey Fierstein was born in Brooklyn. He received a bachelor of fine arts degree from Pratt Institute, Brooklyn, in 1973. While in college he began a career as a drag performer and actor.

Besides *Torch Song Trilogy*, Fierstein is known for writing the excellent book for the Jerry Herman musical about gay life in France—*La Cage aux Folles* (1983). Fierstein has written a dozen plays to date. In his send-ups of heterosexual and homosexual societies, Fierstein can be outrageously hilarious and subversively profound.

Fierstein is concerned with honesty, homophobia, allegiances, the fragility of relationships, the nature of love, the mutability of "family," pride, loss, loneliness, and the relativity of values.

Torch Song Trilogy (1981)

The *Torch Song Trilogy* consists of *The International Stud, Fugue in a Nursery,* and *Widows and Children First!* In *The International Stud,* a two-character plus torch singer play, egocentric Arnold Beckoff carries a torch for Ed, a bisexual. His on-and-off courtship of Ed degrades him, but he loves the suffering of love. Masochism has a sweetness for him, and self-pity proves to him that he is living. As expected he drives Ed away with his overdependency and sharp wit.

Fugue in a Nursery has Arnold and Ed separated a year after the action in *The International Stud.* Arnold is involved with his new lover, Alan, while Ed has married Laurel. The four play on a giant bed. The effect is like prone musical chairs. In keeping with the music implied in the title, the action is accompanied by a string quartet.

Widows and Children First! is a "domestic" comedy-drama with

Arnold in widowhood because Alan has been murdered by homo-phobes. Arnold is castigated by his mother for his homosexuality just as he is concerned for his adopted fifteen-year-old gay son, David. Mrs. Becker thinks that David is Arnold's lover. Ed has left Laurel and doesn't quite know which way to turn, but he and Arnold are maturing with time and responsibilities. The play is a delightfully funny send-up of soap opera.

Tony Kushner (1956–)

Tony Kushner has challenged Terrence McNally for the distinction of being considered the leading gay American dramatist. His seven-hour epic drama, the Pulitzer Prize-winning *Angels in America, A Gay Fantasia on National Themes, Part One: Millennium Approaches* (1991) and *Part Two: Perestroika* (1992) has unveiled the American gay experience via London and Dublin productions and transla-tions throughout much of the world.

Kushner, the son of classical musicians, was born in New York City but was raised in Lake Charles, Louisiana. As a youth he was "treated" with psychotherapy to alter his sexual orientation. The re-sult convinced him that he was naturally gay. Today Kushner is a gay activist. Playwriting as a career was an early choice for Kushner, but after receiving his bachelor of arts degree from Columbia Uni-versity in 1978, he studied directing at New York University with the thought of working in the theater while writing for it. Kushner received a master of fine arts in 1984.

Kushner's earlier work includes *A Bright Room Called Day* (1987), a parable of fascism set in Hitler's Germany and evidencing Kushner's study of political systems; *Hydriostaphia* (1987), which foregrounds Kushner's deep knowledge of English poetry and prose; *The Illusion* (1990), a romantic play adapted from Corneille's *L'illusion;* and *Slavs!* (1992), a discourse on communism in the Soviet Union that premiered with the Actors Theatre of Louisville. In 2001, *Homebody/Kabul,* a prophetic drama about a British woman who disappears in Afghanistan, opened to an enthusiastic reception. Kushner is currently working on a historical drama about the African American experience and the economics of slavery.

Angels in America, A Gay Fantasia on National Themes, Part One: Millennium Approaches (1991) and *Part Two: Perestroika* (1992)

The play observes and comments on the social and political history of the 1980s in America from the perspective of the Left. It presents the impact of AIDS on the gay community. It is a bold and biting attack on hypocrisy, guilt, and selfishness. It expresses fierce anger at the specter of mortality that AIDS has raised for gay men, and it savages Ronald Reagan's politics, conservative Christian theology, and the family values movement.

The date is 1985, when the AIDS epidemic emerged. There are two couples, one gay and one supposedly straight. The gay couple includes Louis, a Jew who talks political correctness but does not act, and his lover, Prior, who has AIDS and is the play's hero. Louis fulminates against the moral dilemma he sees tearing the world apart, but on a daily level he is unable to bear the horrors of Prior's disease. The second couple is made up of Joe and Harper Pitt, Mormons from Salt Lake City. Their marriage is a sham. Harper is on valium because there is no sex in her life, as Joe is really a closet homosexual. He represents all those gay men who are afraid or ashamed to recognize and celebrate their true sexuality.

Louis and Joe become lovers, but Joe finds coming out traumatic. He is torn by the conflict between his sexuality and the social values with which he has been brought up. He winds up back in the closet. An angel informs the audience that God has given up on the world. The demon of the play is the despicable Roy Cohn, the power broker, homophobe, and closet gay who dies of AIDS.

Additional Reading

Geis, Deborah R. *Approaching the Millennium: Essays on "Angels in America."* Ann Arbor, Mich.: Univ. of Michigan Press, 1997.
Vorlicky, Robert, ed. *Tony Kushner in Conversation.* Ann Arbor, Mich.: Univ. of Michigan Press, 1998.

David Henry Hwang (1957–)

Best known for the highly original and successful *M. Butterfly* (1988)—the story of a French diplomat who had a long affair with a Chinese actor who proved to be a male spy—David Henry Huang was born in Los Angeles, the eldest of three children and the only son of Henry Yuan Hwang, a former bank president, and Dorothy Huang Hwang, a pianist and music teacher. His father emigrated from Shanghai shortly after World War II. His mother, who had been born in China, came to the United States via the Philippines.

Hwang attended an elite prep school, the Harvard School in North Hollywood, and then Stanford University, where he received a bachelor of arts degree in English literature in 1979. He had already begun to write plays. After Stanford Huang studied playwriting with Sam Shepard and then attended the Yale School of Drama from 1980 to 1981. For a while he taught creative writing in a California high school, and then moved to New York. In 1985 Hwang married Orphelia Y. M. Chong, a Chinese Canadian artist, but the marriage ended in divorce in 1988.

In 1979 Huang wrote *FOB* (which stands for "fresh off the boat"), a play in which a recent Chinese immigrant attempts, in a ritualized courtship, to win a Chinese American woman. *Family Devotions* (1981) is about accepting one's heritage and engaging the past. *The Dance and the Railroad* (1981) tells the story of a Chinese immigrant in 1867 working on the transcontinental railroad as a strike ensues, caught between his past and the way he wants to perceive his new country. *The Sound of a Voice* (1983) is a one-act play about a bewitched samurai in seventeenth-century Japan. *The House of Sleeping Beauty* (1983) is also a one-act play set in Japan. It is based on a story by Nobel Prize-winning writer Yasunari Kawabata. In it a friendship develops in a brothel between the madam and a client, an aging writer. *Rich Relations* (1986) depicts the conflict between a wealthy Caucasian man and his prodigal son. *Trying to Find Chinatown* (1996) is a ten-minute play, one of the experimental short plays performed at the Actors Theatre of Louisville.

Hwang is concerned with the process of the Americanization of immigrants, which has been going on from the first colonists. Sometimes the process is Westernization as well. Hwang is passionately interested in Chinese cultural history, and his work is often informed by Beijing opera. The experiences, problems, and solutions of his characters serve as models for the struggle of minorities in America to maintain identity. That struggle is in the community and in the individual soul.

David Henry Hwang thinks of himself as an American playwright, not an Asian American playwright, and he eschews the position of spokesperson for the Asian American community.

M. Butterfly (1988)

Set in China and based on the true story of a French diplomat and his Chinese lover, *M. Butterfly* connects to Edward Said's *Orientalism* and *Culture and Imperialism,* works that argue that by seeking the exotic and erotic in the Oriental, the Euro-American male found it easier to believe he had an imperative to rule third world peoples. The initial erotic fantasy of *M. Butterfly*—M. is the French abbreviation of Monsieur, and thus the title is purposely ambiguous—is the same as Puccini's in *Madam Butterfly.* It is the mating of the submissive, compliant, subservient oriental woman and the dominant white male. But Hwang, in an inspired moment, thought to turn the fantasy inside out. In the end it is Gallimard, the protagonist, who is the passive, manipulated one, and it is Song Liling, the Oriental, who has power and control. The Western man, insecure in his sexuality, is acting out *Madam Butterfly* with himself as the handsome, strong, military Pinkerton to the point that for twenty years he has blinded himself to the reality of the situation: his lover is a male and a spy. When at last they are caught, Gallimard and all Westerners learn that the East is not feminine; it does not want to be dominated. Big guns do not make the West masculine per se. Cultural stereotyping is fraught with dangers. Truth must prevail.

Hwang has also written librettos for Philip Glass's *One Thousand Airplanes on the Roof* (1988) and *The Voyage* (1992).

Suzan-Lori Parks (1964–)

Widely recognized as a leading African American woman dramatist, and (along with Tony Kushner) a particularly provocative playwright, Suzan-Lori Parks is a poetic dramatist whose characters are caught up in the sweep of history, economic maelstroms, and other forces beyond their control. She writes about slavery, the Middle Passage, the dehumanization of the African American, urban poverty, loss, sexism, discrimination, American racial history, and the endurance of indomitable black America. In a way language is Parks's central subject. In her employment of fantasy, Parks is influenced by Adrienne Kennedy, and in the lyricism of her work she shows her respect for Ntozake Shange.

Parks loves language. Her dialogue has the density of the best of modern poetry, yet at the same time she beats up on English as if to punish it or to say that it is justly subject to appropriation by those who have to use it.

Suzan-Lori Parks was born in Fort Knox, Kentucky. Her father, Donald Parks, was a career army officer who upon retirement earned a doctorate and then became a university professor. Her mother, Frances Parks, is a university administrator and a storyteller. The Parkses moved from army post to army post when Suzan-Lori was a child and a youth, and while in Germany she attended a German school.

Parks received a bachelor of arts degree in English and German from Mount Holyoke College in 1985. While at Mount Holyoke she had a writing course with James Baldwin, who encouraged her. After college Parks moved to New York City to begin her career as a playwright. Parks has lectured and taught at several colleges and universities, including the University of Michigan, New York University, and the Yale School of Drama.

Although she had previously completed several dramas, including *Betting on the Dust Commander* (1987), a play about domestic harmony (or the lack thereof), Parks's first professionally produced play was the four-part *Imperceptible Mutabilities in the Third Kingdom* (1989), which presents a historical survey of the African American experience from now back to the mythic past. *The Death of the Last Black Man in the Whole Entire World* (1990) is a linguistic romp in which a symbolic African American couple ingest history and rise up by throwing off the shackles of a borrowed language and racial stereotyping. *The American Play* (1991) depicts an African American man in love with the wrong dream. *Devotees in the Garden of Love* (1991) is a one-act tragicomedy on romantic illusion; *Venus* (1996) ridicules the absurdity of pseudo-scientific racial classification in the nineteenth century as it affected an African woman with a physical abnormality.

Top Dog/Underdog, a play about fraternal confrontation; *In the Blood*, a story of infanticide; and *Fucking A* were produced in 2001. Parks has also written the screenplay for *Girl Six* (1996), directed by Spike Lee. In 2001 Suzan-Lori Parks married and received a MacArthur Foundantion Genius Award.

The Death of the Last Black Man in the Whole Entire World (1990)

The last black man is named Black Man with Watermelon. Other characters also have stereotypical names such as Black Woman with Fried Drumstick, Lots of Grease and Lots of Pork, and Yes and Greens Black-Eyed Peas Cornbread. Parks also offers homage to Richard Wright's *Native Son* with a character named Bigger and Bigger and Bigger. Parks turns stereotype around and illuminates it with effrontery. The stereotypes take on dignity, but they also show that Parks has a sense of humor.

Still, Black Man is nearly electrocuted, hanged, drowned, and he almost dies of sheer exhaustion. He is on the run, but he always manages to survive, although vexed with the idea that he has to go on. The play has an epic structure. The present is not good. Better to go back before Columbus to the time of the black Queen-then-Pharaoh Hatshepsut. There is a need to write history correctly or it will be lost, because time is language. Black Man wants to be remembered in his time and in the future. In the end Parks's characters are free, united, in control of their lives, and laughing.

Selected Critical Bibliography

Index

•   •   •

Selected Critical Bibliography

Anadolu-Okur, Nilgun. *Contemporary African American Drama*. New York: Garland, 1997.

Berney, K. A. *Contemporary American Dramatists*. London: St. James Press, 1994.

Berkowitz. Gerald M. *American Drama of the Twentieth Century*. London: Longman, 1992.

Bigsby, C. W. E. *Modern American Drama, 1945–1990*. Cambridge: Cambridge Univ. Press, 1992.

———. *A Critical Introduction to Twentieth-Century American Drama*. 3 vols. Cambridge: Cambridge Univ. Press, 1982–85.

Bordman, Gerald. *The Oxford Companion to American Theatre*. New York: Oxford Univ. Press, 1984.

Brockett, Oscar G. *History of the Theatre* 8th ed. Boston: Allyn and Bacon, 1999.

Brown, Janet. *Feminist Drama: Definition and Critical Analysis*. Metuchen, N.J.: Scarecrow, 1979.

Brown-Guillory, Elizabeth. *Their Place on the Stage: Black Women Playwrights in America*. Westport, Conn.: Greenwood, 1988.

Cohn, Ruby. 1991. *New American Dramatists, 1960–1990*. New York: St. Martin's, 1991.

Couch Jr., William. *New Black Playwrights*. Baton Rouge: Louisiana State Univ. Press, 1968.

Gould, Jean. *Modern American Playwrights*. New York: Dodd, Mead, 1966.

Hart, Lydia, ed. *Making a Spectacle: Feminist Essays on Contemporary Women's Theatre*. Ann Arbor, Mich.: Univ. of Michigan Press, 1984.

Hughes, Catharine. *American Playwrights, 1945–1975*. London: Pitman, 1976.

Kolin, Phillip C., ed. *American Playwrights since 1945: A Guide to Scholarship, Criticism and Performance*. Westport, Conn.: Greenwood, 1989.

Lewis, Allan. *American Plays and Playwrights of the Contemporary Theatre*. New York: Crown, 1970.

Mates, Julian. *America's Musical Stage*. Westport, Conn.: Greenwood, 1985.

Marsh-Lockett, Carol P. *Black Women Playwrights: Visions on the American Stage*. New York: Garland, 1999.

Mates, Julian. *America's Musical Stage: Two Hundred Years of Musical Theatre*. Westport, Conn.: Greenwood, 1985.

Mitchell, Loften. *Voices of the Black Theatre*. Clifton, N.J.: J. T. White, 1975.

Quinn, Arthur Hobson. *History of the American Drama from the Beginnings to the Civil War*. New York: F. S. Crofts, 1923.

———. *History of the American Drama to the Present Day*. New York: Harper, 1927.

Robinson, Marc. *The Other American Drama*. Cambridge: Cambridge Univ. Press, 1994.

Schlueter, June, ed. *Feminist Reading of Modern American Drama*. Rutherford, N.J.: Fairleigh Dickinson Univ. Press, 1989.

———. *Modern American Drama: The Female Canon*. Rutherford, N. J.: Fairleigh Dickinson Univ. Press, 1990.

Vinson, James, ed. *Contemporary Dramatists*. New York: St. Martin's, 1977.

Wilson, Garf F. B. *Three Hundred Years of American Drama and Theatre*. Englewood Cliffs, N.J.: Prentice-Hall, 1973.

Watt, Stephen. *Postmodern/Drama: Reading the Contemporary Stage*. Ann Arbor: Univ. of Michigan Press, 1998.

Index